THE
BURDEN OF
BEING CHAMP

The Dropout, The Legend, and The Pediatrician

JERRY A. MILLER, JR.

CAMPEADOR
PRESS

THE BURDEN OF BEING CHAMP
Campeador Press

Unless otherwise indicated, all Scripture quotations are taken from the New American Standard Bible®, Copyright © 1960, 1962, 1963, 1968, 1971, 1972, 1973, 1975, 1977, 1995 by The Lockman Foundation. Used by permission. (www.Lockman.org)

Scripture quotations marked (ESV) are from The Holy Bible, English Standard Version® (ESV®), copyright © 2001 by Crossway, a publishing ministry of Good News Publishers. Used by permission. All rights reserved.

Scripture quotations marked (KJV) are from the Holy Bible, King James Version (Authorized Version).

Author services by Pedernales Publishing, LLC.
www.pedernalespublishing.com

Cover design: Jose Ramirez and Barbara Rainess

Library of Congress Control Number: 2014951115

ISBN 978-0-9908126-1-6 Paperback Edition
ISBN 978-0-9908126-0-9 Digital Edition

Printed in the United States of America

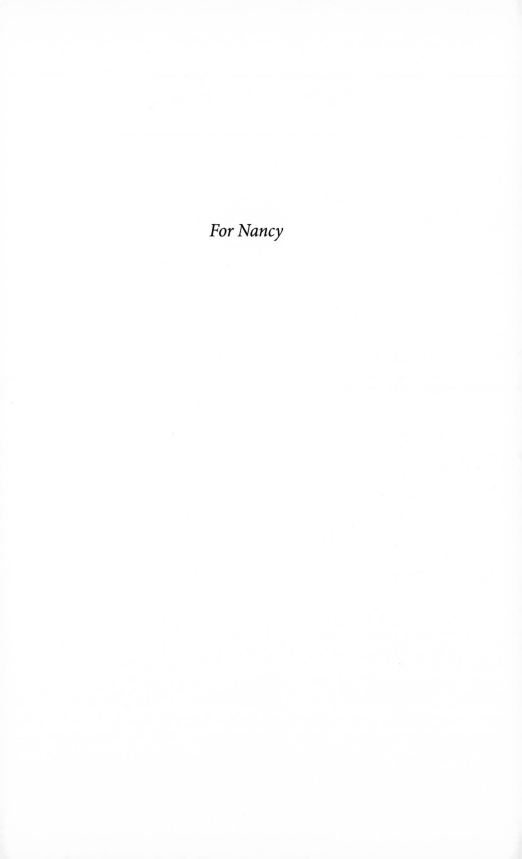

For Nancy

Author's Note

THE ACCOUNTS THAT FOLLOW are true. In some cases, in order to protect confidentiality, I have altered some specific details. In other cases, I engage in a little hyperbole that I hope the reader will enjoy (or forgive). But the essential stories, remarkable as they may seem, are true to life.

Acknowledgements

THERE ARE MANY PEOPLE to thank and acknowledge for their roles in getting this book into your hands.

First, I thank God for being with me all my life, for his constant presence in all sorts of experiences, and for giving me the opportunity to tell much of what he has done for me. These stories are really his stories.

My wife, Nancy, has been a constant encouragement and sounding board during this long project. Thank you, Nancy, for freeing me to find the time to write and for being my best critic.

My children, Rebecca, Rachel, Esther, and Jeremiah, are not only found in these pages but have reviewed much of the book and offered valuable critiques and suggestions. Thank you to my children.

I thank my parents and my sister, Becky, for providing information and for critically reading many of the chapters. They have been great cheerleaders.

I am grateful to the many individuals and families who have permitted me to include their stories in this book. More than that, parents of patients that appear here have allowed me to care for their children, an inestimable privilege. Thanks to all of you.

Attorneys Marcus Hunt (one of my sons-in-law) and Jeromye Sartain have given excellent legal advice. Thank you both. Also, thanks to you, Marcus, for your artistic contributions.

Friends Dr. Aaron Hanna, Rhonda Hatcher, and Kathy Williamson read the near-finished manuscript and offered new insights, things I would never have seen had they not looked on from a different point of view. Thank you.

I thank my editors, friends Ann Robertson and Jennifer Cortez. Ann and Jennifer did not let me off easily. I appreciate their attention to detail and their professional eyes. They pushed me to write better than I would have otherwise.

Pastors Dr. Raymond C. Ortlund, Jr. and Dr. George W. Robertson advised me on the chapter entitled "The Sting." More than that, for many years, they have been true friends to me. I love these men. Thank you.

Thanks to author and friend Karen Jones for her generous and invaluable counsel on publishing a book.

Family friend Mary Donnan Heppert graciously served as an artistic consultant, and I am grateful. Thank you.

Pedernales Publishing has been even better than advertised. Thank you to Jose Ramirez and Barbara Rainess for skilled and professional assistance in bringing this book to published form.

Dr. Jennifer Drake, friend and colleague, proofread the final version of the book just before publication. Her diligent reading and helpful comments strengthened the final product. Thank you, Jennifer.

Finally, thank you to Rachel and Marcus Hunt for allowing me to use the photo of their son (and my grandson), Caedmon, on the cover, and thank you to Robynne and Shilo Robinson for permitting me to use the photo of their son, Aiden (and me), on the back cover of this book.

Contents

Part Four

Introduction: It's All True

I TURNED SIXTY a few years ago. I used to think sixty was old; I still do. Except, of course, when it applies to me. But sixty years *is* a long time to live, and I never thought I would be answering the question, "How old are you?" with a six and another ever-increasing integer. It seems strange.

But it's not so bad.

The past few years, I have been impressed by this one simple phrase: it's all true. God has shown me that everything he says about himself, his promises, his faithfulness, his goodness, his salvation in Jesus Christ, the Bible—it's all true. What I once learned by words I have now learned by experience.

I have learned that if I simply open my eyes and look around, I can see God everywhere: in creation, in nature, in the lives of people, in circumstances. He is there. I need only to look.

This book contains many loosely connected stories taken from my life. Some of them are simply fun; I hope they make you laugh. Others may make you cry. Most of them, I hope, will encourage you because they demonstrate God's faithfulness to me over many years and in many circumstances. I'm not a special case; God holds out his promises of faithfulness to you as well.

As I wrote these vignettes, even without a clear initial intent except to tell a few stories, God's faithfulness ultimately shone through. I find it is impossible for me to tell about my life unless

I also tell about God's faithfulness to me. It is not merely a forced conclusion. I wind up there because God is so real. He is there. God is true and God's promises are true: neither he nor they ever change. God has never abandoned me, and he has never deserted me. Throughout my life—sometimes dramatically, but often almost imperceptibly—God has been with me. He is always there. He is always good.

Have I been lucky? No.

Have I been blessed? Yes.

Has God filled my life with grace upon grace? Yes.

Jesus Christ has never disappointed me. When I die, I want this on my headstone: "He trusted Christ and was never disappointed."

It's all true.

... Whoever believes in Him will not be disappointed.
  Romans 10:11

Jerry A. Miller, Jr.
September 1, 2014

PART ONE

1

The Unbearable Burden
of Being Champ

PARENTS LIKE TO GIVE nicknames to their sons.

I have never understood why they go to the trouble of finding the perfect first and middle names, and then saying, "I know… let's call him _____." Usually it is a sly reference to the original name, sometimes cute, sometimes catchy, sometimes downright silly. Sometimes the nickname has nothing to do with the child's original name. And sometimes it reflects what parents hope their child will be someday.

I was named after my father, so I'm a junior. I've always been proud of that. Even now, I enjoy signing my name "Jerry A. Miller, Jr." But I've always been grateful that my parents never called me *Junior*. Or *Deux*. Or *Dos*. Or *Zwei*.

No. I had a better nickname.

I was Champ.

My father had vision and hope for me. He was dreaming big dreams for me.

Beginning at age four, I became Champ for a year or two. (I admit, it did help prevent some confusion around the house so that when my mom called for Jerry, we all knew she was calling my father.) I even had a Champ jacket. It was a navy-blue windbreaker with the white letters CHAMP sewn on the back for all to see.

When I was five years old, a year into my reign as title-holder, a man came up to me and asked me what I was champion of. Hmm … I had never thought of that. I guessed I was likely champ of the world, or at least of Virginia. But, being the humble person that I've always been, I told him I didn't know. I just knew I was Champ.

By the time I got to first grade, I asked my parents if I could go back to simply being Jerry again. I had no real reason for changing back to my given name, although it *was* true that my Champ jacket both identified me and invited the world to fight me. It was as if I had a target on my back or a sign that said "Hey, you lookin' for a fight?" or an irresistible invitation that said "Hit me!" But no one had ever asked me if I wanted to fight, thus placing at risk my world title, and no one had ever given me a bloody nose.

So, it was not battle fatigue or fear that caused me to go back to my actual name. I think I just didn't like the nickname "Champ." My parents said okay, and I shed my jacket, vacated my title, and retired from the ring all in one fell swoop. I was Jerry once again. My dad was Jerry, and that was good enough for me.

I like the fact that my father and mother had dreams for me. My dad always told me that he wanted me to be better than he was. But to me, that seemed impossible because my dad was my hero. I loved and respected him. I always looked to him for wisdom and guidance. He never backed down from his convictions. He never showed fear. He always did what he had to do. I wanted to be just like my dad. How could I improve on him?

My father wanted me to be more than just Junior, and more than just a "chip off the old block." He wanted greatness for me. I think that's why he called me Champ. It was a fairly unusual name, and I have met only one person since then with that nickname. I believe that all good fathers want greatness for their sons, and they want their sons to be greater than they have been. I have never understood the few fathers I have seen who are weirdly and perversely jealous of their own sons.

I think that I have always felt subconscious pressure to achieve and accomplish. It was not external pressure; it was internal. Although my parents gave me a vision of what I could be, they never pushed me to become the designated symbol of family success. Instead, they helped me to understand the dignity God has given every human being he created; God has made humans a "little lower than the angels," as David says in the Psalms. God has made every person for significance, for eternity, for greatness. God has graced every person with gifts and abilities. My parents instilled in me a healthy sense of destiny and dignity, but they never pressured me, and they never tried to live out their dreams through me.

No, I pressured myself; it was self-inflicted. The pressure I felt was internal. After all, I was the oldest son and the oldest grandchild on both sides of the family. I took my role seriously. I had to lead the way for my sister and cousins and anyone else around who would follow me. Looking back, I believe that as I grew older, too often I was motivated by both fear and pride in my quest for significance. I was afraid of failure, and I was proud enough to desire the praise of those around me, or lacking that, to enjoy the secret pleasure of self-adulation. Fear and pride are not good motivators, and they will take you only so far. Eventually, they will destroy you.

Maybe, deep down, even before I began to feel the pressure, I tried to avoid it. Maybe, thinking that I had to achieve something great, I was wearied and frightened by the thought even before I began. Maybe, in some remote corner of my psyche, I didn't want to bear the burden of being Champ. And, maybe, that's the real reason I dropped the sobriquet and became just plain Jerry again.

Only later would I realize that God in Christ, by creation and redemption, freely offers significance and greatness to every human. We were made by God for greatness, every one of us. And only he can give it. I did not need to be a champion. I did not need to strive to prove to others and myself that I was important.

I did not need to *be* a champion. I *needed* a Champion.

I needed God.

Who knows what goes on in a little boy's mind?

... the LORD is with me like a dread champion ...
   Jeremiah 20:11

Come to Me, all who are weary and heavy-laden, and I will give you rest. Take My yoke upon you and learn from Me, for I am gentle and humble in heart, and you will find rest for your souls. For My yoke is easy and My burden is light.
   Matthew 11:28-30

2

I Was a Kindergarten Dropout

THE RED CHAIR.

Just the memory of The Red Chair still renders me pale, cold, and sweaty.

I don't remember much about kindergarten, but I do remember the Red Chair. It was kind of a cross between today's "time out" and yesterday's stocks on the village green. The Red Chair was for kids in our class who misbehaved—and who were inartful enough to get caught. These miscreants were sent to the Red Chair for a set period of time. It was big chair on a stage at the front of the room, and here, scofflaws were seen by all to be the criminals that they were. Just seeing The Red Chair was enough of a deterrent to keep me out of it.

My young and far-from-rich parents had sacrificed to send me to a nice, private kindergarten in Norfolk, Virginia. There were no public kindergartens in Norfolk then. My father, a World War II veteran, was just beginning his business career with Texaco, and despite the fact that he and my mother could not afford to buy a house, they had committed to sending their five-year-old son to a good kindergarten.

The teacher was a nice enough lady with white hair. I went only until noon each day, and I guess it was fun. But, one day,

I came home with a big revelation and a big announcement: I wanted to drop out. And I had a very good reason. I did not have enough time to play.

Now, to many helicopter parents of the 21st century, this request would seem like heresy of the highest degree. But my parents weren't too concerned about my résumé. I was not active in community service, I did not play for a traveling cricket team, and I was not in the Norfolk Youth Orchestra. Heck, I didn't even take karate lessons. So, they let me drop out—to do important things little five-year-old boys need to do—things like playing with their trucks in the dirt, lying outside on the top of the picnic table watching the clouds, worrying about how to prevent hurricanes from blowing the house down, and just being a foggy little boy.

I wish I could say that first grade was an unmitigated success. My teacher, Mrs. Black, was a tall, skinny lady who seemed emotionally distant from her charges. She always wore a skirt and blouse, along with high heels. She had horn-rimmed glasses, and parted her graying black hair in the middle. I don't recall her ever smiling; maybe somewhere deep in her soul, she harbored some hidden sadness. She did not seem happy.

Mrs. Black had a few disturbing ideas. One of them was this: at break time, all of the children in our class were allowed to use the bathroom in the back corner of the classroom, but, and this was a big BUT, no one was allowed to flush the toilet until every child had used it. I think Mrs. Black was ahead of her time, the first environmentalist, the initial conservationist, a truly "green" person. We never really learned from her stellar environmentalist example, but we did learn a very important life lesson: the preferred place to be is always at the head of the line. I've never forgotten it.

I really frustrated Mrs. Black, though unintentionally. We were on a split schedule because of overcrowding, and thus we were at school each day for only about five hours. We were supposed to bring a snack from home. But I had this great lunchbox—on the side was a painting of a mounted Indian warrior. I loved that lunchbox. Was I going to disrespect my lunchbox by bringing only a few crackers or an apple? Of course not. I brought a four course lunch. It was great. It also took a long time to eat. I was always the last person to finish, and Mrs. Black was always telling me to hurry up and eat. At least *someone* had their priorities straight.

I'm not sure what else I did in first grade. I do remember that my best friend, Stevie, my neighbor and partner in crime, somehow ran afoul of Mrs. Black. (Maybe he had committed the cardinal sin and had prematurely flushed the toilet?) Stevie's punishment was that he was not to come back to his reading group that day. Of course, Stevie misunderstood and didn't show up for reading the rest of the year. Our leader, Mrs. Black, somehow didn't notice. I assume Stevie is still illiterate.

The only other thing I remember about first grade was that a little girl in our class had a huge crush on me, and every time I bent over to drink at the water fountain she would rush up to kiss me on the arm. I learned very quickly to manage to exist in a state of chronic, mild dehydration.

Second grade was even better. Mrs. Lee was a younger teacher who had no weird habits, but I don't think she was a very good educator. The highlight films record two great events during the first half of second grade. The first was that all of the boys at my table decided it would be a good idea if we brought our toy guns to school. Boys are like that: someone comes up with a goofy plan, and then everyone agrees, "Yes! that is a *great* idea!" And someone usually winds up getting hurt or in trouble.

So, of course, the next day we executed our plan. My comrades-in-arms brought their firearms, and I brought my derringer and a miniature sawed-off shotgun (we were real warriors, n'est-ce pas?). Such an act now would find all of us expelled from school and in the youth detention center, needing counseling for the next year for our violent tendencies. But most people back in the 1950s realized what boys are like, and we had no problems until one of our gang refused to put his pistol away to do some real work, thus forfeiting his sidearm.

The other sentinel event was the *Weekly Reader* reading test. *Weekly Reader* was a weekly (surprise) newspaper for little kids. I liked the pictures. The test occurred a few months into the school year. I remember very well taking the test. I also remember my strategy. The setup was for us to read a few short paragraphs and then answer some multiple-choice questions. "Well," I thought after a few scenarios, "this test is too easy." After all, the questions were easy, they were all common sense answers, and I had great common sense. So, why not save some time and just skip the scenarios and go straight to the questions? You know, go straight for the throat. I've always liked a direct approach. It made sense to me. It would save time, it would be efficient, and would leave me more time to play or daydream. So, I took the short-cut. I was the first person to finish, and I proudly put down my pencil and pushed the test to the center of the table to do important stuff while the other dummies played by the rules.

The next month was open house, when all the parents proudly go to the school one evening to meet the teachers and find out how their little darlings are doing in school. The *Weekly Reader* tests were at each student's place at his table. I am sure my parents were stunned to find that little Jerry had distinguished himself by having the lowest grade in the class, coming in with only about twenty percent correct on the test. Strange to me now, my mother and father did not come home and rant and rave. I don't think they even discussed it much except to ask me what had happened. I explained my strategy, they told me that was likely not a winning path forward, and we went on. They were not worried; they had faith in God, and they had confidence in me, that some day I would come in out of the fog. (Many children, boys especially, take awhile to figure out what is really going on in school. I was a fairly typical little boy, a little foggy, kind of dopey, happy to play, not sure why I was in school.)

My father was transferred to Baltimore, and we moved over Christmas break in the middle of second grade. My parents, my little sister, Becky, and I all had a stomach virus (viral gastroenteritis as we say in the profession) just before Christmas. School started in January, and I happily went to Rodgers Forge Elementary School. There I had my first taste of being the new kid and my first taste of doing "the new kid routine." The principal, Mr. Hamilton, took me up to my classroom on the second floor to meet my new teacher, Mrs. Lucretian, and my fellow students. Mrs. Lucretian was a pert little lady with jet-black hair, and she was feisty. She met with us in the hall while her little second graders, told at risk of torture to keep quiet, were excitedly whispering about the new boy. Mrs. Lucretian brought me in with the *de rigueur*, "Class, this is Jerry, our new student from Virginia. Please say good morning to Jerry."

"Good morning, Jerry."

"Now, Jerry, here is your seat. Today, you can look at books and color," she said as she thought to herself, "while I figure out what to do with you."

"Wow," I thought, "this is great." I spent the first two or three days coloring while the rest of the class worked. I'm not sure exactly what they did, but I had fun. I guessed that my privileged position was because I was so far ahead of them academically. That had to be the reason. It would take them at least a few months to catch the Virginia genius.

A few days later, my mother received a phone call from Mrs. Lucretian. "Mrs. Miller, I've spent the last few days looking at Jerry's records and trying to see what he can do. I think we have a problem."

There was a prolonged pause as she attempted to phrase her next words gently and clearly, with just the right tone.

"Jerry can't read," Mrs. Lucretian said softly.

The boy could not read.

My parents were shocked and they were concerned, but they

did not panic. They spent large amounts of time face-to-face and in telephone conferences with my teacher. As I learned, Mrs. Lucretian was very business-like, very professional, and very good at what she did. She suggested to them that they buy the new books by Dr. Seuss; *The Cat in the Hat* and *The Cat in the Hat Comes Back* became nightly fare at our house. Looking back, I am sure I didn't I know why I was suddenly having these books read to me at home, with encouragement to read them myself.

Mrs. Lucretian had been trained to teach reading using phonics, and she began intensive therapy. My parents and Mrs. Lucretian realized that I was at a crisis point in my life and that the reading deficit had to be addressed then, aggressively and quickly. But they bore the concern for me and protected me from knowledge of my danger.

Now I was not very astute, but even *I* knew something was going on. I realized that "the Virginia genius" had been assigned to the lowest reading group, the Robins. It was humiliating. Even worse, the Robins all flew rings around me when it came to reading. There was discussion, unbeknownst to me, about sending me back to first grade. Mrs. Lucretian was patient with me and kept me in her classroom. She gave me time to improve. She was kind and gentle, but she held me to a high level of performance and improvement. Few teachers are able to strike this balance.

I began to sense some pressure and realized that I was a failure in school, not because anyone told me or made me feel that way, but because it was so obvious, even to one as clueless as I was. One day at school, I began to feel nauseated and was sent home sick. Once home, I curled up on the couch with a blanket, ate crackers, sipped Coke, and watched Captain Kangaroo on TV. It was a miracle: I felt better.

I began having more episodes of nausea, but now accompanied by vomiting. These episodes occurred on many school mornings, and *only* on school mornings. Each time I vomited, I stayed home, crawled onto the couch, ate crackers, drank Coke, and watched

Captain Kangaroo. To one so self-unaware, it did not seem strange that I should have so many stomach viruses and have such miraculous healing from the well-known medical regimen of crackers, Coke, and Captain K. I was not faking it. I really was nauseated and I really vomited; I was not sticking my finger down my throat to gag myself.

After a few weeks of this, my wise parents and teacher realized what was happening. I had developed a school phobia (I am not sure they had invented that diagnosis yet but that was what it was). The only treatment here was tough love. I had to face the enemy and the pressure. If I ran now, or was allowed to run, it would be all over. The plan of treatment was clear and straightforward: if little Jerry puked his brains out each school morning, he would be cleaned up and sent to school to face the music.

The first test of my parents' will to send their vomiting son to school came soon enough. Monday morning, my mother and Becky took my father to the airport for a business trip. I was fed and clothed and in my right mind when they left. All I had to do was leave the house at 8:00 a.m. and walk the few blocks to school as I always did. A few minutes before eight, I was seized with terrible nausea, and then proceeded to vomit all over the breakfast dishes in the sink. Doing the only reasonable thing, I went back to bed. At about eight thirty, the phone rang and I sprang from bed to answer it. I was feeling better by this time.

"Hello?" I said.

"Hi, Jerry, this is your dad. What are you doing at home?" (How did he know?)

"I'm sick. I just threw up."

"How do you feel now?"

"I'm better."

With no hesitation, Dad said, "Well, since you're better, go ahead and get your clothes on and go to school. Tell Mrs. Lucretian why you're late, and we'll send a note to her tomorrow asking for an excuse."

There was no discussion. I am sure my father and mother were dying inside, but they stood their ground. And it didn't make me doubt my father's love for me. I knew he loved me, and I did what he told me to do. I dressed and headed off to school.

A week or so later, I left for school at the usual time, got out the back gate into the alley (where I often fell and bloodied my knees and elbows), stopped at the garbage can, and felt sick. I lifted the lid and threw up my breakfast. I turned to go back into the house when my mother stepped out and asked me what was wrong. (She must have been watching.) Of course, I told her I was sick (again). She kept her courage and told me to go on to school. I did. (I wonder how I smelled when I arrived.) My mother and little sister stayed inside watching through tears as I trudged off to school.

Slowly, the battle was being won. I kept going to school, and I don't think I ever vomited again that year. And I was learning to read. I advanced to other classics, such as *How The Grinch Stole Christmas*, and I advanced to the next reading group, the Cardinals. My teacher and my parents were continuing to work with me; they did not give up on me. And I began to actually enjoy reading.

The last few weeks of school, Mrs. Lucretian promoted me to that pinnacle of reading groups, the Orioles (the greatest bird in Baltimore). I didn't really understand that I had gone from being essentially a non-reader to a fairly good second-grade reader, but I did know that I was reading, I was enjoying it, and the pressure was off.

Over the years, I read more and more—some books by requirement, many others for pure enjoyment. I'm grateful that my mother often took us to the library, required us to read extra books besides those mandated by school, and had a summer reading program for us. I love to read now. I'm dangerous in a bookstore or library, and my eyes are always bigger than my capacity to read.

As I look back, I'm grateful to God for his kind providence in moving us to Baltimore and landing me in Mrs. Lucretian's class at a crucial time in my academic life; God's loving hand has been on me all my life. I'm grateful to my parents for not going into a panic over me, for praying for me, for having confidence in me, for being patient with me, and for having the courage to do what was best for me despite the short-term pain for all of us. I'm grateful for Mrs. Lucretian. I have attempted without success to contact her so I could thank her for her impact on my life; she was a very astute lady, she was patient with me, and she would not give up on me. I owe her a lot.

And I'm grateful for the Cat in the Hat.

3

Charlotte

MY NEXT STOP was Charlotte, North Carolina. My father received a promotion and was transferred there just a few months after we had moved to Baltimore. Rather than moving his struggling, emesis-prone, second-grade son again in the middle of the school year, my father commuted long distance from Baltimore to Charlotte for a difficult few months. We moved in June as soon as school was out.

I was well armed for third grade. I could read, I could tell time, and I could write in cursive script. I had all summer to acclimate, make new friends, and get ready for school. My neighbors across the street had ponies, and I fully expected that I would spend all my free time riding them. I rode about two times in the twenty months we were there.

Mrs. Hawfield, my third-grade teacher, was a nice lady and a superlative, experienced teacher. She introduced herself in a good-natured way to the class, telling us to remember her name like this: "Think of someone laughing in a hayfield." The mnemonic device worked.

Third grade was relatively atraumatic, a welcome change. Mrs. Hawfield gave a daily talk on some subject and then had the students write an essay about it. The essay was to be about a page long. To my surprise, all the other kids used only one line to write, whereas I was accustomed to using two lines; the two-line technique was used in Baltimore until children were proficient in cursive handwriting, and to this technique I attribute my present-day near-calligraphic handwriting. Of course, it was easy for me to fill the page since my letters were twice as big as everyone else's. But then, I couldn't understand why I was so fast and the others were so slow. Mrs. Hawfield patiently instructed me to write using single lines and was willing to wait until I could fill the page. The banner day occurred a few weeks later when we were allowed to write on individual subjects of choice. I wrote on Japan since I was an expert on that country, my Aunt Virginia being a missionary there. I wrote a one-page document. I had arrived.

In January, we had about fourteen inches of snow, and it was magical. A week of beauty and tranquillity ensued. Watching falling snow has always been a mystical experience for me. It transports me to a place of warmth, freedom, and peace. Maybe I have been conditioned to realize that snow in the South means everything comes to a stop and that I can't do a thing about it. It is very liberating.

We were out of school for a week, and though we paid dearly for it later by having to attend school on a Saturday, this week was a surprise winter vacation. The McCoys, living just behind us, had a backyard perfectly (though unintentionally) designed for sledding. Their yard was a series of terraces connected by gentle slopes, all descending several hundred yards to the woods. It was a beautiful downhill run for sledders. Each morning, we got up, dressed in layers, left our homes, and walked over the snow as it crunched beneath our feet. I still love the crunching sound and feel of the snow as I walk on it after an overnight hard freeze that turns the upper layer into a thick crust of ice. That ice also makes for fast sledding. We made many runs down the hill each morning and each afternoon, punctuated by lunch and hot chocolate breaks. We built snow forts and waged war with snowballs. It was depressing to see the snow finally melt.

That spring, I played organized baseball for the first time. I was ready. My father had played ball with me since I was little. We often played catch together in the backyard. Dad had pitched to me so I could learn how to hit with my brown, official Jackie Robinson bat. I had learned how to hold the bat, and I had learned the proper batting stance. My dad had taught me how to grasp a baseball and how to throw it. "Get your arm back!" he would say. "Use your whole arm!" (I didn't want the other guys to say that I "threw like a girl.") My father had taught me how to catch using both hands, how to watch the ball into my glove. Now, I even had a new Wilson glove, a Ted Williams autograph model. Upon learning that real baseball players always oiled their gloves to break them in, I decided to do the same. Since I couldn't find any suitable oil, I used some grease off the antenna of my mother's car and rubbed it into the pocket of my glove. It made a mess, but I was ready to play some baseball.

Tryouts were exciting. The best part was when the coach hit fly balls to the guys in the outfield. We were instructed to call for the ball ("Mine!") so all the eight-year-old boys wouldn't collide going for the same ball. The first boy called "Mine!" and then carefully looked skyward at the ascending and then rapidly descending sphere, raising his glove to catch it. He had everything under control, and we admired his sense of cool. After all, he went first. He raised his glove to catch the ball, but the ball hit him right in the nose, bloodying his face and spooking everyone else. He cried, had his wounds tended, and was walked off the field. The second boy did the same thing, with the same result. The next time the coach launched the ball into the air, the guys had a predictable reaction: everyone ran—away from the ball. It hit the ground untouched and unwanted, and then bounced off the hard clay surface. All of us were at least fifty feet away. We were trying out to be ballplayers, not javelin-catchers. When the ball stopped rolling and we were sure it was fully and really dead (like a snake—a snake can never really be dead enough) someone finally picked it up.

I was selected to play for a team sponsored by a local funeral home. I guess there must have been an unfortunate epidemic of excellent health and unusual longevity for the people of Mecklenburg County; this caused the populace to fail to cooperate with the company's business plan. That must have been why we never were given caps and T-shirts like the rest of the teams. At each game, we were promised the uniforms were on the way. They never arrived. I finally made my own uniform using a white T-shirt from my drawer at home. Finding a can of black paint in our carport, I broad-stroked the letters "B&L" on the chest and proudly wore it to our next game; it was a work of art. I wore my favorite (and only) blue baseball cap, bought with my own money earned from weeding a neighbor's flowerbed; it had cost me three dollars. I loved that cap; there was a certain way to curve the bill and crimp the top that made us look like we could play, and my cap was duly manipulated to conform to then-current standards of fashion.

I should have known that being sponsored by a funeral home might be a bad omen. Or maybe we simply took on the character of our sponsor's moribund clientele. Either way, we lost every game—every single game—that season. Maybe that was the real reason our sponsor disowned us halfway through the season and never came through on the uniforms.

Later that spring, I felt a little queasy at school one afternoon. I told my teacher I felt sick, and she thought I would be fine if I just stayed in from recess and put my head down on the desk. (I think that having a child put his head down on the desk is a secret healing technique learned by teachers while pursuing their degrees in education; this position cures most illnesses.) I remember feeling pretty crummy as the other kids came in from recess; I began crying, and the little, cherubic girl who sat in front of me began taunting and mocking me. Then it came. I threw up all over the floor beside my desk. I was tempted to throw up on the sweetheart in front of me, but with great self-control, I beat back the urge. It was really exciting for the whole class. In third grade, few things are as able to elicit the perverse blend of disgust, chaos, *schadenfreude*, and glee as a classmate vomiting in the middle of class; the only thing that can come close is another child with a really good bloody nose.

After this episode, Mrs. Hawfield trusted my powers of self-diagnosis.

My mother picked me up and I went home to bed.

And I remember hardly anything that happened the next three days. I was unaware of much except for turning over in bed a few times. My mother took me to our doctor who probably realized that I had viral meningitis, though a spinal tap was not done. (At least, my retrospective self-diagnosis is viral meningitis.) I was sent home for more symptomatic treatment. It took about two weeks for me to recover fully, and I lost about ten pounds. I was pretty skinny.

The summer was uneventful except for the installation by the older neighborhood kids of a new tree swing in the woods. They tied a rope high in the tree and made a platform about twelve feet high. We climbed to the platform, grabbed the rope, and pushed off. It was a great ride. I was a timid little kid and I have never liked heights; I still don't. It took me a while to work up the courage to take advantage of the swing, but once I did, I was hooked. Interestingly, nobody worried about us. There was no concern about some creep showing up to molest us. There was no concern that one of us might get hurt. There were no legal waivers to sign lest someone should sue the landowners in case of injury to one of the kids. There was not even a sign letting us all know that swinging on a rope swing in the woods might be harmful to our health or result in death. I am shocked now as I think about those backward days and the society's appalling ignorance of the benefits of excessive laws, rules, and litigation.

I became adept at using the rope swing. One morning, during a great ride, I suddenly realized that my left arm was hurting. I looked down, and saw a large, deep gash in my left forearm. I had snagged my arm on a jagged branch. I am not sure how I hung on, but hang on I did, waiting for the pendulum to finally stop swinging. I dismounted and ran home, supporting my left arm with my right hand. My mother and Becky saw me coming and ran to me to lead their bleeding warrior home as they both cried. I am not sure if I cried or not. The yawning wound revealed gaping soft tissue, lacerated muscle, and a lot of blood. I could not see bone. After my mother covered it with a clean dishtowel, we rushed off to see the doctor who was able to close the wound in layers. He sent me home with a big bandage. I had one request as we left his office. My father had tickets to the Charlotte Hornets baseball game that night, and I simply *had* to go. The doctor granted me permission; he knew what was important to boys. I went to the game that night with a bandage, a sling, and a pillow to rest my arm on. I looked like a war hero.

Fourth grade started off just fine. For the first time in my life, school presented no crises. My teacher, Miss Brown, was brand new, fresh from college. She was pretty, vivacious, and kind. All of us loved her. She was engaged to be married, and all the boys in the class were jealous—we all wanted to marry her, if she would just wait a few years. We could tell when her fiancé helped her correct our papers. He was left-handed and so his check marks were always backwards. I could never tell what she saw in that guy.

Miss Brown scooted her chair from student to student each morning, having each of us read aloud to her for a few minutes as the rest of the class read silently. This simple everyday occurrence resulted in excellent readers who loved to read. Miss Brown must have put a few miles on her chair every week.

In the spring, my father was transferred back to Norfolk, Virginia. I remember being picked up after lunch the day we moved. As I left the school for the last time, Miss Brown told me goodbye and tried to say something nice to me. This was one of those awkward moments in life when you say goodbye to someone you will never see again. She told me that she knew I would do well in life and that she hoped I would be able to ... to go ... to go to ... the U. S. Naval Academy ... or someplace good like that. I never made it to Annapolis, but her kindness and her words of hope made a deep impression on me.

We got into the car and drove to Norfolk. It was hard for my parents and sister, because we had loved being in Charlotte. It was hard for me. At about the midpoint of our trip, I pretended to take a nap, lying down in the back seat. I faced backward, pressing my face hard against the seat back.

And there, hidden from the world, I silently and secretly cried, ashamed of my tears.

Yet God still had his hand on me for good.

4

Cuban Missile Crisis:
The View From Richmond

FOR AN ELEVEN-YEAR-OLD boy who loved Civil War history, Richmond, Virginia was almost heaven. In the summer of 1962, I moved to Richmond as my father became the new district manager there for Texaco. We lived a block south of the James River, near the Nickel Bridge.

I doubt if it still costs a nickel to cross it.

I suppose I was a little unusual in my love for history. It felt normal to me, and I just assumed everyone loved it just like I did. I used to read the historical markers on the side of the highways as we whizzed by, learning what battle had been fought here, or who had been born just across the creek. Or at least I read the top line written in bold letters. My parents finally bought me a manual with pictures of every historical marker in Virginia. Then I needed only to identify the number of the marker and refer to my book for the whole story. Living in Richmond was like living in a fantasyland of history, only it was real.

I went to the Civil War Centennial museum. I visited the White House of the Confederacy. I spent time at the Virginia State Capitol. I had piles of books on the Civil War, and I even had a Civil War board game (which made no sense at all to me—the player who became general of the Southern army always lost). I had old bullets, a cannon ball, even Confederate money. I loved all this stuff.

I guess I was a strange little kid.

Life in Richmond was idyllic in other ways. I attended Westover Hills Elementary School. Since we had moved early in the summer, Becky and I were able to go to the day camp at the school and get to know some of our classmates. I spent the mornings playing baseball while Becky did crafts. I enjoyed being with all the new guys, and I had the opportunity to display my baseball prowess all summer.

In September, I did the new kid routine at school (again). I was getting good at this. At the risk of being repetitive, here is where the new kid is brought from the principal's office to his new classroom and made to stand in front of the class like he is in a meat market, enduring the gawking assessments by his new classmates. The new kid is then introduced by the teacher (who must act like she is thrilled to have him) to the class (who is also supposed to be overjoyed he has finally arrived) before he can hide in his desk that is hopefully next to the pretty girl he noticed as he scanned the room.

My summer baseball teammates seemed happy to have me with them again, even if no one else cared if I was there or not.

BECKY AND I RODE OUR BIKES to the school that summer, spent the mornings at the day camp, and then rode back home. My brand new twenty-six inch Columbia bicycle was red and had tires with white sidewalls and a headlight powered by a generator; I have been environmentally sensitive for many years. On the way home, we often stopped by a small drugstore and bought ice treats for ten cents. I'm not really sure what these things were called, but they were a local Richmond delicacy, known only to the initiated. They were paper cups of frozen Kool-Aid with at least twice the usual amount of sugar. There was an art to eating them. You popped the cardboard top off, and warmed the cup a little with your hands. Then came the tricky part. You would gently squeeze the mass of ice upward, grasp it and then skillfully flip it upside down back into the cup. We had little wooden disposable spoons, and as we held the upside-down ice with one hand, with the other we would rotate the end of the spoon in the center of the upended ice; this is where all the sugar had settled during the freezing process. The result was super-sweet ice shavings that we ate with delight. We kept boring down in this way until we reached the bottom, then broke up the rest with the spoon and ate that, as well.

I earned spending money by distributing advertising circulars around the neighborhood for the corner drugstore. They paid my friend and me the princely salary of one cent per circular. It took us all afternoon to get 300 of them on the doorsteps of our neighbors. After three or four hours of roaming the area in the hot summer sun, we had made $1.50 apiece. Pretty good. We heard stories of some of our unscrupulous competitors who would ditch their circulars down the storm drains, lay low for a few hours, and then go and collect their money. We never did that, though, on occasion, after a few hours of alternately walking around in the sun and getting doused with rain, the idea did cross our minds. In the winter we cashed in on our capitalistic instincts by shoveling snow. It seems there were no child labor laws in those benighted times. It was a good feeling to work hard, get paid for it, and have a little cash to spend.

We often rode our bikes to the local library. The delicious feeling of freedom I experienced while riding my bike around the neighborhood and its surroundings was intoxicating; safety was assumed. We never locked our bikes, and we didn't fear being abused by some weird stranger. We never even thought about the possibility of anything going wrong. This was back before the days of "post-Christian America," as it is gleefully described by some now. Our country had not quite yet slipped its moorings;

therefore, we were less open-minded and more judgmental about little things like stealing, child abuse, pedophilia and murder. Back then, the culture was so heavily influenced by the Bible and Christian morals that although crimes occurred, of course, most parents didn't have to be anxious about whether their kids would be kidnapped, molested, or have their bikes stolen. These things were rare, and if they occurred, the punishment for serious crime was severe and swift. These crimes and these perpetrators were not tolerated. The depth and incidence of perversion were far less in those days. I believe children were safer and freer then.

These visits to the library were pure delight for a bibliophile like me. I came home with all sorts of books, especially all the sports books I could find. I remember also the delight of entering the library's air-conditioning on a hot summer day. Our home depended on fans to cool us in the hot and muggy Virginia summers, and many evenings were spent in the screened-porch on the side of our home. Becky and I even slept there at night when it was brutally hot.

SIXTH GRADE WAS A GOOD YEAR. I liked school. Mrs. Fones, my teacher, was a kind lady in her sixties and was patient with all the wild kids in our class. I began playing trumpet that year, and my longsuffering parents had to listen to me toot my horn for hours. It took a long time to finally understand that the notes on the piano did not correspond to those on the trumpet. I eventually learned to transpose the music. My aunt gave me her trumpet, which I played for the next few years. During my first concert. I was so nervous that I could not play a single note; I guess the other kids did, and I'm grateful they covered for me. When I tried to play, no air came out at all, or if it did by accident, I played the wrong note. I was grateful to be lost in the crowd.

I was a safety patrol boy. I got to wear an impressive white canvas belt with a strap that went across my chest. I also had a badge that I wore on the chest strap. (I was disappointed that the badge had recently been changed from a serious, silver professional-looking badge to an innocuous, silly green and white disc, but I humbly accepted it with equanimity.) There was a special technique for washing the canvas belt and then for rolling it up for storage. Each morning, I arrived at school early (a difficult task for me), donned a white pith helmet and picked up my yellow flag with the word "Please" in black letters. (I assume "Please" meant, "Please, don't run me over.")

I rushed to my assigned post and helped little kids get across the street as I walked to the middle and unfurled my flag, stopping traffic. When it rained, they gave us yellow raincoats to wear. I was pretty important. The best part was that during the winter, after had we finished, the school cafeteria ladies made us hot chocolate. Status has its privileges.

In the spring, all the safety patrol boys were given a trip to Washington, D.C., our reward for stopping traffic all those months. We got up early, boarded a Greyhound bus, and arrived in the capital by 9:00 a.m. A key event during the trip was that some of us (the more intelligent ones) decided to walk up all the steps of the Washington Monument—yes, all 897 of them. It took a long time. And I don't want to forget this: I also learned that classic song, "Ninety-nine Bottles of Beer on the Wall." A bus full of rowdy boys sang it all the way home. All in all, the trip was very educational.

Lunchtime at Westover Hills Elementary School brought the expected chaos except for one thing. As everyone finished eating, we were required to stop talking for about ten minutes and listen to classical music. I guess our teachers thought we needed a little culture. Surprisingly, everyone actually was quiet and listened; threats of extermination or time in the principal's office rendered us extremely compliant.

Every week we had square-dancing. I never liked square-dancing much. I never liked all the "swing your partner" and "do-si-do" stuff. I never liked having an assigned partner for the whole year. I would have preferred choosing my own partner, but every week I dutifully filed into the gym and paired off with the girl assigned to me. She was not the prettiest girl in the class, but she was nice and pleasant; in addition, she tolerated me. She didn't talk much. I should have taken a little time to get to know her, but I didn't. I hardly spoke to her except to get our dance moves straight. She wore plaid dresses and a little too much deodorant. She likely thought I wore not quite enough. I have never cared much for square-dancing.

I did my first science project. I decided to do a sundial and demonstrate the fact that we can really tell time by the sun. I had a red fifteen by fifteen inch square of Formica on which I painted Roman numerals. I made an executive decision. Here was my reasoning and my final decision: since sundials were really only old types of clocks, and since actually taking the time to ascertain where on the dial face the sun cast its shadow every hour would interfere with more important pursuits, there could be only one logical conclusion. I simply stuck a stylus in the center of the dial, painted the numerals exactly where they would appear as if they were on a clock, and turned the project in. *Voila!* Project done. Time saved for important things. Everyone happy. Pretty smart. Somehow, and this remains a mystery to this day, my science teacher knew exactly what I had done. She gave me an F but also gave me another chance to do it the right way. My initial voyage into the world of science was somewhat inauspicious.

In Richmond, I had the rare opportunity to study Russian. A couple who had escaped from the Soviet Union taught Russian in the Richmond public schools. From them we learned the rudiments of a language that we thought would prove especially useful, since, at that time, the U.S. was locked in a Cold War with the U.S.S.R. Soviet Premier Nikita Khrushchev had promised the U.S. "We will bury you." These were not pleasant words for us to hear. Relations between the two superpowers were tense, and they would reach a crescendo not many months later. If I had stayed in Richmond, I would have been proficient in speaking Russian by the time I finished high school. I wish I had understood more then what courage this Russian couple had had, and more of the true political climate of the day.

Another sixth-grade highlight: I got the mumps. For me, mumps was a mild illness and I was not very ill with it. (Please do not use my experience to rationalize not giving your child the mumps-measles-rubella vaccine. There was no MMR then. Mumps can be a serious illness and a big public health problem. My case was mild.) I stayed home for a week, watched re-runs of old TV shows like *I Love Lucy*, and took a vacation from school. Dr. Russell Good made a couple of house calls to check on me. He was a nice young GP with a huge doctor's bag full of instruments and medicines. My father tutored me in the arithmetic I was missing that week. All in all, it was a great week. And to top it off, upon my triumphant return to school, sweet and cute Martha Williams came up to me before we filed into our classroom and said, "Welcome back, Mumpy." "Wow!" I thought. "Martha just spoke to me!" From these endearing words, I could tell she was secretly in love with me; I've always had a gift for interpreting subtle social cues, especially from girls. Her greeting made the whole ordeal of suffering worth it.

I played baseball with the neighborhood kids on the vacant corner lot until official baseball season started. It was usually a group of ten or so of us, all of the others older than I. One late Wednesday afternoon, my mother stood on our front porch and called me in for supper. I told the guys I had to go and I asked for my baseball, which happened to be the game ball. They wanted to keep playing and tried to convince me to leave the ball with them. I was not so sure, so I said, "No." This response got one kid a little angry, and he began to taunt me. He was a few years older than I was. I asked him, then *told* him to give me my ball. He wouldn't do it; he just held it in his hand. After a few minutes of argument, I made a fatal error, a miscalculation, a big mistake.

I said, "Do you want to fight about it?"

I still hear the words rattling around in my memory. Who knows why I said that? I certainly don't know; it just seemed like a masculine thing to say. I was not looking for a fight. I just wanted my ball back and wanted to go home. He, however, was not a pacifist. He answered me with a non-verbal message that landed right on my forehead. I'm not always so good at interpreting body language, but I understood this meaning very well. Man, it hurt. So, I hit him back. We briefly exchanged punches until the older boys could separate us. The bigger kid had a bloody nose, and I had a goose-egg on my forehead. The older boys patted me on the back as if to congratulate me for standing my ground. They handed me my baseball, and I went home a hero. My mother and Becky were on our front porch crying. They had seen the whole thing. I was relieved they had stayed there; it would have been humiliating if they had interfered, and my mother had the wisdom to know that. I learned a good lesson that day: never ask a guy if he wants to fight you … unless *you* want to fight, and then, don't ask, just hit him as hard as you can. Otherwise, if you ask, he may just say "Yes" with a sucker punch to your head.

Baseball season finally came around. Our coach was a college student from the University of Richmond. Why would he subject himself to such a coaching experience? My hunch is that his education required him to spend time with a bunch of sixth-grade wild men for a few months. Or maybe he was being punished by his college baseball coach for violating team rules. His punishment: baseball purgatory.

I played first base, mainly because I was a big target, I could catch the ball, I could stretch, and … uh … I didn't move very quickly. In addition, fielding ground balls was not my strong suit. Coach must have thought I could do the least amount of damage here. First base was perfect for me.

I was the best hitter on the team. I often hit to the opposite field. It was a good thing I could hit well because I needed all the power I had to compensate for my lack of, let me say it charitably, mobility. I can still see my coach in the third base coaching box giving me the "steal" sign in one game, and my barely arriving safely at third base. I can still hear him saying, "Jerry, son, you're as slow as molasses." He was right. In those days, it was okay for coaches to say things like that to their young charges. Nobody worried too much that it would affect our self-esteem or offend our sensibilities; the concept of "micro-aggression" had not yet been conjured. I'm glad Coach didn't lie to me and tell me what a speedster I was to encourage me or to try to make me feel good about myself—then I would have had to deal with the disappointment of not making the U.S. Olympic track team in the 100 meter dash. Sports has a way of being an honest meritocracy.

Thinking I might elevate my game by looking more professional, I made some eye-black. I scraped the cork off a Coke bottle cap and burned it with matches; I then applied the charred cork to the area below my eyes. You never know when you might need to catch a pop-fly while looking into the sun. I also bought a pair of professional-grade flip sunglasses at the corner drugstore for two dollars. I was doubly ready for the pop-fly in the sun. Besides, I looked cool. These techniques, however, did not give me much elevation.

Our next-door neighbor was Jesse Reynolds. He was in charge of the Richmond City Recreation Department. One day I noticed his woodpile. It was full of baseball bats! He had a bunch of old wooden bats from the city rec department that he was actually going to burn in his fireplace. This was sacrilege! These bats were a little banged up and were being replaced, but a few were still serviceable. I knew I had to rescue some of these orphaned bats destined for destruction. I asked Mr. Reynolds if I could have some, and he gave them to me. I still have one of them. It became one of my favorites.

Baseball became more than a game. It was my life. Unfailingly, I read the box scores each morning in the newspaper. I knew all the stats. I had baseball cards that required actually investing in gum. I watched baseball on TV, especially the all-star game; this was like a mid-summer's religious holiday for all eleven-year-old boys. I followed the exploits of Mickey Mantle and Roger Maris. At night, I would lie in bed with my transistor radio and secretly listen to Atlanta Braves games, the signal making it all the way to Richmond; no one told me I couldn't do this, but just in case, I never told anyone about it either—there was no reason to divulge all that I was doing. I really liked Felipe Alou because he was a Christian, and as he got up to bat, I would pray for him.

I went to many pro baseball games with my family. The Richmond Virginians were, ironically, the triple-A farm team for the New York Yankees (Yankees and Richmond somehow didn't seem to go together, but I got over it). My father would get off early from work and pick us up. We ate hotdogs at a fine eating establishment near the ballpark just before game time, and then we watched players on their way up to or down from the majors. Joe Pepitone was my favorite; my first-baseman's mitt is endowed with his autograph. I thrilled to being able to talk to these players as they warmed up. The dark night, the bright lights, the sultry summer evening with the pungent smell of hot dogs and mustard, the aroma of freshly roasted "goobers" (peanuts), the white uniforms of the "Vees" and the gray uniforms of the visitors set against the dark-green background, the unfolding drama of two teams seeking a win—this was almost too much for an eleven-year-old boy.

During the summer, we had two events I looked forward to with great anticipation. The first was my father's company picnic, and the second was my church's picnic. For me, the highlight of the Texaco company picnic, Richmond district, was the soft drinks. My mother bought soft drinks for us only when we were sick; they were expensive and they were not good for us. But at the Texaco picnic, there were huge washtubs filled with ice and every kind of soft drink. And I could drink them to my heart's contentment. I began drinking as soon as we arrived at about 9:00 a.m., and by the time of the big softball game at eleven o'clock, I had downed eight or nine Cokes, Mountain Dews, Pepsis, Upper 10s, Seven Ups, or whatever else I found. I drank my year's quota of soft drinks in that one day. I never knew when I might be able to partake again.

The church picnic took place on another hot summer day. This was also the day a total solar eclipse was to occur. Adults warned us not to look directly at the eclipse, but, instead, to make cardboard pin-hole boxes and view the eclipse indirectly using these. I could not resist sneaking a peak at the eclipse and was sure I would go blind; I kept waiting, but nothing happened. I can still see. In the pre-picnic festivities, there were races for the kids in the 100 degree heat, and after I ran as hard as I could, with my usual molasses-like fleetness, I began to feel ill, almost passing out. I lay on the picnic table for a while, and then we left early to take the sick student-athlete home. I don't think I even got a single soft drink.

Life in Richmond seemed idyllic. World events disrupted the tranquillity, however, for a few days in October, 1962. In 1959, Fidel Castro had wrested power from the dictator Batista in Cuba and by now was openly a full-fledged Communist in league with the Soviet Union. Ironically, during the revolution, Castro had been seen as a hero; little boys in America wore Castro fatigues and hats and fake beards in his honor. Much had changed in the ensuing years, and Castro's "good guy" veneer was gone. Now, U.S. reconnaissance had made it clear that Castro was harboring Soviet nuclear warheads in new silos in Cuba. They were pointed directly at the United States. For almost two weeks, our young president, John F. Kennedy, was severely tested by the Soviets as the world stared into the abyss of the frightening possibility of nuclear war.

By this time, I knew all about nuclear war; I had read John Hershey's book, *Hiroshima*, so I was an expert on what an atomic bomb could do. I had heard of atomic bombs that had been tested by the U.S.S.R., and the resulting radiation that had contaminated rain and snow; I had even eaten snow that I was certain had been thus polluted, and was therefore, in secret mental suffering, awaiting my long death sentence from radiation illness. Nuclear warfare was not a desirable event. It terrified me.

During the Cold War, American families were instructed in how to construct fall-out shelters to protect themselves in the event of nuclear war. I knew that one family on our street had built one. Now, training was stepped up to instruct school children on what to do if our country were bombed or went to war. At Westover Hills Elementary School, teachers educated us in how to obey quickly if a crisis arose. We were taught how to use our desks and books as shields from falling debris. (Becky was adamant in thinking that the purpose of putting books over our heads was so that if a bomb hit us on the head, it wouldn't hurt.) We were told how we might have to go into the school's central hallways as a place of relative safety. And we were instructed as to how we were to leave the school and go directly home if the need arose.

It was a time of eerie uncertainty and anxiety. Both adults and children knew there were nuclear warheads directed right at us from only a few miles from our shores; what we did not know was whether the Cubans and Soviets were trigger-happy. In the midst of existential crisis, our country united behind our president, and with each other. We were all scared.

I recall when President Kennedy demanded that Soviet Premier Khrushchev remove the missiles from Cuba. He set a deadline of October 28th. He met the crisis with courage and decisiveness. I remember going to bed on October 27th, my mother's 32nd birthday, worried that the next day would be the end of the world.

October 28th arrived. The exact time of the deadline occurred when I was in band practice. We were all in a state of fear and watchful waiting. We played our scales, we practiced our pieces (if they can be called pieces), and we watched the clock, with each passing minute expecting to be blown to smithereens. Being the sunny, eternal optimist that I am, I expected to die that morning. The clock's second hand kept sweeping, and the minutes dissolved. Nothing happened. The time of the deadline came and went. We kept playing. And, soon after that, Nikita Khrushchev capitulated and announced in Moscow that he was removing the nuclear missiles from Cuba.

No one at Westover Hills Elementary School died that day from a nuclear warhead landing on her head. Life returned to normal. More school, more baseball, more bike riding, more band. And, of course, more square-dancing.

5

The Magic Cadillac

IN 1963, I WAS TWELVE years old and still living in Richmond when my parents decided we (my parents, Becky, and I) would go to a Christian camp in New York's Adirondack Mountains. There was a ranch there for little kids and a conference center for adults.

My parents, who sponsored the high school youth group at church, mentioned it to others and eventually the news spread. Soon, other parents asked if their children could accompany us. My father, of course, agreed that they could come with us, but this presented a little problem. Besides the four of us in my family, thirteen more were going with us. Our travel party had swelled to seventeen strong. How would everyone get from Richmond to New York?

My father asked around about different possibilities, and someone suggested that we go in a Cadillac.

"A Cadillac? What do you mean 'a Cadillac?' There are seventeen of us. How will that work?" my father asked incredulously.

"Yes, a Cadillac. It will suit your needs perfectly. Here, call this number. I think he'll let you use it."

My father followed the lead and made the call. As promised, the Cadillac would function well as our mode of transport, and permission to use it was granted. We never expected to travel in such luxury.

It was a 1951 Cadillac. That had been a black hearse. That was now a "school bus" for a private school. And had been painted "school bus yellow" so it would look like a real "school bus."

The "school bus" looked like it had been hand-painted by the first-graders as part of their service project to the school. You could even see the brush strokes. It was a true *objet d'art*, at least in relative terms.

It could not have gotten any better than this.

Yes, our group of seventeen would travel the fifteen hours from Richmond to the Adirondacks in a yellow hearse. It was a Magic Cadillac.

People would see us coming. That was for sure.

Now, my father ordinarily has very good common sense. Something got him a little off kilter this time. I'm not sure what got into him. Did he have a brief lapse into temporary insanity? Had someone dared him to do this? Did he feel that his manly pride demanded he accept this challenge? Had someone thrown down the gauntlet? Had his good common sense been overwhelmed and overruled by the sense of adventure, the sense of going where no one had ever been before, the sense of discovery, the adrenaline rush that would be his when he arrived?

Why drive to New York in a yellow hearse packed with seventeen people? Because he *could*. Because New York was *there*. Maybe Dad wanted a place in *The Guinness Book of Records*. Maybe Dad was a secret extreme sports junkie.

I'm not sure why Dad did it.

Yes, I am.

Necessity. You may have met Necessity yourself. I know I have. Necessity is very demanding. He wants it his way and is never in the mood to compromise or negotiate. Necessity is rigid, kind of a control freak.

Necessity now demanded that my father take the hearse.

It was not pretty, it was not comfortable, and it was a little humiliating. But there was no other way to get all these kids to New York on a shoe-string budget.

The Magic Cadillac was well-equipped with first class and business class seating, as well as other amenities. Four of us would sit in the front seat, my parents on either end and two smallish kids in the center. This was first class.

Business class was in the rear, where in former glory days, caskets had traveled. No one had to ride "economy class," mainly since there *was* no "economy class." We rotated seats at every rest stop, thus enabling everyone to travel in both first class and business class at least part of the time. We were a very egalitarian bunch.

Business class seating consisted of two long benches, actually 2 x 12s going the length of the rear cabin. These were secured to the tracks previously used to slide caskets in and out of the compartment. It was extremely intelligent and creative repurposing, refurbishment, redesigning, and upfitting. Business class could easily accommodate thirteen in the coffin compartment. Passengers traveled comfortably face to face and knee to knee. Excuse me, did you say, "Thirteen in the coffin compartment?" "An unlucky number," you say? No. It was a Magic Cadillac. It was *not* unlucky.

Seatbelts? What seatbelts? Who needs seatbelts? "Unsafe," you say? No. I respectfully disagree. It was *not* unsafe. It was, after all, a Magic Cadillac

Our luggage compartment was a trailer hitched to the rear of the Magic Cadillac. We threatened any troublemakers with having to travel in the trailer. There were no takers.

As for the amenities … ah, well. Yes … the amenities. There were lots of amenities. The Magic Cadillac had a trailer hitch, windows that actually cranked up and down, an engine, a gas tank, and headlights. There may have been a radio, too. I'm not sure. If there was, I don't think it worked. All in all, we traveled in ostentatious luxury. It was, after all, a Cadillac. A Magic Cadillac.

We lacked cabin attendants, but one of the girls brought along a pitcher of Tang as part of the beverage service.

Everyone gathered at our home at 3:00 a.m. on Saturday, the day of departure. In the moon-glow, the Magic Cadillac was positively radiant and phosphorescent; it was unspeakably soul-stirring. My father strategically packed and stacked everyone's suitcase in the trailer. He is a master packer. All was secured, tied down, closed up, and ready to go.

We moved out by four o'clock. I was in the coffin compartment ... er ... I mean ... business class.

The Magic Cadillac was a rolling coffin. A yellow tube of sheet metal hurtling down the highway at top speeds of 55 mph. Containing seventeen victims.

Sometimes we went straight ahead and made good time. At other times, if the wind caught us just right we went sideways, which slowed us down a little.

We meandered northward. A few hours after departure we made our first stop, somewhere in Delaware. Everyone got out, stretched, used the restrooms, and ate breakfast. My father filled the tank with gas, and fed the hungry engine its quart of oil. The Magic Cadillac enjoyed its oil; every tank of gas required a quart of it. It didn't use the oil for lubrication as much as it used it for fuel. But, boy, did it use oil. And the oil-rich diet gave it a little indigestion.

As the day dawned, all of us began to realize how ridiculous we looked in a yellow hearse. The growing light made the yellow look more hideous, though the brush strokes gave it a "primitive art" kind of look. We briefly thought about wearing paper bags over our heads, but it was too hot.

Before we left the first pit stop, one of the ninth-grade girls emerged from the restroom, crying. A disaster of high order had just befallen her. The toilet had overflowed, and her shorts and undergarments were all wet with (how do I say this delicately?) *eau de toilette.*

Now, of course, as one might expect, her clean clothes were all in her suitcase in the trailer. And of course, she could not travel another twelve hours in wet, smelly clothes. So, my father patiently undid his packing and stacking, looking for her suitcase. And of course, as one might expect, it had been the first one in, and therefore, now, was the last one out. My father retrieved her suitcase, she changed her clothes, and my father repacked and restacked the suitcases in the trailer.

We finally got back in the hearse, and only with great difficulty was my father able to restart it. But start it he did, with great belches of smoke, and great blasts of what sounded like gunfire—from the indigestion. I noticed that several men hit the ground. The hearse backfired every time we began a new segment of the trip and every time my father turned it off. It was so bad that the service station attendants begged us to leave quickly so as not to scare off other customers who thought they might be in a war zone.

We finally made it to New York.

After dropping off the kids, with great relief, my parents drove to the conference center. It was dinnertime. Formal dinnertime. There were nicely dressed couples on the veranda, men in blue blazers and women in dresses. My father drove the circular driveway all the way to the main entrance of the lodge. As if staged by a Hollywood director, the Magic Cadillac emerged with great pomp from a cloud of black smoke and the din of firecrackers. The setting sun gave it a luminous glow. The couples on the porch just stared, mouths agape. As Dad parked the beautiful yellow hearse, everyone saw the black and white license tag and it all made sense to them. "Ohhh—they're from Virginia!" That explained everything. These were Southerners. *Southerners.* Of course, all Southerners drive old yellow hearses, especially when they travel to the Adirondacks. A yellow hearse is our preferred mode of transportation, our vehicle of choice. I experienced the same reaction when I later attended a northern college; when I said I was from Georgia, students wondered if we had indoor plumbing, if we still had cannons in our front yards, and whether I had ever worn shoes.

My father and mother got out of the Magic Cadillac, completely exhausted, both wearing shorts. My father was limping; he would have knee surgery just weeks after this trip. The beautiful people on the porch gawked at these refugees from the South. They were paralyzed with disbelief at the spectacle before them. They could not move, and they could not take their eyes off the Magic Cadillac.

Except for one person: Paul Johnson. Paul watched the proceedings from the porch and immediately admired the grit, guts, and determination he saw in my father. He wanted to meet this man. He descended the steps and stuck out his hand to shake my father's. And Paul Johnson invited my parents to dine with his wife and friends. It was the start of a long friendship that would span the next fifty years.

MEANWHILE, BACK AT THE RANCH, my little sister, Becky, always fun-loving and always fun, was having a ball. Becky somehow was always able to carry her party around with her, and life was always good. She loved camp. Not me. I was miserable. I hated camp. I was homesick all week. It was cold. Besides, my counselor didn't like me; he was more interested in body-building than his campers. I wanted to go home.

I didn't think I needed to bathe or shower there, it being so cold and all in the Adirondacks, and since I don't sweat much in cold weather. Swimming everyday in the icy lake would take care of my personal hygiene.

I fatally underestimated the pungent power of the apocrine gland in a pubescent boy.

I noticed after a few days that someone in our cabin really stunk. Because I'm a southern gentleman, I didn't want to accuse or embarrass any of these northern boys. They couldn't help it. But the smell was really getting to me.

Soon, though, I had a great realization. In the immortal words of that great southern philosopher, Pogo: "We have met the enemy, and he is us." In my case, the enemy was me. I was the stinker in the cabin.

I had a slight problem. I had gone through all my clean clothes by the time I realized the harsh truth about myself. All my clothes smelled like B.O.

What to do? Being the resourceful boy that I was, I hatched a plan. I would scrub my armpits and shower every day, use deodorant (a lot of it), and buy some new clothes at the trading post, well, actually only one new article of clothing. With five dollars, all the money I had, I bought a short-sleeved blue sweatshirt and studiously avoided sweating for the remainder of camp. I wore the sweatshirt every day. When my parents picked me up on the final Saturday, I was still wearing it, and I wore it home. I think it smelled fairly fresh.

When we piled into the Magic Cadillac for the homeward voyage, I was happy to see the old friend that would carry me back to Old Virginny. As we pulled out of the camp, the Magic Cadillac belched and backfired; its diet at the conference center had been far too rich. Newly arriving campers ran for cover. And fifteen hours later, we pulled into Richmond, safe and sound. It was nice to be home again.

What was so magical about the Magic Cadillac?

For one thing, how many Cadillacs do you know of that died as black hearses and then were reincarnated as yellow school buses? And later, as rolling coffins? The Magic Cadillac reinvented itself every few years.

For another, how many Cadillacs do you know that can transport, with style and class, seventeen people?

But, most importantly, how many Cadillacs do you know of that have birthed a fifty-year friendship?

Besides, if I had called this story "The Yellow Hearse," would you ever again take me seriously?

6

Coach Orr

NOBODY ADMITTED IT, but we all feared Coach Orr.

He was 6'1" and weighed 225 pounds, but in our eyes he was a full 6'5" and weighed 250. He was all muscle. He shaved his head long before it was stylish. He said very little; we thought it was natural gruffness, but I think it was really natural shyness. We heard that he was a former Marine drill sergeant, but no one knew for sure. Some called him Mr. Clean—just not to his face.

Coach Orr's mystique lay somewhere in the blurry region between reality and legend. To a bunch of scrawny fifteen-year-old boys, he was fearsomely awesome. We respected him and we wanted him to respect us. He never yelled at us, he never cussed at us, and I can't remember him even raising his voice. He didn't have to. We would have done anything for Coach Orr, mainly so he wouldn't think we were a bunch of pansies.

Tenth-grade physical education at Winter Park High School was a test of manliness. We had a choice. We could take regular tenth-grade boys' PE where you did the typical stuff: flag football followed by basketball followed by volleyball followed by softball. No sweat, no suffering, no gain. Just fun. And no self-respect.

Or we could take PE with Coach Orr. With Coach Orr, there was plenty of sweat and suffering. We all hoped there would be some gain. Real men, the guys who thought they had manly testosterone levels, took PE with Coach Orr. We all knew going in it would be hard, and we knew that he would work us. What we did not know was how hard. In Coach Orr's class, it was all conditioning. We lifted weights, and we did innumerable pull-ups and dips. We also had "Fun and Games" day periodically.

At the beginning of the year, he laid down the rules. Besides the obvious Rule Number One that we were to do exactly as he said (and be happy about it), there were only two other rules. Rule Number Two: To get an A in the course, you had to be able to lift as much or more than Coach Orr. We all resigned ourselves to getting a B at best—all except Wendall, that is, a misplaced senior in our class. Wendall looked like he had been shaving since he was seven years old. He was in a category all to himself. He could out-lift Coach, and the two became lifting partners.

Rule Number Three: To pass the first six-weeks, we had to complete the one-mile carry. Each of us paired up with another man (boy) in the class whose weight matched ours. So far, so good. Then, we were told that each of us, before the six-weeks ended, must carry his partner piggyback … for a mile … without putting him down … in forty-five minutes. Now, that might seem like an easy assignment. But if you think so, try it sometime. We practiced this drill several times a week. If you did it once, you could quit and you got your B. If you did not do it, you got your F.

My partner, John, and I were about the same size. For a few weeks, we attempted to do our mile carry and just couldn't get it done. Each time, about half way through, we were so sweaty and slippery in the blazingly hot September Florida sun that we couldn't hold on to each other. (Surprisingly, the main obstacle to our success was not the delightful aroma of our unwashed T-shirts with three weeks of sweat, mould and bacteria firmly embedded in the cotton fibers.) We finally hit upon an ingenious way to carry each other: the guy on top would drape his arms over the shoulders and chest of the carrier; the carrier would hook his arms beneath the thighs of the carried and then grasp his extended wrists. This worked pretty well for both of us. We were both able to do our mile. We passed.

Coach Orr did not take it very kindly when some of the boys hid in the woods at the end of the field until forty minutes had elapsed, then reappeared with a dramatic finish, huffing and puffing as if they had walked the whole mile instead of a fifth of the distance. I'm not sure what happened to these guys. Rumors of their untimely demise were likely not true, but I'm not sure I ever saw them again.

Once we had proven our manhood, we went on to doing serious lifting and conditioning. We worked out on the field outside the field house, though we also spent some time in the antiquated weight room inside. The field house was a pale-green stucco, just like the rest of the school, and it showed its age. Ironically, this was also where the "smoking bench" was. Yeah, that's right, the smoking bench. This was the designated area for the school's student-smokers. They were allowed to smoke on campus before school and during lunch. None of us real men smoked.

A lot of the guys worked out shirtless. A tenth-grade English classroom overlooked the field, and I think these guys wanted to give the girls a thrill. I always wore a shirt—the one that smelled so good.

Our workout regimen consisted of first climbing onto the ladder. The ladder was just what it sounds like: it was a steel ladder built parallel to the ground, similar (except for its heft) to the ones children on playgrounds use to "walk" across hand over hand. Here we did our pull-ups and dips. We did five types of pull-ups. We did dips without number. But simple pull-ups and dips were not enough, not for us; they were too easy. Coach Orr instructed us to tie ropes to twenty-five and fifty pound weights. While one man climbed onto the ladder and readied himself for dips, his partner looped the rope and weight around his feet and recorded how many up and down motions he could do. The girls in tenth-grade English loved to watch this one: whether from admiration or from hope that we would crash, I am not sure.

Of course, we did all the routine weight lifting: bench presses, military presses, cleans, curls, reverse curls, dead lifts, squats, and so on. We worked on our biceps, triceps, deltoids, lats, pecs, quads, hamstrings, and every other muscle not mentioned. We kept a record of our growing prowess as we worked out with our partners.

"Fun and Games Day" did not mean we played badminton. "Fun and Games" was a euphemism—Coach's quaint and ironic expression for whatever creative and inventive torture he had dreamed up the previous weekend. One of the favorites was to utilize the hill next to the field house. The hill was there—why not use it? It was the perfect place to grab your partner and wheelbarrow up and down it for forty-five minutes.

One day Coach Orr had something new for us. A deep-pocketed booster of Winter Park High School had bequeathed to us a gift of unspeakable value: a telephone pole. This was soon laid on the ground, and it became our sit-up pole. We began by doing sit-ups while sitting on the pole, our bodies perpendicular to it. This arrangement gave us an additional forty-five degrees of extension each time we went back and pounded our shoulder blades to the ground. Of course, we progressed and added weights. Most of us held a twenty-five to fifty-pound plate behind our heads as we went down and came back up. If you weren't careful, you would mash your fingers or give yourself a bad headache.

Coach Orr's class went on like this all school year. He showed us we could do much more than we thought. By June, we were still skinny kids, but we were muscular and well-conditioned skinny kids. We all had a certain respect for each other for sticking it out all year. And every one of us had a healthy self-respect.

So what was the point of the one-mile carry? How about all the other stuff? Was this all just a test of will or strength? Was

Coach Orr a mean-spirited, sadistic misanthrope? Was he trying to break us? What was in the back of Coach's mind?

One obvious answer is that Coach Orr wanted us to know the benefits of conditioning our bodies, a lesson he hoped we would carry with us all our lives. He wanted us to realize the greatness of the human body and what it could do, especially when well cared for over a lifetime. And this answer is a true one.

But as I grew older, I believed there may have been a deeper answer, possibly so deep that it was buried within Coach's subconscious thoughts, yet there just the same. This answer to all the questions was spelled out in just one word: Vietnam. Coach Orr was preparing his guys. He knew that at least some of us would wind up in the jungles of Vietnam. And that it was very likely that a few of us would have to carry a fallen buddy to safety.

He wanted us to know that we could do it.

NOTE: I am grateful to Coach Orr for allowing me to include this chapter about him. He actually was and is a Marine—once a Marine, always a Marine. During World War II he fought in the Pacific theater. He was called back up to active duty during the Korean War.

He is now a healthy and vigorous ninety years old. He still pumps iron and pushes his body three times each week in the gym. He is clear-minded and perceptive—a good example of someone whose life mirrors his words.

7

The Legend: Playing Near the Shadows of the NBA

I WAS BORN to play basketball.

I was twenty-four inches long at birth and weighed over ten pounds; my birth brought my mother and me close to death.

I ultimately grew to be 6'4" (almost).

My parents took me in utero and as an infant to Emory and Henry College basketball games. This early exposure gave me a sharp eye for the game, much like the Mozart effect in music.

When I was four years old, we lived in a little house just outside Appomattox, Virginia. We had a small, old, unpainted, wooden chicken-house in the backyard. Like a latter day James Naismith, my father nailed a bottomless half-bushel basket to the side of the chicken-house, and that was my first basketball goal. Small, unimpressive beginnings can portend great things.

Later, an elderly neighbor of ours in Norfolk looked at me, commented on my size as a six-year-old and predicted that I would become a good basketball player. I would be so big, she said, that I would not even have to jump to dunk the ball. I never forgot that comment. I knew I was destined for basketball greatness.

Between the ages of nine and twelve, I had a basketball goal in the backyard of every place we lived. It was a little tough to dribble on the back lawn with its hillocks and valleys, its grass and mud puddles, but it improved my ball handling skills. And it was here that I began to learn to shoot. My dad taught me the hook shot and two-hand set shot. I patiently honed my game, unobserved by the rest of the world.

In Orlando, Florida, I came into my own. As a thirteen-year-old, I played by the hour in our driveway; the goal was just above the garage. I usually played barefoot. My feet were tough, but I admit that it hurt when on occasion I came down from leaping for a rebound only to land on a pebble that had loosed itself from the pea-gravel normally confined to the flowerbed. Looking back, I would say that foot toughness is inversely proportional to common sense. I taught myself how to do a jump-shot. I was embarrassed to keep doing the two-hand set shot because none of the other guys were doing it. I began to teach myself how to shoot with my left hand; I began to do lots of things left handed just to train myself to use both hands playing ball. Later, I would shave with my left hand; the results were not always pretty, as I emerged from the bathroom with nicks and cuts, often with bits of toilet paper absorbing the blood. But, then again, I still can't shave, no matter what hand I use, so nothing was lost and much was gained.

In eighth grade, I got my first big chance. I played for Coach Dale K. Rider's Maitland Junior High School Golden Hawks. Coach Rider was the ideal first basketball coach. He knew the game. He stressed fundamentals and conditioning. And there was one more big thing about him: he loved us.

We loved Coach Rider because we knew he loved us.

Coach Rider was into body sculpting, way before it was chic. He was ahead of his time. He told us tales of childhood dissatisfaction with his own height. He and his twin brother had invented a stretching system using their beds whereby ropes attached to their legs and arms at night would predictably result in a future adult height of at least 6'5". (It was much like the rack of medieval times.)

It did not work; he was 5'11".

Coach Rider was also concerned that he might be a little overweight; he wore a dark-green nylon sweatsuit during our PE periods so he could lose weight. He lost a lot through sweating in the Central Florida oven, but he only lost water and electrolytes.

It did not work.

But what did work was his love for all his little junior high basketball players. He decided to go with a no-cut policy for his junior varsity team (seventh and eighth graders). We had twenty-five guys on the team. We evoked terror in the hearts of our opponents when we ran out of the locker room to begin our warm-ups: twenty-five boys running out of the locker room onto the hardwood gym floor, arranged from tallest to shortest. It was a never-ending circle. It took a long time for us to get the whole team out of the locker room and onto the court. By the time we finally got around to warming up, the buzzer usually had sounded for game time.

We practiced in the Winter Park High School gym for an hour each weekday. We shared court time with the high school players, another junior high team, and the Rollins College team. I still remember the drab-green locker room, the locked gym baskets stacked five high, and most of all, the delicate composite aroma of sweat, mildew, sour towels, and liniment.

Occasionally, we practiced outside on the asphalt court near our school locker room. Afterwards, mature junior high boys got into the eighteen head common shower room and used the floor as a Slip 'N Slide.

Rick Barry of the University of Miami led the nation in scoring that season. He rarely missed a free throw. His technique? The granny shot. That's correct—he shot his free throws grasping the ball with both hands and beginning his shot from between his knees. Coach thought that if it was good enough for the nation's leading scorer, it was good enough for eighth-grade boys. And so it was that all season long, every Maitland Golden Hawk JV basketball player shot free throws granny style. It was required, and we followed orders. We all abandoned that method the next season.

Coach Rider tried to play all the boys at least a little. We knew that only fifteen would make the varsity team the next year, but it was nice knowing that we were official ballplayers for now.

One slight disadvantage to having such a large squad of sweaty, grubby junior high boys was that we had a uniform issue. We were fine as long as we played in our red uniforms. But there were some times when the opposing team wore red. No problem. We had gold jerseys to go with our red shorts. But we only had ten gold jerseys. What to do? Also, no problem. Coach Rider had it all figured out. When Coach went deep into his extraordinarily deep bench, anyone deeper than tenth man on the team participated in an unusual drill. As he entered the game, he simply traded jerseys with the guy he was replacing. The guy coming out of the game was rewarded with a fairly clean red jersey, and the guy going into the game was rewarded with a soppy, sweaty, stinking gold jersey. And when the substitute came out of the game, he and the starter would again exchange jerseys. We changed our jerseys right there on the bench. This whole process was much better entertainment than the game, and the crowd loved it. It also drove the scoring table crazy.

I almost forgot Charlie. He always sat at the end of the bench. One of the parents asked us why he never took off his warm-up jacket. I'm glad she asked that question. It was a good question, but it never occurred to us to ask it. The answer was obvious: Charlie had no jersey at all, not even a red one. So, Charlie always had to use someone else's jersey, whether red or gold, if he ever entered the game. Having a team of twenty-five boys did have its downside.

I worked hard on my game during the summer between eighth and ninth grades. I made the varsity team and wound up being a starter. I loved it. I loved being able to play basketball better than my friends. I loved beating other guys in one-on-one situations, either overpowering them or faking them out. I loved the physicality of the game, especially rebounding.

I also loved the adulation.

Our first game of the year was like a dream even as I played it. I was scared stiff. It is intimidating to get out in front of your friends as you play an opponent who wants to beat you as much as you want to beat him. Somehow I scored eleven points and was high scorer for my team. I went to bed that Saturday night completely happy. I looked forward to the next morning and could not wait to see the box score in the Sunday newspaper. And *The Orlando Sentinel* did not disappoint. There it was, a three-line article with a box score in microscopic print, alerting the world that I had done something great the night before.

I tried to act humble at church that day.

We had a good season. Several times, Coach Rider took us to Steak 'n Shake after games, I am sure at his own expense. One game, he could not accompany us, and our substitute coach decided to bring his ninth grade daughter on the bus with us to an away game. That was a bad idea. In the raucous celebration after we won, the bus ride home was rampant with male adolescent humor. We had forgotten that a female was on board. The interim coach finally stood up with a red face and yelled at us about how we should act like gentlemen.

COACH RIDER LOVED winning, and after we had won three or four games in a row, he became as giddy as a little kid on the bus rides home. After a long winning streak culminating in a tough win, he taught us a new cheer on the way home. Coach was from Michigan, and I guess they did corny cheers there when he was growing up. But, here he was, standing at the front of the bus, teaching his varsity and JV junior high basketball teams the corniest cheer you have ever heard. We were cool teenagers. "Are you kidding, Coach?" we thought to ourselves. But soon, we were following his lead and we loved it. Soon, we were doing the "boom-chick-a-boom" cheer after games. It became our trademark. Our cheerleaders adopted it and used it often during our games. It was our school's signature cheer.

My good friend Wayne Kerr and I developed the flu (the real thing—influenza) late in the season, just before our last game. Wayne had befriended me soon after my move from Richmond in seventh grade, and had been my loyal *compadre* ever since. He had taught me all about DNA and RNA when I had never even heard of them. He had made sure my ridiculous seventh-grade science fair project on clocks was nominated to go to the school-wide science fair, much to the consternation of our teacher who recognized a dud when she saw it. (Wayne's projects always went to the state science fair, and he usually won.) He and I had run against each other for junior high student body president; he had shellacked me, and yet, our friendship had survived the election. In addition, we were both renaissance men, as proven by the fact that we had been in band together, he on trombone, and I on baritone.

So, Wayne Kerr and I had been through a lot together, and now we had the flu. Together. We were both starters for the team; we were the twin towers. The afternoon before the last game, our team practiced in the cold, half-darkened Winter Park High School gym, Wayne and I with fever and chills, coughing and achey, running through plays at half speed. The next night, we were barely able to play, but play we did—both of us with fever—and we won. It was a great game that came down to the buzzer. We exited the post-season tournament quickly, however, losing in our first game. I knew something was wrong with me then: as we came out of the locker room after halftime, I barely had the strength to run, and I had no energy to warm up at all. I could not get my arms above my waist to shoot. I was exhausted.

I began having night sweats and could hardly practice as

basketball season seamlessly turned into baseball season. I could not understand why I was unable to keep up with my teammates on the baseball field.

The reason soon became clear: I had developed a secondary pneumonia and wound up in the hospital for four or five days. There, my youth pastor visited me and smuggled junk food to me, notably real hamburgers and fries. While hospitalized, I sold my baseball cleats to a friend; no longer would I enjoy the clicking sound they made as we walked on pavement to the field for games. Thus ended my illustrious baseball career—with a whimper.

Football: A Lost Opportunity

I made a brief foray into football as a sophomore at Winter Park High School. As a little kid, I had played catch with my father and we had developed many passing patterns and routes over the years; he was Johnny Unitas to my Raymond Berry. I was not very fast, but I had good hands, and he often threw the ball over my shoulder as I sprinted (or, to be truthful, lumbered) down the sideline en route to an imaginary touchdown.

Since I was 6'4" (almost), I knew I owed it to the team and the school to be their primo wide receiver.

We began two-a-days in the Central Florida August heat. We ran only drills the first week, but it was brutal. Water breaks were rare and only for weaklings anyway, and since we were tough, we had only a few gulps of water all morning. At the end of the first practice, I vomited after the tenth windsprint, but I was not the first or last that morning to reveal to all what had been breakfast a few hours earlier. I guessed this was a team-building exercise, a way to get us to bond.

I noticed some of the veteran players getting some pills after practice and heard that they were salt and dextrose tablets to improve their performance. I knew salt was okay but I didn't know what dextrose was; I figured it must be similar to Dexedrine, so I avoided it. I had heard about drug use in sports, and "dexies" in particular. I wanted no part of performance-enhancing drugs. Later, I found that dextrose was sugar, so I tried a few salt and dextrose tablets without any noticeable effect. It was all unsupervised, and we received no instruction on why or how to use these medications.

I enjoyed riding home from practice with my tenth-grade friends; since none of us could drive, our mothers took turns carpooling us to and from practice. We nursed our aches and pains to the sounds of the latest Beach Boys, Beatles, Donavan, and Kinks songs. I didn't like the rides to practice nearly as much.

We finally got around to skills and positions. Our head coach was also our school's track coach, and he therefore placed a high value on speed. Speed was never one of my vices, but I was not worried; I knew my hands would carry the day. One of our coaches was a genius in discerning our skill-sets. He gathered all the would-be receivers and quickly realized he had far too many. He easily weeded out the non-receivers. Each of us went out for a pass. A successful reception kept you on as a receiver. Failure to catch the ball sent you to the line. Brilliant.

I caught his pass without any difficulty and trotted back to the group, feeling exuberantly confident. But there were still too many receivers; somebody had to go. The survivors went out for a second pass. My turn came, and he heaved it over my head; not even Ray Berry could have touched it. I was demoted immediately to the interior line.

Did I mention that I was 6'4" (almost)? And that I weighed 165 pounds?

I was beginning to feel that my skills were unappreciated. Practice uniforms were handed out, and by the time they got to me, the only helmets left were leather. "Leather?" I thought, "Oh, this is a joke. I get it. I can take a joke." It was not a joke. I had never even *seen* a leather helmet. It must have been a Jim Thorpe autograph model. I thought they had hauled it out of the Winter Park museum. It was so old that I was afraid to touch it, thinking it must be a valuable antique. I saw it had no face-mask but they told me not to worry; they would attach one later.

There I was as a tackle—in my leather helmet. I was third string on the varsity depth chart—for about fifteen minutes. The first drill involved Coach Orr's telephone pole lying on the ground. Coach Orr was our line coach. One of the linemen stood at the end in a box painted on the turf. Another ran down the length of the pole, feet churning on either side, and hit the guy in the box as hard as he could. Almost immediately, a man in the box broke his femur. We hauled him off, and we went on. Coach Orr instructed us to run hard and stay low as we ran down the pole. I guess I didn't hear the "stay low" part, and as I got to the end of my attacking run, I rose up and the big guy in the box crushed me.

I lasted until a few weeks into the start of school and finally put away my dreams of being Raymond Berry II. I told my coach I was quitting. He didn't seem too disappointed. Winter Park High never knew what they were missing.

I waited for basketball season.

Basketball: Again

My tenth-grade basketball experience at Winter Park High School was almost as bad as my brief football career, and it was not noteworthy—not at all. Our junior varsity coach lost control of the team early in the season and I was glad when, mercifully, it was over. Early in the season, I showed up for practice and found that my basketball shoes were gone—stolen. I asked around, and found that one of the varsity guys had forgotten his shoes and had conveniently liberated mine from my gym basket. I walked into the gym in my socks, and sure enough, my shoes were on the feet of another player. I walked up to him and asked him what in the world he thought he was doing. He smiled and told me the story, suggesting that he wear them until his practice was over, and then turn them over to me. It was not a fight worth having, so I went along with him. He returned the shoes, and I wore them the rest of the year without sharing them.

I MOVED to Virginia Beach, Virginia for eleventh grade and attended Princess Anne High School. I had lived here twice before for a total of four years, and would know at least a few of the students I used to go to elementary school with.

I loved Princess Anne High School. I was proud to attend PA. It was the largest high school in Virginia at the time with about 2,800 students.

These were heady times for American basketball. The Boston Celtics were the reigning NBA dynasty. I never tired of watching Bill Russell, Bob Cousy, John Havlicek, Don Nelson and Bailey Howell play on TV on the Boston Garden's parquet floor. John Wooden was in his prime at UCLA, winning ten national collegiate championships and, during one stretch, winning eighty-eight straight games. Lew Alcindor (later Kareem Abdul-Jabbar) was the UCLA center. Elvin Hayes played at Houston. In my mind, basketball was *the* game, and I was happy to be a part of it.

I was always reserved and introverted and had to be pushed often to do things, especially in new situations. My mother pushed me go to the Princess Anne gym that summer before school started to see if there were any of the basketball guys hanging around. There were. I played an hour or so with them and shot the ball better than I ever had up until that point. Everything went in, no matter how far or how difficult. I could not miss from anywhere on the court. I casually acted as if this were my normal game. I forgot to mention to the guys that I was not usually that good. They believed they were experiencing the second coming of Bill Bradley. It was not to be.

Basketball tryouts went pretty well. The first day we spent a lot of time doing suicides. For the uninitiated, suicides are like wind sprints, only worse. You stand at the end of the court at the baseline, the coach blows the whistle, and you run to the free throw line, bend and touch it, then run back to the baseline and touch it. Then, you run to the halfcourt line, touch it, and run back to the baseline. From there, you go to the far end's free throw line, and then back to the baseline. Finally, you sprint to the end of the court and back. I think that's why they call it a suicide. We did suicides over and over again. Guys throw up, some pass out, some give up. Coaches use suicides for at least three reasons: 1) to assess conditioning 2) to assist in conditioning 3) to weed out the guys who only *say* they want to be basketball players. The main idea the first few days is to have a bunch of guys quit so the coach can deal with the serious players.

Tryouts went pretty well, that is, until the football players finished their season by winning the state championship. Then, the school's great athletes came to practice—the great football players were also great basketball players. Bob German, Jack Spence, Bob Gerloff, and others suddenly appeared at practice. Gene Alley and Mike McCully, friends from my fifth-grade class, were trying out as well, and they ultimately made the team. Our coach had several cuts. Lots of guys went out for the PA team, and only a few would make it. Each week we went to the bulletin board outside the coach's office to see if we were still a part of the team. It took courage to finally look at the typed names and hope to find yours there. I survived until the very end. Then, the coach brought two of us, Jimmy and me, into his office. We were the number fifteen and sixteen men on the team, he told us, and he could not decide whom to keep; so, he was keeping us both. I was relieved. There was one trivial problem, however: there were only uniforms for fifteen players ("I've seen this movie before," I thought). His solution: he would let us alternate. I would dress out one game, and Jimmy would dress out the next game. I was selected to dress the first game. I was thrilled. Jimmy, not so much. I think our coach was hoping one of us would quit.

Immediately thereafter, Coach walked me into the supply closet and told me to try on a navy-blue blazer with a "PA" patch on the left breast pocket. I found one that fit and took it home, happy to be wearing it to school the next day before the game. In those days, athletes wore a coat and tie to school on game day, then arrived at the gym later that evening dressed the same way. It was a way of showing unity, honoring our school, and giving due dignity to the game.

I remember my excitement in walking into my home that evening with my official PA blazer. It was a happy day, and I was grateful to God that I had made the team. I had arrived.

I went to school the next day and happily received congratulations on making the team from my friends or new admirers; the PA blazer made it obvious to all that I was somebody.

I went to the game that night and watched the junior varsity guys play their game until halftime. The job of the varsity players on home game nights was to stroll casually into the gym, a little after the JV game had started, with our PA gym bags slung over our shoulders; then, we were to lounge around on several rows of bleachers, cheer for the JV team, and basically act cool. We were good at the last thing.

After the JV halftime, we strode into the locker room to get dressed. I was surprised: this was a very high-class school. Each player was given his clean uniform (including socks), a warm up shirt, *and* a red or white long-sleeved sweatsuit. This was living. We ran onto the floor as we warmed up looking like red or white snowmen, depending on the occasion. I quickly learned that the starters were the starters, and guys like me were only there for show and to rebound for the starters during warm-ups. I was just a schmoe. One hazard of warm-ups was the steady stream of balls heading for the basket; I had to be careful not to get bloodied. Those of us on third string (or worse, in my case) had our own competition to see how many points we could score during warm-ups, it being unlikely that we would score many in actual competition.

I think we won that first game. I am sure that I did not play.

I think we won our second game. I am sure I did not play. However, by that time Jimmy had decided he did not believe in uniform timesharing, and he had quit. Coach was ecstatic that he was now down to fifteen men (and didn't have to make a decision about cutting someone else) and I was ecstatic that I was officially the number fifteen man on the team. I would bide my time patiently; patience is one of my primary virtues.

The third game was a home game, and it was a blowout for our team. We won by twenty or thirty points. I thought, "Surely now is my time." Coach began substituting five guys at a time. I kept waiting for my call. The clock ticked down: eighty-nine seconds left in the game. I heard Coach call, "Miller!" Now was my time to shine, my big chance on the big stage. I'd show them what I could do. I threw off my warm-up shirt and ran to the scorers' table where I crouched until the next time-out. I finally got in the game. Nine seconds later one of my teammates came in to replace me. I had touched the ball once. I felt humiliated, betrayed, and angry. I sat down and went to the locker room as soon as the game was over. I took the world's fastest shower and got out of there, pronto. I went straight home.

Walking into my home, I let my frustration out. I ripped off my beloved navy-blue PA blazer and threw it to the floor. My parents and sister tried to encourage me, but I was livid with rage. I could not believe the coach would subject me to playing for nine seconds in a game in which even I could do no harm to the final score. My pride was deeply wounded. How could I face my friends?

I finally simmered down. I became patient again. As I said, patience is one of my greatest virtues. Just ask my friends and family.

So, I waited.

As the season progressed, I endured the humiliating questions at church from well-meaning friends who had seen in the newspaper that C. Miller had scored thirteen or fifteen or twenty-two points in last night's game. "Is that you?" they asked. "No," I said with embarrassment, "that's another Miller on the team. He's the real player; I'm just the fifteenth man. I didn't get in the game." I also endured the lack of any feedback at all from my friends at school—what do you say to a guy who never plays? "Great warm-up!" or "You were the best guy on the bench last night!" somehow doesn't sound quite right as a compliment.

Finally, something happened. We had not been playing well for several games, and then we lost a close game in the last few seconds. We should have killed this team. We had some great players on our team, and I had to admit, they were better than I was. Bob German, in particular, was an amazingly gifted athlete. We were a big team. I was, at 6'4" (almost), one of the little guys on the team. The team picture shows me on the front row kneeling with the small guys; our team had some size. But, here we were, not playing nearly as well as we should have been. We had size and we had skills. But we were not winning.

It was time for a big shakeup.

At Monday's practice, Coach walked in and announced that he was changing things. Everyone's job was up for grabs. He would try various combinations of players until he found the right mix. At practice, he put me with the starting five, I guess for shock value. I did pretty well. Bob German had befriended me earlier in the season, and he kept encouraging me.

I sprained my ankle badly in practice on Tuesday but didn't tell anyone. Very likely, in retrospect, it was fractured. It was colorfully bruised and grapefruit size. I had the student trainer tape it and I kept practicing. And I kept quiet about it. It hurt to walk and play, but I tried not to limp. I was not about to let my big chance slip away.

During Thursday's game, things were going only fairly well. Coach called my name: "Miller, get in there!" I looked around to be sure he was talking to me and not the real Miller. But he was looking right at me. I ran to the scorers' table and checked in. Very soon, I was taking down an offensive rebound and putting it back in. In all I had five points that game, and I felt I was finally playing some real basketball. I was no longer ashamed. We won the game, and things began to turn around for our team and for me. I became the sixth or seventh man on the team, the first or second off the bench, and had a fantastic season considering my inauspicious beginning. In my grandiose way of seeing life, I became the John Havlicek of the Princess Anne Cavaliers.

We wound up going to the regional championships but lost in the first round, finishing in the top sixteen in the state. God gave me the gift of allowing me to play well in that last game, scoring a few points in the last meaningless minutes of a bad loss for us. Still, I was playing and I was happy. God even gave me a bonus gift the next day: the Sunday sports section of *The Virginian-Pilot* (the Norfolk area newspaper) ran a big picture of me shooting the ball. Who knows if I made the shot or not? I guess they needed a photo of someone, anybody, even me, to verify that their reporter had really been there. They randomly chose me. I was stoked. I was ready for my senior year.

Only one thing remained for my junior year. I needed to get a letter. Boy, I really needed to letter. Not the kind that you write to your friends. No, I needed the big red and blue PA letter to wear on a white sweater to proclaim to the world that I was for real. The problem was this: the other players told me that in order to letter, a player had to have played in half of all quarters for the season. I had not done that. I created endless solutions and concocted elaborate schemes in my mind for how our coach could justify giving me a letter. I figured if he added my quarters played and my points scored, that new total would surely merit a letter for me. Or maybe they could come up with some other weird formula just for me. Maybe the coach would simply be merciful to me. I prayed a lot about it and asked God to grant this gift to me. It really bothered me. I needed that letter for my senior year.

Awards day arrived the last day of school. I went to the gym with all the other kids; it was not air-conditioned, it was packed, and it was steaming hot. I remember exactly where I sat. I could not stand the suspense. They gave out all the academic awards. They gave out all the awards to the state champion football team, the girls' field hockey team, the golf team and so on. Then they got to the good stuff—the boys' basketball team. Our coach began handing out stars for guys who had previously lettered in basketball. Then he began handing out letters for first time letter earners. I could barely contain myself. At last, I heard my name called out, and as if dreaming, I walked down the bleachers to the center of the gym and received the cherished letter. "Thank you, God," I thought. I'm sure my friends were clapping for me, but I did not hear. I went back to my seat in my fugue-like state and sat down. Hold on—was that my name being announced again? I had already been given one letter, and I wasn't greedy. One was enough. Yes, they announced my name again. I couldn't tell what it was for, but as if in a trance, I went back down. Awaiting my arrival was a large blue and silver trophy. "Uh-oh," I thought, "this must be for the other Miller, the real one." How embarrassing—I had shown up for another guy's award. But no, it was really for me. I was named the team's most improved player. God was giving me much more than I had asked for. I went home as happy as I had ever been. My parents had been at the awards assembly to see me receive my letter, having been invited in a very general communication to come to see their son "receive an award." They had left the sweltering gym after the letter presentation, not knowing about the trophy, and thus, had missed that award. They were as surprised and elated as I was about the double gift that day.

I positively loved wearing my letter sweater and my varsity club jacket. The PA letter was a thing of beauty, worn on a white sweater, the big red and blue PA on the left side. The varsity club jacket was all red wool, and on the left chest was sewn a blue and white round PA patch; the jacket was even reversible so that I could wear it in the rain by turning it inside out. (The designer had been a genius.) Mike McCully and I spent an entire Saturday afternoon in September finding the only athletic supply store in Norfolk that sold these jackets. The effort, time, and money were well worth it. My mother sewed the patch on it for me while she was recovering in the hospital from serious lumbar spine surgery.

I wore my letter sweater the first chance I had, which was to PA's first football game of my senior year. Despite the heat and humidity of a Tidewater fall, I wore that sweater. I don't remember how hot I was or how sweaty I got. (I am certain that my date noticed and probably wondered to herself, "What kind of moron is this guy?") I only remember being proud to be a letterman at PA. I would have worn that sweater during the summer if I could have done it without looking ridiculous.

My senior year was a year of change. Our coach retired from coaching, and we had a new coach, a young guy named Leo Anthony who had had a stellar All-American college career at Old Dominion College (now University) and a successful coaching career at an archrival across town. Coach Anthony had played for and coached with already-mythical college coach Lefty Driesell. He was serious about basketball and gave us a summer workout schedule which I adhered to assiduously. I spent many hours at night skipping rope with work boots on. I ran around the neighborhood. (I still hate to run.) I learned new drills and new moves. Our new coach involved us in summer ball at our gym and arranged for a few of us to play unofficially at the Old Dominion gym with college players. Earl "The Pearl" Monroe of the Baltimore Bullets came to our gym that summer for a clinic. What a ball handler! Once official practice started, we scrimmaged with a local Navy team; these were men who had played high school or college ball and now played for the Navy in Norfolk. They routed us; the competition was good for us, though. We scrimmaged a local college team and won.

Coach Anthony exuded cool. He had long sideburns. Soon, all of us had long sideburns. He began to give us Gatorade at games. Gatorade was a new product, and before this, our coaches had given us slices of oranges at halftime. We got new home uniforms, white double-knit with surfing stripes. We had a new warm-up ball (straight from the ABA?) that was red, white, and blue, our school colors. We wore black, low-top Chuck Taylors, just like the Celtics.

All we needed was to win a few games.

We had a good team, and we had high expectations. I was somehow elected co-captain, along with Skeeter Whitlow, our lightning-quick point guard. Our center was 6'9" Ernie Seiderman: "Big E." Ricky Michaelsen, our leading scorer, and Don Maskell completed our starting five. Don Maskell and I had sharpened our skills by playing one-on-one many hours at "Miller Stadium," our affectionate name for my driveway and home basketball goal. We had a deep bench with guys like Gene Alley, Mike McCully, Rudy Tucker, and of course, burly Bob Gerloff.

I lost my starting job for a few weeks over Christmas break because of poor play but was able to win it back soon. I was loving being a basketball player at Princess Anne High School, a member of a winning team. I loved everything about it. I even loved practicing over Christmas break early in the morning so we could have the rest of our day free. I loved shooting free throws at practice for a six-pack of Cokes. I loved driving my little VW bug home from games. I had some breakout games in which I was the star, but I was never a real star player—I was simply a solid, aggressive, physical high school basketball player, a team player.

My aggressive play on the court led to my having a lot of fouls called on me. I went hard for the ball, and I was not afraid of getting hurt. I loved to bang around under the basket going for rebounds, and I loved to go after loose balls on the floor. What can I say? If you play hard, and you play aggressively, you will get a lot of fouls, right? So fouls were a badge of honor. If I didn't get at least a few fouls called on me each game, I wasn't really playing—or so I thought.

Coach Anthony also had a name for the source of my foul trouble, and it was not aggressive play. He called it "clumsiness." Yes. Clumsiness!!! He threatened me with forced ballet lessons to improve my agility and grace on the court. I have never aspired to becoming a *danseur*, and now I suddenly had great incentive to ramp up my agility. I improved quickly, and by the end of the season, I was able to play both with powerful abandon and without silly, unnecessary fouls. I was positively balletic. I was a genuine gazelle—almost.

Our team was considered a contender for the district title, and as we unreeled victory after victory, we began to play like contenders. Deep into the season, we knocked off two previously undefeated teams. In one of these games, we shot 100 percent from the floor in the first half. We were rolling.

In January, my father was transferred to Atlanta. Because my father himself had experienced a move during his senior year of high school, my parents allowed me to remain in Virginia Beach with close friends, the Bungards, to finish my senior year. It was especially important to me that I finish out the basketball season.

Thus, my father, mother, and Becky all would move to Atlanta as I stayed behind. I would miss my biggest fans, the ones who loved me the most. I would miss my father's trenchant game analysis and my mother's completely biased favoritism. And I would miss my little sister. Becky was always and has continued to be the ultimate little sister: loyal to a fault and proud of her big brother. She remains one of the few people on earth who can really understand me; this may be a dubious distinction, but I am grateful she does.

The Bungards allowed me to become part of their family for a few months, and Libby and Clif, their two children still at home, adopted me as their brother. I was even adopted by their wonderdog, Pepper. They were all very good to me. They took care of me, and in exchange, I taught Clif the fine art of choosing pretty girls to date, using the PA yearbook as our only resource.

The Friday night before my family moved, we played and lost to a team we should have easily manhandled. As my parents and sister watched, I played one of my worst games of the season. I had wanted to give them a parting gift, but I was disappointed. I think my parents were very sad over our impending separation. We spent the night together at a motel and there my father and I dissected the game as we always did. Early the next morning, I drove my family to the airport and saw them off to Georgia. Afterwards, I hopped into my VW, stopped at Krispy Kreme for breakfast to drown my sorrows, and moved in with the Bungards.

After my family moved, our team recovered from the surprising loss and regained our previous high level of play. One of our last games was against our cross-town rival, the Maury Commodores. It was a big game, and we played at the Norfolk Arena to accommodate the crowd. We lost the game as they ran away from us in the second half. A fight erupted in the final minutes, and it turned into a bench-clearing brawl. Unchecked emotions ruled when one of the Maury players was injured in some rough play. Coaches exchanged angry words, and Leo Anthony stood up for his players, as always. As Coach Anthony appeared to lose the argument, cheers went up from the Maury side. Coach returned to our bench and told Bob Gerloff to go into the game. Bob was 6'4" (really, not almost) and weighed 240 pounds (again, really, not almost). He was a high school All-American football player who just happened to be an excellent basketball player, as well. Bob tore off his warm-up shirt and tossed it high into the air. A roar of cheers rose from the Princess Anne side of the arena. As soon as Bob entered the game, one of the Maury star players flagrantly gave him an elbow under the basket. Bob turned to him and said, "Don't do that again!"

Running down the court, the Maury player shoved Bob. And Bob Gerloff turned around and clocked him. As he went down, players and fans ran onto the court. Bedlam ensued. I don't remember what I did except that I know I raced to the aid of my teammates and was later told that I landed a good blow to the head of one of the Maury players. I guess adrenaline is strong stuff—you know, fight and flight. As the buzzer sounded, Coach Anthony quickly herded us into the dressing room, and we waited for a safe exit strategy. We finally left the arena escorted to our team bus between two lines of policemen and their German shepherds.

The district tournament began, and we were to play a team we had already beaten twice. They would be a pushover. My parents made plans to fly up for the weekend games, hoping to see our team win the district tournament or at least qualify for the regional tournament.

We arrived at the Norfolk Arena later than planned for the first round game and had to rush to get dressed and ready for the game. I hate to rush; it's bad for me psychologically. I'm not sure we even had time to say the Lord's Prayer together. One other disconcerting thing happened to me in the locker room. I was talking to Tony, our selfless trainer, about nothing important. He then turned to me and said, "Jerry, my name is Jon. You've been calling me Tony all year, and I just thought I should tell you. Please call me Jon." I apologized and felt like a dummy. It was the start of a bad night.

We lost the game 68-66. I played poorly, scoring an anemic seven points. I called my parents from the arena and told them we had lost. My senior season was over. Just like that. No farewell tours. No parties. It was over. I thought I would never play competitive basketball again, despite a little very vague encouragement from a couple of college coaches. (Lefty Driesell had sent me a letter, as I am sure he did to all men who were applying to Davidson College and who met the stringent criterion of having seen a basketball at least once.)

THE LEGEND | 69

Stoked on Surfing

Virginia Beach was one of the best places to surf on the east coast; they even held the East Coast Surfing Championships there. Lots of my friends were surfers, at least one of them having "surfing knots" on his knees from knee paddling. I was really impressed with him; surfing knots were like the ultimate symbol that you had arrived as a true surfer, a badge of honor. They were boney knots just below the knees. Only one thing: they are not surfing knots at all, but something called Osgood-Schlatter's disease, a benign cause of knee knots, usually in teenage boys. Anyway, Virginia Beach was a great place to surf, and there were plenty of guys who did it. Of course, there were also poseurs who bought racks for their cars, or even a board to go along the racks, and then cruised the area looking like they were the real thing, I guess hoping to impress the girls. They never got their boards off the car.

I was determined to become a real surfer. I had surfed before, but now I bought a surfboard from a friend for forty-five dollars. It was a ten-foot Hobie, a Gary Propper model. I became a surfer for the next few months before I graduated. I hot-waxed my board by melting paraffin and painting it on. (For those of you in Iowa, wax goes on the top so you can gain a little traction, not on the bottom to make the board go faster.) It was a good thing I had a VW bug with a sunroof. Since I was a non-traditionalist (and a fiscal conservative), I did without surfboard racks. I took my board to the beach by sticking the nose in the far back reaches of the bug, letting three feet of the board and the skeg hang out the front through the sunroof, and tying it in to a front seat grab-bar. Clif Bungard sat in the back and held onto the board and rope. We became airborne a few times as we cruised Virginia Beach Boulevard at 55 mph.

The maiden voyage occurred in late April, early on a Saturday morning so as not to embarrass myself or hurt anyone. The sun was out, but the water was cold. Really cold. Of course, being a non-traditionalist, I would never think of wearing a wetsuit. So, I didn't. I paddled out beyond the whitewater and looked for a wave. I was so cold that when it came, I could not hold onto the board to get up. I was blue, and I was numb. I had to get out. I got to the beach, wrapped up in a blanket and tried again fifteen minutes later. Same story. I tried three or four times without success and finally went home, doing wheelies when the wind caught the board just right. But, despite my failure, I was a real surfer. No one could dispute the fact, since no had seen me except Clif, and he was not talking.

My surfing ability improved. Sometimes I went surfing after school. It was a great life. That spring I also worked at Sears as a salesman, ten to twelve hours per week, usually evenings. Since they couldn't figure out what else to do with me, they naturally placed me in the drapery department, that being my area of expertise. It made perfect sense. I don't think I messed up too many blinds as I cut them for customers. Sometimes I showed up for work just after an afternoon of surfing. Once, I served a nice lady who asked me for some curtains on a lower shelf. As I bent down to retrieve them, a flood of water came rushing out of my nose onto the plastic-wrapped curtains. I had spent more time that afternoon under water than on top, and had taken a good deal of water into my sinuses, now flooding the merchandise. I did my best to act as if nothing had happened, and I don't think she noticed. Or maybe she just thought I had severe allergies.

Graduation

I pretty much checked out of studying the last month or so of my senior year. My place in the history of Princess Anne High School was assured: I had become The Legend by now—in my own mind. (Just ask anyone there now if they know my name.)

I hardly studied at all for my physics exam, and it showed—I bombed it, but passed the course. I wasn't too upset about it until I saw the pained and disappointed expression on my physics teacher's face at the commencement exercises.

I was designated to give an address at commencement. I wanted to include in it this verse from Philippians: "For me to live is Christ, and to die is gain" (Philippians 1:21). One of the teachers broke out in hives over this, and he did me the great favor of toning it down for me. He re-wrote my speech into an unrecognizable mass of words with ridiculous drivel like "as we all drift down the river of life" and so on—the usual graduation nonsense—very inspirational. I stood my ground, and the teacher kicked the problem upstairs to administration who also said "No" to my version; they still wanted me to talk about the river of life. Eventually an administrator of Virginia Beach schools ruled on my case and gave the same answer: I could not give my speech as written. My family arrived in town for the graduation, and my father, a very persuasive man, discussed the situation at length with the administrator at the Virginia Beach schools office. Still "No." I was ready to cave, but my father encouraged me to stand fast. I did. If I couldn't give the speech I had written, I would give no speech at all. And so, on graduation night in the Princess Anne football stadium, not a word was heard from The Legend. I had my two-page typed speech in hand (just in case someone had a change of heart) as we sat down in alphabetical order. As usual, my good friend from fifth grade onward was seated next to me, as she almost always was in these alphabetical affairs. She acted confused as it came time for me to walk to the rostrum and address the crowd because I just sat there, the program progressing without any explanation despite my name appearing in the printed order of events. She leaned over and whispered to me, "What is going on?" I handed her my crumpled speech. She read it and perceived immediately what had just transpired. And Ina Mirman, my sweet and loyal little Jewish friend, began to weep hot tears of grief and anger at the sudden realization that my freedoms of speech and religion had just been unjustly and summarily trampled.

After graduation, I rejoined my family in Atlanta and decided I would definitely not pursue basketball in college. At Camp Westminster where I worked that summer, I met a distractingly beautiful sixteen-year-old brunette named Nancy. I was completely and thoroughly undone by her.

Without effort, without intention, and without difficulty, Nancy disarmed, overwhelmed, and captivated me. What was it about Nancy that conquered me? At the risk of appearing shallow, I readily admit that the first thing I noticed about her was her beauty that she bestowed on me with her smile. But soon I realized that here was a girl who wholeheartedly loved Jesus Christ. Here was a girl I could freely talk to, a girl who understood me. Here was a girl with whom I could share my deepest hopes and anxieties without fear of rejection. Here was an intelligent young woman with uncanny good sense. She balanced my pessimistic bent with optimism. She was my equal in every way; the question was whether I was her equal. She completed what was lacking in me. I loved that girl. I wanted to share life with her.

And that beautiful girl became my beautiful wife two years later. She is still beautiful after forty-three years of marriage.

Nancy had me doing all kinds of crazy things, things like playing tennis with her at five in the morning. Still, I carried on with my assigned jobs at camp, counseling and teaching the campers the finer points of basketball in the barn-gym—when I wasn't too busy with my newfound love.

Uh-oh. I was getting basketball fever again.

Basketball: Yet Again

I worked out some that summer but mainly romanced the cute girl I had met at camp; she was my number one priority.

I knew what was important in life, and her name was Nancy. I also decided I would give basketball a shot at Wheaton College (Illinois). I felt the northern guys deserved to see how we played the game in Virginia. It was the least I could do for them. After all, I was born to play basketball. And besides, I was 6'4" (almost).

When I arrived at Wheaton, I was in the throes of withdrawal from my new love whom I had left behind in Georgia, but I pulled it together and went on. Knowing I was pre-med, it seemed reasonable (to someone) to give me a Bible professor to advise me. He believed that I needed to be a chemistry major, and because I was a chemistry major I would need to be able to read all the German chemistry journals, and therefore, German was a must. It made sense to me. In addition to chemistry and German, I had a little calculus, PE, ROTC, and a few other courses. The net result: there I was, taking a very heavy load, an unnecessarily heavy load. But, hey, no problem. I was just following my advisor's counsel, and he must know or he would not have been an advisor. Right? And, besides, I was a legend. I met some of the Wheaton freshman basketball guys. Five of our freshman players had been all-state in their respective states—guys like Robin Cook and John Woolmington. These were nice guys, and I thought I would be fine. After all, I was a Virginia high school legend.

I was a little intimidated.

Early in orientation week, I casually and coolly strolled into Centennial Gym just to check it out. Inside were some of the biggest, strongest, quickest basketball players I had ever seen. And they were running impossible drills. I suddenly felt very discouraged with my basketball aspirations at Wheaton College. These guys were far better than I thought they would be, and I knew at that point I could not even stay on the court with them. My legendary status was quickly fading in my mind. I watched for a few minutes and then walked out. I was likely very pale. As I left the gym, a friend walked in and I said to him, "The Wheaton varsity looks pretty good. I don't think I stand a chance with these guys. They are just *too* good!" He looked at me quizzically at first, then seemed to understand. "Wait a minute, Jerry. Who do you think is practicing in the gym?" "The Wheaton varsity, of course. Who else?" I answered. "Jerry, you idiot, that is not the Wheaton varsity! They're the Chicago Bulls!"

Unbeknownst to me, "Da Bulls" were holding their rookie camp at Wheaton that summer, and some veterans showed up for a little extra practice. I immediately felt better about my prospects.

Appearances are often at odds with reality.

Tryouts began, and I enjoyed playing for the Wheaton coach, Lee Pfund. I found the Wheaton guys could play some basketball, and some of them were completely out of my league. Tom Dykstra, Robin Cook, and John Woolmington were standouts. I was able to hold my own and made the freshman squad, sometimes practicing with the varsity. Coach Pfund was no-nonsense. The player who dogged it at practice or who didn't play aggressively enough had the honor of wearing a pair of woman's pink underwear at the next practice. I successfully avoided that punishment.

I played a few lackluster games for the Wheaton freshman team at places like DePaul and the University of Wisconsin at Kenosha. However, I was not enjoying it, and basketball was interfering with my studies. I decided over Christmas break that it was really time to leave my basketball career behind. I knew that I would never be an NBA player. I knew my future lay in medicine and that I needed to apply myself to studying. I was lovesick, I was depressed, and I was getting only a few hours of sleep each night trying to keep up with all my coursework. In addition, there was always the ultimate negative motivation for doing well in college: Vietnam. I feared flunking out of college because I knew that if I did, my next stop would be Vietnam, likely in the infantry. I did not want to go there.

I went in to talk with the freshman coach (not Coach Pfund) in January to tell him I was leaving the team, and he seemed to understand. Surprisingly, he was not too upset; he definitely did not go into mourning after I left. Another coach (of another sport) drifted in, overheard our conversation and tried to talk me into staying, calling me a quitter. These types of psychological tactics don't work well with me. He didn't even know me. I stuck to my guns. It was over. Really over.

So, just like that, The Legend's basketball career ended. Again, there were no farewell tours or goodbye parties. It was really over this time.

Wayne Kerr attended Georgia Tech and eventually became a dentist in the Atlanta area. He travels widely, giving lectures to his dental colleagues across the country.

Bob German went on to start at quarterback for Virginia Tech where he had a great career; he received an offer to play for the Denver Broncos. I always wished he had played college basketball, as I think he could have played ultimately in the NBA. I have never seen a finer athlete.

Ricky Michaelsen led all Virginia school boys in scoring in 1969-1970 with an average of 39.6 points per game. He poured in 69 points in one game, and scored more than 50 points four times that season. All this was done without the benefit of the three point arc. He still is the third leading single season scorer in Virginia high school history.

Bob Gerloff played football for three years at the University of North Carolina.

Gene Alley and his brother Jerry became part of pro golfer Curtis Strange's posse in the late 1980's. Curtis was a couple of years behind us at Princess Anne and became PA's most famous graduate. He won two U.S. Open Golf Championships.

Skeeter Whitlow played college basketball and then became a paratrooper en route to a successful business career. He has always found time to coach basketball.

Tom Dykstra tried out for the Baltimore Bullets (NBA) and was the last man cut. For many years, he and Robin Cook got together each year to be certain that each of them could still slam-dunk.

Coach Leo Anthony finished his basketball coaching career with more than 400 wins and left a legacy of joy for his players. It was a privilege to play for this man. He still coaches high school golf in Virginia Beach. He and Lefty Driesell attend Old Dominion University basketball games together.

As for me, I can still shoot well—as long as no one guards me too closely. And the closest I have come to the NBA since college was one Easter Sunday morning at our church in Augusta, twenty years ago. It was the final day of the Masters Tournament. The whole world comes to Augusta that week every year. A tall, handsome man walked up the steps. He was even taller than I was, a very weird and disorienting thing for me, something that does not occur often. He looked familiar.

I greeted him and shook his huge right hand. It was Julius Erving. "Happy Easter" said Dr. J to me as our eyes engaged.

Jesus is risen. He is risen, indeed. Alleluia.

There are more important things in life than basketball.

8

Life with Rocket Nan

EVERY TIME I HEAR Elton John's song, "Rocket Man," I think of my wife. You may not realize this, but the song is about her. As only Sir Elton and I know, a typographical error caught too late irreversibly changed the name of the original title of the track from "Rocket Nan" to its well-known current form. If you listen closely, though, you will hear that clearly he is singing "Rocket Nan," not "Rocket Man."

My wife, Nancy, is a rocket. I, on the other hand, am a B-52 bomber.

Nancy bounds out of bed each morning ready to charge into the new day, happy at the new prospects and adventures in front of her, running and bumping and thumping around the house. She makes a lot of noise, especially for such a little person: 5'4" (almost) and 113 pounds (max).

I wake up thinking, "Oh, no, I'm awake!" I roll out of bed, stumble to the sink to wash my face, throw on some clothes, and head for the coffee. For the next two hours I try to wake up. I get up early because I know my biorhythms. I don't do mornings. It takes me a long time to achieve cruising altitude. And during my two-hour ascent, all I want is a little peace and quiet. Just leave me alone, don't ask me any questions, and keep the volume level turned way down.

At T minus 0, there is ignition, and Rocket-Nan lifts off and soars through the stratosphere, though never quite escaping the pull of gravity. And then she comes crashing down to earth. She gets a multitude of things done when she is soaring. She is the consummate multi-tasker. She does her work well and efficiently. She does it neatly and in an organized fashion. It doesn't hurt that she is pretty smart too. But when she crashes, she is gone. If she begins to lose altitude in the afternoon, she may take on a little high-octane rocket fuel such as an "energy drink," that great invention of post-modern science with all natural (and secret) ingredients: you know, lots of amino acids and other secret stuff like sugar and caffeine. It acts as her booster rocket and keeps her flying for a few more hours, but after dinner, the rocket comes in for her final crash landing. Her energy and her rocket fuel are spent. If she sits down, she goes to sleep—for the night. She can sleep anywhere. Most rockets have post-flight narcolepsy.

The B-52 slowly, gradually, and deliberately rolls out of the hangar, onto the runway, and into the air. Then he can cruise around all day long. He is not fast, and he is not flashy, but he can endure just about anything and he can fly almost forever if he has too.

The B-52 is not too worried about making a mess. To the untrained and unprofessional eye, my desk may appear disorganized, but I know where everything is, as long as Rocket Nan leaves things as they are, that is. Rocket Nan has this peculiar need to get all my things neat and orderly, while it really doesn't matter to me much what things look like as long as I can do my job. I often invoke Proverbs 14:4 to justify myself: "Where no oxen are, the manger is clean, but much increase comes by the strength of the ox." In this word-picture, I am the strong ox, and my workspace is my manger … uh … which is not especially neat. To any thinking person, it is obvious that I am so messy because I am so productive. It also follows that messiness is necessary for productivity. Just ask any extremely productive genius. It is a basic understanding of the way humans work, and I don't see why everyone doesn't understand this concept.

I have analyzed Rocket Nan, and I have deciphered the code, the key to her inner type A: I know why she is like she is.

She's running.

She is running away from entropy.

That's right. Entropy. Rocket Nan knows all about the Second Law of Thermodynamics. After all, she *is* a rocket, and rockets know all about this scientific stuff. Besides, the concept of entropy is simple—it is not rocket science. Entropy is the idea that all things left to themselves tend to become random and disorderly; energy must be put into the system to maintain order or to reverse the process of disorder.

Entropy is terrifying to the Rocket. Why? Because she has seen its ravaging effects. It can destroy systems, societies, and lives. She has experienced what it can do. So she fights against any encroachment of entropy anywhere. She will not let entropy gain a foothold. Not in her life, my life, or our family's life—not in anything she is responsible for.

There is a reason Rocket Nan gets up each morning ready for her mission, ready to push back disorder, randomness, and the creeping kudzu that would otherwise envelop, strangulate, and destroy her life and mine. She refuses to let entropy catch her.

And I love her for it.

He who finds a wife finds a good thing and obtains favor from the Lord.
   Proverbs 18:22

PART TWO

"My profession is to me a ministry from God."

Dr. Crawford W. Long

9

Gross Anatomy and Beyond

IT BECOMES EVERY PERSON who purposes to give himself to the care of others, seriously to consider the four following things:

First, that he must one day give an account to the Supreme Judge of all the lives entrusted to his care.

Second, that all his skill and knowledge and energy, as they have been given him by God, so they should be exercised for his glory and the good of mankind, and not for mere gain or ambition.

Third, and not more beautifully than truly, let him reflect that he has undertaken the care of no mean creature; for, in order that he may estimate the value, the greatness of the human race, the only begotten Son of God became himself a man and thus ennobled it with his divine dignity, and far more than this, died to redeem it.

And fourth, that the doctor being himself a mortal human being, should be diligent and tender in relieving his suffering patients, inasmuch as he himself must one day be a like sufferer.

Thomas Sydenham (1624-1689)
Puritan Physician, "The English Hippocrates"

I MET HER SOON after classes began at the Medical College of Georgia.

After a brief orientation, our professors led us into the gross anatomy lab where we would spend many scores of hours learning human anatomy—by dissecting a human cadaver. Entering the lab, we inhaled the distinctive atmosphere of formaldehyde and death, taking care not to breathe too deeply. We noticed twenty shiny stainless steel rectangular boxes. Eight to a team, we approached our assigned caskets and awaited instruction. Opening the hinged steel doors on top and allowing them to drop to the sides, we gazed with wide eyes into the vat of preserving chemicals and met our cadaver for the first time. She was lying on her back on a steel panel, her features distorted as light bent its rays through twelve inches of the toxic solution. Using the hand-cranks on each end, we slowly raised her up out of the fluid and saw her face to face, allowing the preservative to drip back down into the vat below. We hid our sense of mystery and fear beneath a carefully crafted veneer of nonchalance, as if we had done this every day of our lives.

One of our group recognized this little woman as being from her home town. Another decided early on that he would not help with the dissection, and in fact, would not even touch her; he would learn his anatomy from lectures, books and atlases, and would show up for review sessions just before the practicums. (He had an aversion to getting his hands messy; this aversion became more apparent in our second year as we teamed up for physical diagnosis. He suggested that I do the exam and leave the history-taking to him. He didn't like to touch patients, dead or alive.) The rest of us divided into two teams and worked together in the careful, meticulous dissection of the upper extremity. Here is where we began, and we would keep at it for the next six months, eventually dissecting her entire body.

Most of us did not wear gloves while dissecting; we saw no need to, and no one recommended it. Just after I had spent my first morning with my cadaver, I went home for lunch with Nancy. We sat down in our little kitchen to eat. She had made me a fresh tuna fish sandwich, but I simply could not eat it in the normal fashion. Since my hands smelled like my new friend, I had to eat the sandwich with a knife and fork. The toxic odor from my hands was just too strong, and besides, the tuna fish was too much the same color as the flesh I had just been dissecting. I could barely choke the tuna down.

It was in this kitchen that I would take advantage of a big blackboard hanging on the wall. I used it to help me memorize biochemistry. Depending upon what we were studying at the time, you could always see some biochemical pathway on the board: the Krebs cycle, glycolysis, gluconeogenesis, the urea cycle, etc.

Our apartment then was in a very old, decrepit Augusta home, a fine mansion in its day, but it now looked like a haunted house. Our parents thought it looked like a firetrap. We lived in three large rooms upstairs and paid seventy dollars per month, including utilities. It was close to school for both of us, which helped since we had only one car, a dark-green Volkswagen fastback with genuine Corinthian vinyl white seats. It was reliable car, when it actually ran, which was only about half the time. That VW was a major source of financial and emotional stress. It required many major repairs.

I hated that car.

Once, after I had barely coaxed the sputtering fastback to the repair shop, in rage and frustration I walked the five miles home, fuming at the car and at life in general. "Why do I deserve this?" I thought. No one offered to pick me up as I walked, and that was just as well. I was so mad, I would not have accepted the ride. Besides, I wanted some time alone to feel sorry for myself. I made the walk home in record time. And my young wife, Nancy, as always, was able to calm me down and help me to see that this was not such a huge crisis, not really.

It's nice to have a wise, understanding wife. It's also nice when she's pretty.

A FEW OF THE STUDENTS in our medical school class were pros. They were the ones we "normal" med students (is any medical student really normal?) referred to as "gunners." Gunners sat on the front rows during lectures. They gunned for straight A's. (In fairness and honesty, I was likely a gunner too—I was just a little more subtle, less overt and obvious—I didn't want anyone to know.) These guys must have had fathers who were doctors. They wore cool lab coats, snowy white and starched; I wore my old scruffy, yellowed, stained one from college biology. They had great dissection kits, some with real scalpels; I used my dissection kit from college, the one with the cheap blue plastic case that didn't quite close, the one with the dull, non-replaceable blade that didn't quite cut. This kit had served me well in the past dissecting frogs and cow's eyeballs, but now it seemed pedestrian and obsolete.

The gunners even wore surgical gloves when they dissected. We "normals" could not believe it. Surgical gloves! It made the rest of us feel like amateurs. Their wearing of gloves was the penultimate insult to those of us who barehanded it.

But the thing that really got us the most about the gunners, the ultimate insult, was their name tags. Yes, name tags on their lab coats. Someone had gone to the expense to have customized name tags made for these guys. I think they wore them just to demonstrate their superiority. We "normals" laughed at them. Economic necessity (most of us were financially challenged) and pride kept us from following suit.

In mockery and defiance of the gunners, I did what I could do. I had an old name tag at home, one I had worn when I was the high school drapery expert at Sears. I took it out of mothballs and wore it to gross anatomy lab, right there on my left breast pocket to announce that I was somebody, too. In bold green letters on a white background, it said "Welcome to Sears!" And just below it, in bright white letters on a black background: "Mr. Miller."

We dissected for many hours every week. Between two and

four of us worked together, during officially designated lab times, and at night, on weekends, anytime we could get together. The lab was always open. It was not just the dissection. We had to learn all about the anatomy of the human body and memorize it. We had to know it cold. Origins and insertions of muscles, names of tendons, ligaments, and bones. Normal anatomical variants. Names and locations of heart valves, names of coronary arteries. The aorta and all its tributaries. We had to know it all cold. We carefully dissected as we propped our anatomy books and atlases up on the corners of the tank, trying not to stain the books. We taught much of this to ourselves and to each other; we depended upon each other to learn, and in our class, we had great *esprit de corps*. We had many very smart students, and we were willing to help each other, cooperatively collaborating in one another's education. Before medical school, I thought I was fairly intelligent. Once I got there, though, I realized that everybody else was just as smart as I thought I was, and some were actually brilliant. It was a great bonus having unselfish geniuses who were willing to teach their fellow students.

Our class president, Frank Farmer, helped foster this great spirit of unity. He was a Vietnam veteran, and, in Frank's mind, cooperation was the only reasonable course. We had heard stories of other classes in which students stole or conveniently "misplaced" or "liberated" textbooks from the library so as to deprive their fellows of the books prior to exams. This never happened in our class, I think, in large part thanks to Frank. Dr. Farmer practiced internal medicine for many years, later serving as Surgeon General of the State of Florida before he retired.

Another unselfish leader was Julian Hutchins, our class VP. Thinking ahead for the class, he stood in the rain several hours one April Sunday afternoon and collected seventeen Masters Tournament badges as patrons left town. The downpour that day had forced the final round of the Masters to be delayed until Monday—an unprecedented thing. Hutch had anticipated it, and on Monday morning, he stood in front of 160 freshman medical students and freely offered the tickets to anyone who was willing to miss physiology and microbiology for the day. It was a hard choice, but immediately, seventeen freshman medical students willingly sacrificed their classes that day to attend the final round. It was important not to allow medical school to interfere with one's education.

Hutch was also a shrewd judge of people. Knowing my proclivity to immerse myself in details and my self-torture in attempting to master them all, he once predicted I would become a great pediatric enzymologist. Unfortunately for me, and maybe all of us, there was and is no such sub-specialty. But he had a good point. I might have inflicted less pain on myself and others if I had narrowed my field and lost myself in some remote corner of esoteric pediatrics.

As one example of a student who personally helped me, Rick Kemmerlin took me under his wing and tutored me in histology just before our first exam. He realized that I had no idea what was going on. He did not have to do that for me.

Our class even initiated a note-taking service that provided lecture notes to those who wanted them. Two of our brightest students, both of them women, each with a decidedly un-physician-like handwriting, were our designated note-takers.

Several other students in our class also went on to greatness or fame. David Johnson, who won our class's "Physician's Physician" award—he was voted by his peers as the one person in our class we would most like to attend us if we were sick—is now Chairman of Internal Medicine at the University of Texas Southwestern Medical Center.

Andy Norman, on faculty at Vanderbilt University School of Medicine, has spent decades as a missionary gynecologist in Africa.

Eddie Cheeks endured and surmounted years of racial discrimination with his intelligence, hard work, and joyful demeanor, becoming a successful obstetrician-gynecologist; he also served as chairman of the Georgia Composite State Board of Medical Examiners. He is still on the Board today.

Tom Kendall practiced family medicine for thirty years before becoming president in 2013 of the Association of American Physicians and Surgeons, a conservative cultural counterweight to the liberal American Medical Association. He continues in private practice.

Edwin "Flip" Homansky achieved fame as an expert in combat sports, authoring books, testifying before the U.S. Senate, serving as Nevada's Chief Ringside Physician, and working to make combat sports safer.

Most of my classmates, however, have not become stars in the public eye; they have simply practiced good medicine quietly and in obscurity, never becoming famous. They are unheralded and often unrecognized, but they have faithfully cared for sick patients every day over many years; these are not insignificant accomplishments and contributions. Friends like Charlie Davis, Danny Bramlett, and George Williams—people like Rick Kemmerlin—these all come to mind. Few know the magnitude of their lives apart from their grateful patients—and God.

EVERY FEW WEEKS, we had gross anatomy exams. The practical exams were like this. We all lined up and were assigned to different stations. Each station had a numbered tag tied to a certain part of the anatomy. Our job was to identify the part of the body that was tagged. We then rotated through the lab with our answer sheets, spending a few defined minutes at each station, recording our answers, and then moving on. Each exam took about an hour.

Beginning in the winter, we added neuroanatomy to our repertoire. Here, we learned about the anatomy and physiology of the central nervous system, and we were assisted by actual human brains that had been removed from cadavers. Some brains were whole, some were sliced in various types of sections. We handled them, dissected them, and delved into the profound, labyrinthine secrets of the human brain—secrets concealed from most but opened to us as privileged doctors-in-training. We learned about the frontal and parietal lobes, the cerebellum, the corpus callosum, the ventricular system, the cerebral aqueduct, the amygdala, the locus ceruleus (what a great name). We were treading on sacred ground.

Our sophomore year, we would progress to pathology. Our professor and course director was the legendary Dr. Teabeaut. In pathology we built on our knowledge of gross and microscopic anatomy, and in this course we learned what could go wrong with the human body, which is just about anything. We learned about disease and disease processes.

We spent many hours in lecture, and we spent many hours in the lab. In groups of four, we were required to do two autopsies and then turn in complete reports of our findings. At autopsy time, we were notified without warning. We dropped everything else we were doing, and rushed to the morgue. Later our team presented our findings and discussed them before the entire class of 160.

Dr. Teabeaut began to teach us how to think like doctors. In the lab, great carts of metal pots were wheeled in. And in the pots were the mysteries of disease—human organs from dead humans that had undergone autopsies. There are hundreds of ways to die, and we studied almost all of them. As we handled (again, *sans* gloves) these diseased organs, Dr. Teabeaut interrogated us, always beginning with the question: "What do you see?" He would remove the lid from a pot, take out an infarcted heart (or a diseased liver, or an atherosclerotic aorta), hand it to one of us, and ask: "What do you see?" It was never enough to robotically recite what we had learned from our pathology textbooks the night before. He wanted to know what we saw. He wanted us to think. What did we observe? And from that observation, what was wrong with the organ? What was the immediate problem in front of us? What was the underlying disease process? What was the cause of death? There was intense pressure to perform, to stay calm and not panic, and to think under heavy scrutiny. It was strangely good for us. We would have to do this the rest of our careers.

A remarkable thing began to happen.

We started to think like physicians.

The first pathology exam did not go well; at least it did not go well for about seventy-five percent of us in the class, and it did not go well for me. I bombed the exam, as did all three classmates I carpooled with. We all commiserated with each other as we rode to and from class. Possibly the cause of all four of us doing so poorly was that we had carbon monoxide poisoning from my VW. Maybe. It sounded like a reasonable explanation. But I had another good excuse. Nancy was in her last few days of pregnancy with our first daughter, and she had gone into false labor the night before the exam. I was a little distracted that night as I tried to study. I suppose misery loves company, but I would have preferred the carpool company of students (including me) who had aced the exam.

The pressure to master pathology built after this first disastrous exam because I had to make up for a poor start. I was in a deep hole, and I was trying to shovel my way out like a man who feared being buried alive.

Our daughter, Rebecca, was born a few weeks later. She arrived in early November, and we decided to stay in Augusta by ourselves for Thanksgiving. I had four days out of class and gave myself a vacation from studying on Thanksgiving Day. I tossed the football around with our neighbor, enjoyed holding Rebecca, and tried to help Nancy. We kept things simple that day and had hotdogs for Thanksgiving dinner. They were some great hotdogs, and the Pilgrims had nothing on us. We watched some football games on our eight-inch black-and-white TV that afternoon. I got back to work Friday, finishing the day at school viewing pathology slides that afternoon and evening. I was surprised to see a couple of the party guys in our class studying there as well. It is amazing what a little fear can do to motivate a medical student.

Besides the fact that we began to think like doctors, something else occurred, something very odd and insidious. The toxic combination of stress and new knowledge of disease seemed to produce in some of us the very same illnesses we were studying. Strangely, just about every disease we studied found its way into our class—only temporarily—and then amazingly vanished as we moved on to the next unit. It was an unusual epidemic.

The intense pressure to perform while stressed, though good for our long-term development as physicians (being a doctor is all about performing well under pressure), produced other symptoms in us as well. Nervous tics developed in some. Others dreaded even showing up in class for fear that they would be called onto the platform and questioned in front of the entire class. I myself developed what my wife and I called "tight chest." Every time I walked into pathology lectures, my chest painfully tightened up as if in a vise. It was all stress induced. "Tight chest" miraculously began to disappear as I became more proficient in pathology and was gone completely when the course ended. Strange.

We took our knowledge of the human body and the diseases that ravage it to the next stage when we began our junior clerkships. Here, we would actually care for real patients as part of the team. As third-year students, we would help treat patients who suffered the things we had just studied. We were the lowest players on the depth chart, but we were finally in the game, and we would need every bit of knowledge we had just mastered in our first two years of medical school.

Our final two years of medical school we would learn by seeing and doing, both bolstered by constant reading and studying. We would help care for hundreds of patients. We would learn to think even when sleep-deprived, dead tired, hungry, and pressured. We would gradually acquire more skill, knowledge, and judgment. By graduation, we would be proficient enough to enter our residencies for further training, ready to care more independently for these complex beings of infinite value called humans.

The learning would continue all our lives.

THE HUMAN BODY is beautiful. It is well-conceived and well-designed. It is well-created. It works. The general uniformity, consistency, and symmetry are remarkable. Yet, the specific differences and great diversity among humans are also beautiful. Can there be any doubt that God created us?

Some would say that the body is not important, that it serves only to house the human soul. And others would say that there is no such thing as a soul, and that only the body matters. God would not agree with either. God created humans to be both body and soul, an integrated whole. Jesus, the Son of God, came to earth in the flesh, signaling not only the dignity of the human body, but also his intention to redeem both body and soul. He healed multitudes of the sick and maimed, *and* he died to make possible the forgiveness of our sins and our reconciliation to God. His resurrection and promised future return guarantee the ultimate redemption of the bodies and souls of those who love him.

The human body and the human soul are both important to God. He created the first humans: living, eternal souls in beautiful, well-crafted bodies. And Jesus entered history to redeem humans, body and soul, an integrated whole, incapable of being compartmentalized.

The human body retains dignity even in death. This is why we instinctively treat dead bodies with respect. Only in backward or darkened cultures are human corpses desecrated or cannibalized.

It is a great privilege and responsibility to be a physician, to care for the physical, emotional and spiritual needs of humans created and loved by God. I am thankful for this privilege.

I am thankful for all who will their bodies to be used to train future physicians and surgeons.

And I am especially thankful to the petite woman whose unselfishness helped to train me in gross anatomy.

> *I praise you, for I am fearfully and wonderfully made. Wonderful are your works; my soul knows it very well.*
> *Psalm 139:14 (ESV)*

WHAT IS YOUR ONLY comfort in life and in death?

That I, with body and soul, both in life and in death, am not my own, but belong to my faithful Savior Jesus Christ, who with His precious blood has fully satisfied for all my sins, and redeemed me from all the power of the devil; and so preserves me that without the will of my Father in heaven not a hair can fall from my head; indeed, that all things must work together for my salvation. Wherefore, by His Holy Spirit, He also assures me of eternal life, and makes me heartily willing and ready from now on to live unto Him.

Heidelberg Catechism, Question 1

10

Dermatology

My senior dermatology elective started unimpressively. I was late to the first lecture, scheduled for 8:00 a.m., and my tardiness was not well received.

I had been late before to other things—occasionally. Well, really, I have been late all my life, ever since I was born three weeks after my due date. It's a good thing I'm a doctor. People expect me to be late; they graciously forgive me because I must have a good excuse, like saving someone's life. And because of doctor-patient confidentiality, they can't ask and I can't tell. It's a nice arrangement.

I had been late before in medical school as well—occasionally. As a junior medical student, I worked as a phlebotomist (a blood-drawer). I arrived early in the morning at University Hospital or Talmadge Hospital, and picked up my lab tray full of specialized equipment: needles and bandaids, alcohol swabs and tourniquets, vacutainers and tubes. The most important thing was my stack of lab orders: these were my marching orders for the morning. They told me where to go, which patients to stick, what lab work to draw, what tubes to use. It was important to get there early in order to get the easiest, most pleasant, and most cooperative patients. We all tried to do the post-partum floor.

Here were new mothers, just having given birth, who were full of contagious joy. They were also young which meant they had "good veins." They almost always could be relied upon to be an "easy stick." Older patients had either very sclerosed veins or very thin-walled collapsible veins—either way, it required much more skill to draw the needed lab work, and often, it was almost impossible.

My phlebotomy job provided some needed money to support my young wife and daughter. One morning, just after having finished my blood-drawing, I rushed out of the hospital and ran to the student center where I was supposed to arrive at 7:00 a.m. I was running late. My attending physician was having breakfast rounds with his four students who would be in his clinic that morning. The general idea was to review the charts of patients to be seen that day so that once in clinic, we would neither be in the way nor come across as a bunch of incompetent buffoons. It was a good idea. The bad idea was this: no one else could afford to eat breakfast there except for the attending, so we all sat there and watched him eat his eggs, bacon, and toast while he discussed the patients. It was highly instructive. I learned that if I were ever in the same situation as he, I would either forego breakfast or buy it for my young charges.

I arrived at this breakfast meeting at 7:10 a.m. With a glare and measured tones, my attending physician helpfully informed me, "Doctor, this meeting starts at 7:00. Sharp." I think I might have given him a little heartburn. I offered my abject and humble apology and sat down to watch him down his eggs.

So, now, as a senior student, when I arrived at my first dermatology lecture a little late, I was ready to be excoriated; I knew I deserved it. And the lecturer did not disappoint me. I had attempted to slip in unnoticed, in stealth mode; however, no one has ever accused me of being stealthy or subtle (or cute, for that matter). It has always been difficult for me to be any of these things. The lecture stopped as I "slipped in." There was an eternal moment of silence. "Uh-oh," I thought. "Here it comes."

"Doctor … do you know what time it is?" came the words from the front.

I tried to think quickly about how to answer his question. Did he really want to know what time it was? Had his watch stopped? Should I coolly glance at my own watch that said it was 8:02 and reply with that fairly favorable answer, or should I use the time on the wall clock that gave me an inconvenient 8:07? Should I break out into a cheery rendition of Chicago's hit song, "Does Anybody Really Know What Time It Is?" And if so, should I ask my classmates and the housestaff to sing along? Or was this merely a rhetorical question?

True to form, I was too late. Before I could get my answer out, I heard the lecturer say quietly: "Doctor, this lecture starts at eight o'clock. Sharp."

I had no excuse, so I mumbled an apology, slunk off to my seat, and slouched down as low as possible. I was humiliated at my inauspicious beginning.

After the initial embarrassment, I recovered quite nicely. I was fortunate that by now I was a senior medical student, and thus had attained a level of higher consciousness, an exalted state of being. I, like all good fourth-year medical students, had reached the point in my career where I had achieved near-omniscience, an aura of invincibility, and an air of imperturbability. (Little did I realize how insufficient I would feel many times just a few months later as an intern.) Therefore, as a senior medical student, I was not too badly rattled by my humiliating entrance into the realm of dermatology. It took a lot more than this to destroy my confidence. I had seen much worse—like the time my surgery attending had extended his telescoping pointer and placed the cold metal point, rapier-like, on my neck just over the carotid artery, demanding an accurate description of a chest X-ray. He was just kidding (of course!). He was quite a jokester. But stuff like that would not be tolerated in our med schools today. Now, he would likely be shipped off for anger management counseling, boundary therapy, or some other type of charm school to assist him in tamping down his hostility. Things were not quite as kind and gentle then in medical school as they are now. Nowadays, attendings must endure an uncomfortable meeting with the dean if they simply question their med students too thoroughly. It is not nice to hurt a medical student's feelings.

Dermatology went well after that. I enjoyed it, and despite my best attempts to derail myself the first day, eventually got my A. I realized, though, how extraordinarily difficult dermatology can be. The skin is a complex organ and its diseases can be difficult to diagnose clinically because of the mystery and ambiguity of their presentations. Diseases of the skin can also be extremely debilitating and sometimes fatal.

The dermatology clinics were housed in the middle of a gravel parking lot, a cluster of pre-fabricated buildings that are often now euphemistically referred to as "cottages" or "temporary offices." They looked like trailers to me.

Our routine each day consisted of a morning lecture (at eight o'clock sharp), and then seeing patients that we examined and subsequently presented to faculty and residents. We broke for lunch, had another lecture, and saw patients again until the late afternoon lecture.

I liked the routine, the predictability, and the relative calm of each day (not counting day one). Dermatology was a nice gig for a fourth year medical student.

Routine, predictability and calm have a way of changing very quickly.

One day in clinic, our patients were prisoners bused in from Reidsville State Prison, *the* Reidsville State Prison where the original *The Longest Yard* had been filmed. Burt Reynolds had starred in this classic movie.

The morning went well and fairly routinely, at least at first. It seemed rather exotic to treat state prisoners, but I had done it before in the hospital where their beds were in a special unit behind locked doors and a chain link fence. Armed guards secured the area in the hospital, and armed guards secured the dermatology clinic now.

Clinic progressed as it usually did for the first couple of hours. Suddenly, though, just before lunch, everything changed, and all the medical students were instructed to move to the conference room—immediately—and to stay there. There was a good reason.

At about 11:30, one of the prisoner-patients had been escorted to an exam room by his guard. His doctor, a resident, had turned to him and asked him, professionally and pleasantly, "What kind of skin problem are you having today?" As the doctor turned away for a few seconds to open the chart, the prisoner answered that he had a rash on his arm. Still studying the chart, the doctor asked him to expose the skin beneath the jean jacket he was wearing so he could examine him. As the prisoner meekly complied with the request, and before the doctor turned on his stool to face the patient, the prisoner completely removed his jacket, along with his handcuffs, and produced a gun from within the jacket. He wrapped his left arm around the doctor's neck and pointed the nickel-plated pistol at the back of his head, jabbing the barrel into his scalp; the young physician could feel the cold steel of the barrel, and it gave him chills. "Get up!" the prisoner snapped. He got up. Then the prisoner demanded that the guard surrender his service revolver to him. He pocketed the little pistol and pointed the new gun at his hostage's head. This gun was bigger and colder.

It seems that just before his examination, the prisoner had begged to be allowed to use the facilities. As he went into the men's room alone, he quickly lifted one of the ceiling tiles, moved it aside, and found the expected two inch .38 caliber Smith and

Wesson pistol waiting for him, resting just above the next tile, planted there by an accomplice. There just happened to be a key for the handcuffs as well.[1]

This particular prisoner had nothing to lose. He was already serving a double life sentence for the execution style murder of two police officers in Forsythe County. There was no death penalty in Georgia at the time. He was desperate, and he had counted the cost to himself—no matter what happened, it would cost him exactly nothing to attempt to escape and shoot a few more people if needed. He could not lose.

The prisoner shoved his physician-hostage into the hallway, not sure where to go from here. Several armed guards were in the hall, and the prisoner commanded that each one drop his gun to the floor. They obeyed.

Next door, the dermatology chief resident was in the middle of examining his assigned prisoner, with his exam room door barely cracked. He heard some noisy commotion coming from the hallway, and through the small aperture, he saw his friend and colleague being pushed down the hall with a gun to his head and a chokehold around his neck. Quickly and quietly, the chief closed the door. As he did, his own prisoner-patient stood to leave—he was obviously part of the conspiracy. The chief stood up, and having no other weapon, he drew his ballpoint pen from his shirt pocket and raised it just over his shoulder, wielding it like a knife. "Sit down—now!" he growled. The prisoner feared being stabbed with the pen, and he sat down, at least for the moment. The power of words is often underestimated.

The first prisoner kept making his way down the hallway, still exploring his options, and still choking his human shield. They

---

1   This paragraph is based on supposition and on my own best theory from reading the newspaper articles and interviewing actual participants in this incident. From my research, it was never clearly proven how the prisoner accessed the pistol.

arrived at the front office where a pretty, young secretary was talking on the phone. "Hang up!" he shouted, waving the point of the gun at her. She became pale, her heart raced, and she almost passed out—she was hysterical. She sat there, hung up the phone, and waited. She could not move from her chair—the weight of terror immobilized her.

As the prisoner and resident-hostage left the hallway, the chief resident saw his opportunity and quickly ran to the lab where he phoned campus security and informed them of the emergency. He then found a desk and took refuge under it until the ordeal was over.

The gunman kept his hostage and found another one—a medical student from Texas who was there to interview for the dermatology residency. He was dressed in a suit and tie to make a good impression. He did make a good impression—on the convict. The murderer thought he would make a fine hostage. He pointed the gun at him and said, "Come on!"

As they got to the exit that led into the parking lot, the resident-hostage knew that if he were forced out of the building, all would be lost. He told the prisoner, "I feel faint. I think … I'm going … to pass out," at which time he slumped to floor. As he collapsed, the prisoner shoved him into an exam room doorway. There was no way the prisoner was going to carry him out. The doctor was crumpled on the floor, limp and lifeless; he would be dead weight. Just to be sure he wasn't faking, the prisoner kicked him in the back. Seeing he didn't come around, he kept going. It was the acting job of the year.

The Texas medical student saw how effective a good syncopal episode can be, so he did the same thing. "I feel faint. I think I'm going to pass out." He collapsed to the floor, and the prisoner had no hostages. (Of his imitated fake fainting spell, the Texan later said, "It looked good to me, so I thought I would try it.") Good acting ability seems to be a highly valued trait in dermatology.

The original hostage saw the convict exit the building,

recovered quickly from his feigned faint, scooted completely into the exam room, and got behind a desk. He thought a second: "Maybe I should lock the door." He got up to lock it, then realized it had no lock. This was not a very safe place to be. With the Texan, he ran, without knocking, into the chairman's office, slammed the door behind him, and locked it tight. He slumped on the couch there, drenched with sweat, hair disheveled, pallid, and looking like he had seen Satan himself. "A prisoner has escaped and he's armed!" gasped the resident. They called security and stayed in the locked office.

By this time, the convict had run out into the parking lot, and two other prisoners had joined him. Awaiting them was a circle of police cars, rifles and pistols trained on them. There was a burst of gunfire. The murderer fired away with both of his pistols. The resident-hostage heard the guns as if they were cap-guns. The chief resident thought his friend was dead.

The gunfight in the parking lot lasted a few minutes and ended quickly. No one was injured and all three escaped prisoners were rounded up. The only casualties were six cars in the parking lot, including a Porsche that was pockmarked with bullet holes.

The police said afterwards they were glad the convict-murderer-escapee was not a good shot.

Several people came close to death that day, and even more could have died—all because a doubly convicted brutal murderer had not been given the death penalty. It was a terrifying day in the dermatology clinic.

The Texas medical student never returned to Georgia. He only *thought* Texas was the Wild West. He realized it was pretty calm there compared to Georgia.

The dermatology resident taken hostage informed his superiors that "No matter what—even if you fire me—I will not see prisoners again." He never did.

And I learned a lot in dermatology. I learned about papulosquamous disease. I learned about eczema and contact dermatitis, about scabies and ringworm. I learned the rudiments of how to diagnose melanoma, squamous cell and basal cell carcinomas.

I learned that a ballpoint pen can be a good weapon—especially if accompanied by strong words.

I learned that fainting is a good strategy to avoid becoming a hostage.

I learned that dermatology can be a very hazardous profession.

And I learned that I should probably show up for 8:00 meetings at 8:00. Sharp.

ACKNOWLEDGEMENTS: I thank Drs. David Hood and Anthony Meyers for generously providing me their firsthand accounts of what they survived that day.

11

Haiti Cherie

REBECCA ALWAYS RAN high fevers when she was sick: 105 degrees was her temperature of choice. And now she was doing it again in rural Haiti. I was worried she might have malaria already.

We had just arrived in Haiti a few days before, landing in Port-au-Prince, spending two days there, and then flying westward to Aux Cayes. We would spend the next three months there working in the *Dispensaire Lumière* (Dispensary of Light), a small Christian medical clinic, with Dr. and Mrs. Dudley Nelson. Nancy and I had great interest in international Christian medical missions, and this would be our first taste of trying it for ourselves. We hoped to spend time abroad during my medical career as either long-term or short-term missionaries. A medical doctor has opportunities all over the world to offer the gospel of Jesus Christ to people while treating their medical needs in the name of Christ. Everyone needs a physician. Everyone needs the Great Physician.

I was a fourth year medical student and Nancy was now an RN. Rebecca, our only child, was two years old. I had been awarded a Medical Assistance Program/Readers' Digest International Fellowship to spend three months of my senior year in an undeveloped country doing medical work. I had prepared for this mission for months before we departed. I had finished my junior year, and as a senior had taken strategic electives in emergency medicine, dog surgery, dermatology, and obstetrics. I had finished the interview process for my residency to follow a few months later. I had even signed my will, drawn up at no charge by good friend and attorney Ashby Davis; I'm not sure how important this was since my net worth was about $734.

I was as ready as I could be to care for patients in Haiti, or so I thought.

Before we left, one of my med school classmates asked me, "Aren't you afraid of taking Rebecca? What happens if she gets sick there?" I answered that I believed God would take care of her (and her parents) just as easily there as in Augusta, that we are always safe in God's hands. So I wasn't worried. It was an honest and natural answer, not canned or rehearsed or forced. It was what I believed.

Now, only days after our arrival in Haiti, and only hours after our arrival in Aux Cayes, I had the opportunity to demonstrate that I really trusted God as much as I said I did. When Rebecca began her fever, I realized it was not likely that she would have malaria already, but I didn't like her being sick so far from home. We prayed for her, we gave her fluids and fever medications, and we watched her carefully. In addition, many were praying for us at home the entire three months. Rebecca was well within a few days; it had been just another virus. We were relieved and we were grateful to God for protecting our little blonde, curly-headed daughter. This was the last illness any of us experienced while there.

We were shown to our living quarters on the mission compound: a one room apartment with a bed (actually two twin beds pushed together) and mosquito net, a portable crib for Rebecca, and a table and chairs for meals. Our little apartment came complete with two other roommates: a tarantula and a mouse. The tarantula introduced himself to Nancy one morning while she was doing laundry. He plopped himself on the bed as he dropped from Nancy's shoulder and gave her a hearty greeting. Her screams didn't make him feel very welcome, and he disappeared for good. The mouse, however, liked living with us, and we could never convince him to move.

Luxurious red bougainvillea bloomed outside our door, and a set of outside stairs led to the flat rooftop that gave us a panoramic view of the azure Caribbean to the south. We had dinner there with friends on one occasion, hauling a table and chairs up the stairs, along with our meal.

After being in Aux Cayes a day or so, Nancy turned to me and said, "I want to go home." Nothing had really happened to prompt this statement. Simply put, Nancy is a homegirl; she likes to be in her own home, and she has always made our homes into places of peace, beauty, and refuge. Now, she just wanted to go home. And I had to disappoint her: "You can't go home, Nancy. Not for three months."

We weren't in Kansas anymore.

In fact, in this remote corner of Haiti, we were so far away from Kansas (or Georgia) that we may as well have been on a lunar colony. We had to travel to town thirty minutes away to use a phone; we used it exactly once in three months. We had no newspapers, and in our isolation, we were shocked when visitors from America told us of the remarkable peanut farmer from Georgia who was running away with the Democratic presidential primaries.

On Match Day in March, when all the other fourth year medical students gathered at their respective medical schools to hear where they had been assigned for their residencies, I would be absent. My friend and classmate, Charlie Davis, was my proxy. He sent me a telegram to the town of Aux Cayes with the words: "Houston, TX." Houston would be our home for the next four years, and I found out about it a few days after it was announced. So much for real time communication.

Our family transportation was a cool orange Honda 90. Yes, no fooling, a Honda 90cc motorbike. Sorry—what did you say? Um ... me neither ... I don't know how we did it either. It was fine for one person on level ground, but didn't work so well for all three of us going up the steep gravel roads of the compound. After all, Haiti is a mountainous place.

Each morning I took the Honda to the clinic, my white coat flapping and my *panier* (a woven basket-like bag) hooked over the handlebars. The *panier* was full of reference books from home, including *Harrison's Internal Medicine* and *The Washington Manual*. With its more than 2,000 pages weighing in at twenty pounds, *Harrison's* was almost a deal-breaker.

I had to get creative for the Honda to accommodate Nancy, Rebecca, and me all at once. We utilized a brilliant strategy. I drove, Nancy sat behind me, and Rebecca was sandwiched between us. I got the little Honda going as fast as I could, ran it downhill even faster, and then hoped the engine and momentum would carry us up the next hill.

It rarely worked. Nancy usually gave up and hopped off to walk the hill, more from fear than from frustration. We provided such great entertainment for the missionaries and for our clinic patients that we thought about selling tickets. On market days, we went into town on our little Honda, yes, all three of us, fording a creek and a river while keeping our feet clear of the water (sometimes). Continuing further, the road would carry us to the beach through sugarcane fields with cane higher than my head. Once, a donkey darted out from the sugarcane and got his rope tangled up in our motorbike, causing a slight delay but no real casualties.

We were given a crash course in Creole. Nancy and I built on our high school French. Rebecca picked up the Creole well and soon was speaking it appropriately, even using the idiom *"mes amis!"* (my friends) when a wave crashed over her at the beach. *"Mes amis!"* is an all-purpose term to express excitement, surprise, or joy. Our Creole lessons served us well in the clinic and in other areas. We were able comfortably to go to town ourselves and bargain at the local market. On our way out of Haiti, we bargained in Port-au-Prince's Iron Market and surprised the vendors that we spoke to them in Creole, and not French as most "blancs" did.

During the evenings, we heard the voodoo drums from the village just next to us. It was a haunting sound and sensation, a chilling experience to know that overt demonic activity was occurring a few hundred yards away. It made us pray all the more for God's protection. A German missionary couple, Johannes and Luise Schürer, pointed out to us a verse from Revelation that became a favorite of mine: "And they overcame him [the devil] because of the blood of the Lamb and because of the word of their testimony, and they did not love their life even to death" (Revelation 12:11). Satan can never do any ultimate harm to followers of Christ.

On weekends, we visited Haitian churches. One church was situated on a particularly beautiful spit of land just beside a mountain and extending out into the Caribbean. There was no electricity in this remote village. Because he knew Americans liked ice with their drinks, one of the brothers there spent hours traveling to buy us some ice in order to offer us cold drinks with our lunch. We were humbled by the Haitian believers' sacrificial generosity.

Another Sunday, we left early in the morning and went with missionary Carlyle Herring and his protégé, Jules, to a church they had started high in the mountains. We drove for about two hours, and then, leaving the jeep, hiked up the mountain for another hour. The believers there greeted us and we worshiped together. They gave us roasted goat, rice, and red beans for lunch, and for dessert, one of the men climbed a palm tree and cut down some coconuts for us.

Dr. Nelson allowed me to work independently in the clinic from the start, yet he was always there for consultation early on. Soon, however, I was manning the clinic by myself at times. Dr. Nelson was very kind to me and a good teacher. He was a true pioneer missionary doctor, one of a generation of Christian physicians in the 1940s and 1950s who aggressively carried out the Great Commission by starting clinics and hospitals in remote locations around the world.

I treated patients with malaria, syphilis, parasites, malnutrition, and pneumonia. I saw patients with tuberculosis and meningitis. I saw children vomit roundworms twelve inches long as I caught them in the trashcan. I even cared for a young man with a subdural hematoma (a blood clot on the brain), courtesy of a falling coconut that had landed on his head.

On one occasion, most of the missionaries and support team from the compound left for the groundbreaking of the new hospital (*L'Hôpital Lumière*) at Bonne Fin, high in the mountains. Nancy and Rebecca went with them, and I stayed behind to give what supportive care I could to a man dying of tetanus. At the groundbreaking there was the sudden arrival of a bus; fierce, blue-uniformed men with machine guns stepped off. Nancy was frightened at first. Were they the dreaded *tonton macoutes* (President Duvalier's brutal secret police)? It turned out they were only soldiers who were serving as guards for the festivities—and as spies. Besides, they didn't want to miss out on the refreshments.

One afternoon, after a busy day in clinic, we were winding down when a nineteen-year-old Haitian girl was brought in to see us. She had been severely ill for two weeks, and now she was near death. She was a believer in Christ; her parents were not. They had called for the voodoo witchdoctor as her condition deteriorated. Knowing he was satanic, the young woman had repeatedly refused the incantations and potions offered by the witchdoctor. She could not and would not submit herself to the devil, even if it meant death: she belonged to Jesus Christ and she trusted him. She knew he would not disappoint her. As long as she was conscious, she would cling to her Savior. She worsened.

Because it was obvious that she was dying, her parents finally relented and brought her to us for help.

Our assistants wheeled her on a gurney to the back room where the sickest patients were taken. When Dr. Nelson and I saw her, we knew that, short of a miracle, she would not survive. She had a 105-degree fever, she was comatose, and she was convulsing. She was short of breath, and her skin was wet with sweat. We listened to her lungs with our stethoscopes, and she had râles (or crackles) on both sides.

She had severe and advanced bacterial pneumonia.

It was too late. We did all we could for her, but this young follower of Christ died thirty minutes after she arrived, true to her Lord until the end.

I had just witnessed the death of a martyr for Christ.

And she was just as safe in the arms of her Savior as my daughter was.

Precious in the sight of the LORD is the death of His godly ones.
Psalm 116:15

12

Life Flight

PEERING OVER THE UN-RAILED edge of a sheer cliff face to the valley 800 feet below, I felt it again: that noxious mixture of nausea, dread, and pain in my gut. It is not a pleasant sensation. I suffer this visceral, gut feeling every time I find myself high above my surroundings. Here I was, experiencing it again in Banff, Canada as I "enjoyed" Tunnel Mountain with Nancy.

I do not like heights.

Do I have acrophobia? No. I don't think so. I don't have a neurotic, irrational fear of heights. I don't have a reaction that is disproportionate to the height. People can get hurt from heights. I think it's really quite rational to not exactly cherish the idea of falling several hundred feet to my death. So I don't have acrophobia. I just do not like heights. I'd rather not call it fear—I'd prefer to say I have a healthy respect for heights, a sort of reverence for their mystery, a feeling that I don't belong there.

All right, I admit it: I'm afraid of heights.

When I was nine years old, a pilot friend of ours once took my dad and me up in his plane for a joyride in Charlotte, North Carolina. The pilot, Captain Larry Montgomery, was a missionary with Wycliffe Bible Translators and their aviation unit, JAARS. The plane was a small heliocoupe, designed for flying people and supplies into tight spaces such as jungle airstrips, sandbars, or riverbanks. My father and the pilot sat in the front seats, and I sat in the back seat by myself. After a very tame takeoff, we flew over Charlotte and took in the view as our captain pointed out familiar landmarks. So far, so good. If it had only continued like this. Suddenly, however, he banked the plane to about forty-five degrees and turned; I was certain I was going to fall out the side door. And then he turned again ... and again. I made sure my seat belt was fastened securely. It was so secure it was in asphyxia mode. I took no chances. I was not going to fall out of that plane. I sat in the back seat terrified, trying to pretend that I was enjoying the fun, but in reality, I experienced the mysterious gut feeling for the first time. I prayed that we would land soon. Despite the cold weather outside, I emerged from the plane drenched in sweat.

I never liked even climbing trees much above ten feet. I did not like the high dive or the high sliding board at the pool. I didn't like being in the nosebleed section of a football stadium and looking outward over the outer wall; here, you could feel the stadium swaying and feel the wind blowing—the sensation of imminent collapse terrified me (of course, not neurotically, mind you). And, oh yeah, let's not forget rollercoasters—I hated them too; being chained to some machine that uncontrollably whips me straight up and straight down is not my idea of having fun. The gut feeling was always there. But I put on a smile and a brave face—a boy must at least *act* courageous, even if he is scared to death.

So why was I spending New Year's Eve in a helicopter, high above Houston, Texas?

ALONG WITH MY growing retinue (Nancy and Rebecca), I had moved to Houston in 1976 just after completing medical school. I began my family practice residency, but after a year, took an elective pediatric rotation at Hermann Hospital. I was hooked. After a short time, I talked with Dr. Rod Howell, the chairman of pediatrics, about changing to a pediatric residency. With his approval, I sat down with my family practice chairman, Dr. Frank Webber, for what I thought would be a difficult conversation. He let me off easily, as he always had in the past, and allowed me to change to Dr. Howell's pediatric program. I have always appreciated Dr. Webber's many kindnesses to me.

There was only one problem with the pediatric residency: Life Flight. An air transport service at the Texas Medical Center—yes, I said *air transport*. I was going to be able to fly again. You can imagine how overjoyed, how thrilled, how delighted, how ecstatic I was at the prospect of being a frequent flyer on a helicopter.

I got over it pretty quickly.

Life Flight was conceived and instituted by Dr. James "Red" Duke. Dr. Duke is a living legend, a famous trauma surgeon with a stellar career. Red Duke was a surgery resident at Parkland Hospital in Dallas on November 22, 1963, when John F. Kennedy was assassinated. Dr. Duke saw the president come in and realized at once that he had sustained a fatal wound. As a neurosurgeon futilely attended President Kennedy, Dr. Duke noticed that over in the corner on a gurney lay another man who was not breathing. He walked over and saw it was Texas Governor John Connally with a gunshot wound to the chest. He had a pneumothorax. Dr. Duke inserted a chest tube and saved his life. John Connally went on to become the U.S. Secretary of Treasury, and the two men became lifelong friends.

There were at that time many other luminaries at the Texas Medical Center, among them Dr. Denton Cooley, Dr. Larry Pickering, Dr. Ralph Feigin, Dr. Dan McNamara, and of course, Dr. Howell. I loved being around these men, even from a distance. We young residents were awed by them; it was a heady experience to work with them or just to walk the same halls with them.

Houston was a hotbed of young guns then. Much of the best, young medical talent in the world came to the Texas Medical

Center to work: physicians like Frank Simon, Gene Adcock, Frank Morriss, and Bill Bartholome.

I felt privileged to be there.

Very quickly, Life Flight had acquired three French helicopters, Alouettes, originally designed for search, rescue and transport in the Alps. We used them to fly to outlying hospitals or accidents within a 120 mile radius of the medical center and then transport patients back for intensive care. Surgery residents manned adult transports and pediatric residents handled sick babies or children.

I don't like heights; I may have already revealed that little-known fact about myself. But I was able to suppress my fears and act like the flying didn't bother me. I beat my fears deep down; I submerged them; I buried them. Very quickly, the flying really didn't bother me. I actually kind of enjoyed it. I even prided myself in being the Life Flight doctor—the guy flown in to handle the big problems. I would stride into the smallish hospitals in my green scrubs and white lab coat, wearing either my cowboy boots or blood-spattered Wallabees. I knew what to do because I had been trained in intensive care. I could intubate patients, I could place chest-tubes, I could insert an umbilical artery catheter. I could start an IV in the smallest premie. I thought I was pretty good; all of us were pretty good at this. I felt sorry for the local doctors who couldn't handle these problems. My descent from the sky to come to their aid likely symbolized my arrogant attitude toward them. Only later, after I had been in practice for a while, did I gain an understanding of their lives. The local pediatrician I was helping had seen forty patients that day. He did not have the back-up to care for these seriously ill patients, nor did he have the recent hands-on experience of caring for them. In addition, he could not be in several places at one time, seeing patients in the office, caring by phone for someone in the ICU, etc. He had the humility and the grace to admit that the patient was better off in a big referral center, and his role now was to keep the patient alive until the cavalry arrived by helicopter. These guys were usually exhausted and simply relieved to hand their patients off to us; later, I understood how overworked, overburdened, and stressed-out they were. But then, all I knew was that I had the skills of an intensivist. I thought I could take care of anybody. No brag, just facts.

I enjoyed being the expert from the Texas Medical Center.

I had some unusual experiences flying in these helicopters. Once, I was called stat to the helipad in a severe storm, rain pelting us as we emerged from the elevator, thunder booming, lightning flashing, gale-force winds blowing (or so it seemed). We made a difficult and unpleasant run to a nearby hospital (I don't like heights, and I especially don't like heights in a hurricane). When we arrived, our cute little patient was sitting in her hospital bed and playing, barking like a dog but happy as a clam. She had viral croup and was *not* very sick. She had scared her doctor, but the transport was not necessary. We couldn't decide who needed more care, the patient or her doctor. When we returned, my supervising doctor was livid that this ridiculous mission had jeopardized our lives for nothing.

Another time, on a very dark night, we flew to a hospital an hour away for a little child who was in shock. We approached a field about 100 yards from the hospital, obviously in the midst of a construction project. Sheriffs' cars had encircled the field, and they shone their headlights into the center to guide our landing. We noted numerous drainage ditches crisscrossing the field. After safely arriving, we negotiated our way around the ditches with our equipment and made it to the emergency room. After stabilizing our patient, we rolled him out the front door of the emergency room and into the field. Fighting our way through the field and dodging the ditches, with fifty yards now separating us from the chopper, the boy arrested. We had to stop and stabilize him right there and then. In the middle of a dark field with our only light the headlights of the cars, we began CPR. The little boy was dying.

His heart rate was dropping. I pulled every drug I had out of our equipment chest and gave them all IV. He kept going down. I had one thing more I could do: I gave him intracardiac epinephrine. I carefully felt his left ribs near his sternum, placed a large needle between two of them, and plunged it into his heart. I drew back on the syringe to be certain I was in the right ventricle, and seeing the red flashback, I rapidly injected epinephrine directly into his heart. "Thank God," I thought, "he's responding." We began moving quickly again toward the helicopter. We loaded him on board and lifted off. Never since have I done a resuscitation in a dark field.

On another occasion, we flew to a country hospital to pick up a premature baby. The hospital had no newborn nursery. When we arrived, we were taken to a kitchen; I was hoping they were going to give us some coffee and homemade breakfast cake, or at least doughnuts, before we went to work. But no. There in the kitchen they had our premature newborn, and there we stabilized the baby before loading her into the helicopter for the flight back to Houston. I never quite understood why she was in the kitchen. And they never gave us any doughnuts.

NOW, IT WAS New Year's week, and I was on call every other night for a week. I had been off the previous week for Christmas, and my fellow residents had covered me. Now, it was my time to pay. I would work a thirty-six hour shift, go home and sleep like I was dead, and then get up and do it all over again the next thirty-six hours, all week long. Earlier in the week, my father-in-law had flown into town for the Bluebonnet Bowl, and he and my wife had gone to watch the Georgia Bulldogs play as I stayed home to "take care of the girls." What that meant was that my girls and I all went to sleep at the same time. Nothing would have awakened me. Nothing. I was worth very little that night as I "took care of the girls."

My week was almost over, and it would end like this, in the

helicopter again. As the most senior pediatric resident in the hospital, my job was to oversee the other residents and interns as our team ran the inpatient service, the term nursery, the intensive care nursery, the pediatric intensive care unit, and the emergency room. In addition, if an outlying hospital called us needing an emergency transport, I was the designated in-flight physician.

It was about 7:00 p.m., December 31. My beeper went off. I hated it when that happened: it was never good news. A call had just come in about a near-drowning victim. I headed to the emergency room as the crew gathered, then boarded the helicopter on the pad just on top of the emergency department. I knew exactly what to do as we lifted off.

My headset was on as I silently surveyed the lights and houses below me. My company in the cabin were the pilot and the flight-nurse. I was in the front seat beside the pilot. I was tired. I had worked all day, and would work until 6:00 the next night. The time in the helicopter was actually a break for me. I had time to think—and rest. Most normal people were preparing for New Year's Eve celebrations. My devoted wife and two sweet daughters, Rebecca and Rachel (born after our move to Texas), were at home by themselves, without husband and daddy. And I was here in the air. The only sound was the thumping whirring of the rotating blades above us. I thought and I prayed. I remember thanking God for the beauty of the cold, quiet, winter night, and thanking him for blessing me in the year now ending. I asked him for his blessing in the New Year. And I asked him for help for this new mission. I was too weary to be worried, but I knew that I was going to a small Texas town to try to save a young girl's life. By this time, I was used to this. I was too tired to be anxious even about heights.

My reverie and rest were interrupted by the pilot announcing through our headsets that we were five minutes out. Time to get myself ready mentally and psychologically. We landed safely in the parking lot near the little hospital, and the nurse and I jumped out as soon as we touched the ground. We kept our heads down, crouching low so as not to be rudely and inconveniently decapitated by the still whirling helicopter blades. Others were waiting for us there and helped us unload our equipment and stretcher.

We ran into the emergency room and, pulling back a curtain, found our little patient. She was a beautiful four-year-old little girl who had wandered away from her house and fallen into a creek on their ranch. The creek ran through an isolated, remote section of the land, and, in the thirty-five degree weather, the child had discovered the polluted, contaminated, slowly moving water. Playing for awhile, she had most likely tripped over a root and fallen in. Who knew how long she had been submerged?

My patient was comatose.

We secured her airway, made certain we had a large-bore IV in place, stabilized her, and loaded her onto the gurney and into the helicopter. En route to the Texas Medical Center, the nurse and I took turns "bagging" her; that is, we breathed for her using mechanical ventilation by hand, positive pressure breathing, through her endotracheal tube. We alternated because of fatigue; you can do this for only so long. Our intention was to hyperventilate her to decrease brain swelling.

We arrived back at the hospital and unloaded her, wheeled her across the helipad to the elevator, descended to the ER, quickly made certain that she was stable, and rapidly transferred her to the pediatric intensive care unit.

I phoned the attending physician to ask him to come in. I consulted a neurosurgeon to request that he place a bolt in the girl's skull to enable us to monitor intracranial pressure. We did all we could to prevent the dreaded and fatal outcome of brain herniation.

Just after midnight, the girl's parents and grandparents arrived at our hospital after a three-hour drive. In the hallway just outside the Pediatric Intensive Care Unit (PICU), we discussed the little girl's serious condition with the distraught family. Grief, fear, fatigue, lack of food, our very guarded words, and our grim prognosis had their combined effects on the crushed grandmother: she passed out completely, lurching and then crashing to the floor like a felled timber, landing on her face. We helped pick her up and assisted her to a chair; she was uninjured except for slight bruising.

I flew again a few hours later on New Year's Day to pick up a baby boy who had been discovered in a trashcan at a shopping center. He was a few weeks old and had been discarded like a piece of refuse. He was covered with fleas. He was emaciated and cold. His blood sugar was low, so we gave him an IV bolus of D10W. We warmed him and brought him in good condition to our PICU. As we walked in with him, I looked to my left and saw an empty bed: my four-year-old patient who had nearly drowned was not there. She had finally succumbed to the assault on her brain. My fellow residents had pronounced her dead while I was away.

What did I feel? Deep, crushing despair? Profound sadness? Extreme helplessness? Sudden weariness? A humble sense of my own weakness?

Or was I too numbed by fatigue and repeated exposure to death and suffering to feel anything?

I don't know. I didn't have the time or luxury to process what I felt: there were too many needs among the living, and I had to keep going.

I knew only one thing: I had not been able to save her life. The whole team had not been able to save her life.

Only God can heal. Only God can save a life.

I have never liked heights. I have always been afraid of them.

... to the LORD your God belong the heaven and the highest heavens ...
Deuteronomy 10:14

*LORD, my heart is not haughty, nor mine eyes lofty: neither do
I exercise myself in great matters, or in things too high for me.*
   Psalm 131:1 (KJV)

*For my thoughts are not your thoughts, neither are your ways
my ways, saith the LORD.*
*For as the heavens are higher than the earth, so are my ways
higher than your ways, and my thoughts than your thoughts.*
   Isaiah 55: 8-9 (KJV)

*For I am convinced that neither death, nor life, nor angels,
nor principalities, nor things present, nor things to come, nor
powers,*
*nor height, nor depth, nor any other created thing, shall be able
to separate us from the love of God, which is in Christ Jesus our
Lord.*
   Romans 8:38-39

NOTE: Life Flight is a registered trademark of the Memorial
Hermann Health System in Houston, Texas.

13

The Unreal Pediatrician

OOH—THE DREADED three a.m. phone call—3:00 a.m.—in the morning—*that* three a.m.

Was it real?

Yes, the phone really was ringing; I was not just having a bad dream.

I slid out of bed and ran quickly to the kitchen phone, hoping the rest of my family was still sleeping.

I grabbed the phone after the fourth ring. Not too bad for a slow guy in the middle of the night.

"Hello?" I mumbled.

"Uh, hi … uh … Dr. Miller? Yeah, hi … this is Brenda Smith. I've never met you, and you've never treated my children. But my four-year-old son has had this 104-degree fever for the last three days and I just can't seem to get it down. You're not his real pediatrician. His real pediatrician is in Augusta. But, I thought I'd call you to see if you could help me out."

She seemed to emphasize the "real" part. Was she subtly hinting at something?

I politely (I'm *always* polite, especially at 3:00 a.m.) ran through his symptoms, assured her (and myself) that it was nothing serious and nothing that demanded immediate care, and gave her instruction in fever management. She told me she planned to take him to his real doctor in Augusta, thirty miles away, later that morning, a few hours after the roosters began crowing.

As I hung up the phone I realized I had just been used. It took me a few minutes to figure this out. I'm not always aware of subsurface issues, especially at 3:00 a.m. Mrs. Smith had called me to avoid long distance charges, and to avoid awakening her son's real doctor—who needed his sleep.

And I wondered to myself: "Am I not real? Are the real pediatricians only in Augusta?"

Was I therefore an unreal pediatrician?

I WAS TWENTY-NINE years old when I arrived in Thomson, Georgia with Nancy and our three little girls. I was fresh from my residency in Houston, Texas, a newly minted pediatrician. The people of McDuffie, Warren, Wilkes, Glascock, and Talliaferro Counties took us in and welcomed us. I was the only pediatrician between Augusta and Atlanta; I was the law west of the Pecos. And I admit I spent a lot of time on the phone discussing difficult cases with my mentors in Houston and Augusta.

I was busy from the very beginning. People brought their young children to me for care, and they trusted me. I've always been grateful for the way the people of Thomson and the surrounding area gave me a chance and a start. They were very good to us, far better than we deserved. I still see many Thomson children, most of them now children of my former patients.

I was idealistic. I printed my phone numbers, office and home, in the phone book. I actually *wanted* a beeper; I was the only MD in town who wore one. The older doctors saw no need for a pager. They had been doing fine for years without one; they were available by phone, and in a small town, people would show up on your front porch if they really needed you. The other physicians in town really took good care of the new young guy and seemed happy to have me there. My youthful zeal and eagerness likely amused them a little, but they never showed it.

I was very comfortable handling most of what I saw. I could handle the big stuff, the serious stuff, because I had been trained to do it. I had committed myself to a big goal during my year as chief resident: to become the consummate pediatrician. I had made good progress, but I was not there yet. I still had a lot of work to do in the everyday little things, the things that won't kill patients, yet are still important. I was still developing what we call "clinical judgment," a concept that sounds nebulous to medical students and that comes with experience. I was still learning the art of medicine. All of this would take a while.

Unintentionally, the 3:00 a.m. mother had made a good point. I don't think she was trying to show me any disrespect when she told me I was not her son's "real doctor." But it got me thinking. It was true that there were some very good pediatricians in Augusta then: Drs. Billy Wilkes, Herb Harper, Joe Green, James Bennett, Beryl Tanenbaum, Gene Tanner, and George Echols. And I had to admit, they were real pediatricians. They were more real than I was. They had cared for many more sick children for many more years than I had. I looked up to them all. They were real.

I began to see that several things make pediatricians real. First, we love children. I love children. I always have. I don't know—I just like children. I like being with them, I like their honesty, I like their hopeful view of life, I like their beauty. I like seeing things through their eyes. I like their deep and searching questions.

I like it when children tell me they love me, and when, after a difficult exam or some shots, they hug me. I like to make children laugh and giggle at my ridiculous stories and "witty" comments. I like it when they give me pictures they have drawn or colored for me. I like it when they tell me they pray for me—I tell them I need it. I like it when they sing for me. I like it when they tell me they love Jesus.

I just like children. If kids scare you or annoy you, then pediatrics is likely not your field.

Second, of course, real pediatricians need to be well trained and well educated; that allows patients and their families to have confidence in our abilities.

Third, we need to have integrity in dealing with our patients; that allows people to trust us.

Parents need to know two things when they hand over their most precious possessions, their dear children, to me for care. They need to know that I will do what is best for their child, and they need to know that I will do whatever it takes to do my very best for their child. It is all about trust and confidence.

The fourth thing that makes a pediatrician real is time. Yes, time. Time takes time. Time cannot be rushed. This final ingredient is essential to becoming a real pediatrician. It takes time, years of building mutual trust and confidence. Offering care year after year, persevering in practice, not going away, hanging around, consistency (not perfection)—these simple things are not easy, but they yield credibility.

Time also produces humility. Years and years of caring for sick children will make even the proudest physicians humble. Why? Because we are forced to realize that we are not really in control: God is. Things can happen that completely surprise doctors. Taking care of sick children can be humbling, even humiliating. Decades of pediatric practice erode away even the most arrogant pride and replace it with a humble awareness of our own fallibility and a gentle understanding of human suffering.

It has been a long time since I began my practice in Thomson. Most people there trusted me even then. Now, more than ever, people actually think I know what I'm doing. I treasure that trust and confidence, and I realize these are gifts families give me. I never want to abuse these gifts or disappoint my patients and families.

Somehow, over the years, time has slowly done its work,

and I hope I've been gradually transformed from being an unreal pediatrician to being a real one. Maybe now, after more than thirty years and more than 160,000 patient encounters, I'm finally almost real.

If you hang around long enough, people start to think you know what you are talking about.

And reality starts to set in.

14

Ben

JOSH AND LESLEE were newlyweds, a great young couple joining our church family. They explained to me how they had met and how they had come to Christ. They had graduated from college in Milledgeville, Georgia and during their time there had been greatly influenced by a young campus minister named Ben. Ben sounded very impressive, and it was clear from their description that they loved and respected him. Josh could not stop talking about Ben. I finally asked him, "Josh, who is this Ben? What's his last name?"

"Ben Thigpen," Josh responded.

"Ben Thigpen? Really?" This was getting interesting.

"Yeah, Ben Thigpen. Do you know him?"

"I might. Is he deaf in one ear?"

"Yes. When you talk to Ben, he always turns his left ear, his good ear, toward you, so he can hear you. He can't hear out of his right ear. How did you know?"

It was a long story.

IN 1985, I was a young pediatrician and had been in practice for five years. I was at an early morning breakfast meeting for the

University Hospital pediatric department. I always had a love-hate relationship with these meetings—mainly hate.

I hate early morning meetings: they mean I have to get up an hour earlier, do everything I ordinarily do each morning, and still try to get to the office on time. I do not like early mornings. I do not like meetings. And I do not like to rush around. Early morning meetings make it tough on someone like me to be punctual. I can be thankful that people usually give doctors a pass on being late to things; they very generously assume we are late because, of course, we must have been at the hospital caring for some acutely ill patient. Sometimes that's true, but not always.

I loved these meetings for one reason, and one reason only: breakfast. University Hospital makes gourmet omelets, and their doughnuts are twice the size of Krispy Kreme doughnuts, covered in a whitish, sugary, translucent glaze. I was usually in a coma for a few hours after I ate breakfast there.

I had just arrived at the meeting (a little late, of course) and had just begun to take a few bites of my two-egg cheese omelet, and my two deluxe doughnuts. The meeting itself was boring, as usual. (I hate meetings.) But the price for admission to the breakfast, and for staying on staff, was attending the meetings.

My beeper went off a few minutes after I sat down, right on cue. It never failed me. I can't tell you how many meals, how many nights, how many basketball and soccer games, how many piano and violin recitals, have been interrupted by my faithful pager. This was routine.

I got up, exited the meeting and called the mother of my patient.

"Hi, this is Dr. Miller," I said. "I think someone there just paged me." I'm pretty flashy early in the morning.

"Dr. Miller, this is Brenda Thigpen." She was always calm.

"Good morning, Brenda. Is someone sick?"

"Yes. Ben. Ben has meningitis again." Brenda was always calm.

I almost choked on my doughnut.

"Wait a second, Brenda. There's a lot of noise here. I thought for a second you said Ben had meningitis again."

"Yes, that's what I said. Ben has meningitis again." She was always calm.

Certain words or phrases have a magical quality in their ability to terrify me. "Meningitis" is one of them. Others that get my undivided attention and put me on high alert are things like: "He can't breathe" or "She's turning blue" or "I can't wake him up" or "Her temperature is 107." And lest I forget: "He has a 103-degree fever and kind of a purple rash" also gets me. I never like to hear things like these, and especially not early in the morning.

I thought I was going to throw up.

Ben had had pneumococcal meningitis three years before and had made a nice recovery. He was fine. Now, his mother was calling me saying he was giving an encore. I knew she was probably right. I told her to come quickly to the emergency room and that I would meet them there.

Ben was now six years old. When he and his parents arrived at the emergency room, they gave the history of fever, vomiting, and increasing lethargy over the past few hours. On examination, his temperature was 104 degrees. He was responsive only to pain. His neck was stiff.

Yep. He had meningitis.

He was pretty sick. I was pretty scared.

I performed the needed lumbar puncture (spinal tap); his spinal fluid was obviously full of pus, not the clear watery fluid normally seen. He definitely had bacterial meningitis. Meningitis is a serious infection of the central nervous system, and it can be fatal or cause long-term disability even with the best, most aggressive treatment. It is one of the diseases I hate the most. The stakes are very high. It is also a disease which in 21st century America we do not see often, thanks to three very effective vaccines.

I began Ben on high dose IV antibiotics. He spent the next few days in the pediatric ICU and gradually became more responsive. I was beginning to be relieved. His blood and spinal fluid cultures grew out pneumococcus and he completed a ten-day course of IV antibiotics in the hospital. All was going according to plan. I was worried, though, about why he had had two episodes of pneumococcal meningitis (this was unusual) and we began a big work-up to try to determine the reason.

Oddly, he began to say after a few days that he could not hear out of his right ear. I hoped it was because of the ear infection that had preceded the meningitis; we see a lot of temporary hearing loss from middle ear infections.

Ben kept complaining about his loss of hearing, even though, by now, his ear appeared totally normal. Each day on rounds, I asked him about his hearing, and each day I rubbed my fingers near his ears and held my Accutron tuning-fork watch to his ears; he could not hear in his right ear. Audiometry confirmed my fears. The meningitis had extracted its toll on his right auditory nerve. He was deaf in that ear.

I could never explain his recurrent meningitis despite aggressively looking for an answer. We took steps to be sure, as much as possible, that it never happened again, and it never did.

Ben grew up and stayed relatively healthy. I lost track of him after high school, but he was always an engaging, joyful, delightful child and young man. I never heard him complain about anything, not even his hearing loss.

God formed Ben into a man who was to influence many college students for good. And now, here were Josh and Leslee telling me that a young boy whose life I had been privileged to touch had become a great man.

God's ways are often hidden and often mysterious. I often misunderstand God. Yet, there are times when he rolls back the mist of mystery a little and gives us a glimpse of his secret workings in our lives. I think God does this for our encouragement. He is telling us: "Keep on. I'm with you. Trust me that I'm doing something great and eternal with your life."

In our seemingly ordinary, everyday lives, God is weaving an intricate tapestry, writing a poem of unspeakable beauty, working his artistry into us to create his own handiwork for his glory and our good. He keeps on working in us, around us, and through us whether we are conscious of it or not, whether we see it or not, and even whether we acknowledge it or not. God is not thwarted in his purposes, and he will fulfill all his sovereign, good will.

God grants his followers the privilege of participating in his story as it plays out under his active direction.

For we are His workmanship [poiema], created in Christ Jesus for good works, which God prepared beforehand, that we should walk in them.
Ephesians 2:10

15

A Hand on My Shoulder

DIAGNOSTIC CHALLENGES can be fun, as long as the patient in front of me isn't dying for lack of a diagnosis.

Diagnostic puzzles are interesting when they occur at an early morning case conference. Here, far removed from reality by several layers, physicians are insulated from time pressures and patient outcomes. As doctors and med students sip their high-intensity black coffee and eat their coma-inducing doughnuts, nothing much is at risk except a little pride—no one wishes to appear unintelligent. It's an educational game. The purpose is to prepare doctors for the real thing. It's a dry run or a drill so that when it happens in real time and real life, you're ready.

Diagnostic dilemmas are also entertaining and educational when presented in journals. The patient may be real, but to the doctor reading the journal it's all theoretical, and there's no pressure to be right.

Diagnostic puzzles can be intellectually challenging and satisfying when treating actual patients. With plenty of time to think and observe, these puzzles may be a great exercise in thought, imagination, and creativity. The reward for the patient is often rich, and the process for the physician fulfilling.

The process of making a diagnosis can be challenging, educational, exciting, and even fun.

But diagnostic ambiguity is not so much fun if the real patient lying in the real bed before you is near death and you *must* know *now* what is wrong and how to treat quickly. I have never cared much for ambiguity anyway. I'm a pretty straightforward kind of guy. Give me the facts and data, let me think about it, let me arrive at a good differential diagnosis, let me come to the likely diagnosis, and let me go ahead and treat my patient. Cut and dry. Carve away anything extraneous and get to the problem. Cut to the chase. And get out of my way. No ambiguity.

To be certain I'm clear and that there is no ambiguity about it, I don't like ambiguity. And I definitely don't like ambiguity when I have a dying patient in front of me. Here, it's not a game, it's not fun, it's not a sterile ivory-tower exercise, and it is not theoretical. It is real life; the pressure is enormous, and the consequences of a wrong diagnosis can be catastrophic for the patient and family.

Mary Winn had been admitted at about 7:00 a.m. by one of my partners. She was a cute little seven-month-old baby girl who had suddenly developed fussiness alternating with lethargy. Her symptoms demanded that she be evaluated for infection and metabolic disease. A complete work-up had been done which had revealed nothing helpful. I saw her a few hours later. She was alternately moaning in pain and sleeping. Something was dreadfully wrong. I examined her and reviewed the lab work. I couldn't come up with anything to explain her symptoms. I talked things over with her worried parents and explained that I was not sure what was wrong but that we would watch her carefully, continuing to evaluate her. I planned to come back later to check on her. "It might just be a virus," I said (and hoped). Many things are viral, and viruses can cause a myriad of diseases and manifestations, often masquerading as other illnesses. Besides, this diagnosis is always a good back up when we can't quite figure out what else to say. If it were viral, it would go away by itself;

I have never understood the mystery of where viruses go when they go away, but they usually do. I didn't really care where this one went, as long as it left the building.

But I was not really convinced it was viral.

I left the room worried and frustrated. I was worried that I was missing something bad, and I was frustrated with myself for not knowing Mary Winn's problem. After all, I was a doctor, and doctors are supposed to know these things. And I really wished that Mary Winn had been a little more considerate. She was not cooperating with me. She was stubbornly resisting all my efforts to come to a diagnosis. Patients should be easy to get along with, have a little consideration for their doctors' feelings, and serve up an easy diagnosis. I don't like ambiguity, especially in a very sick patient and when I'm scared, and I really didn't know what was wrong with Mary Winn. The problem was that she was not some theoretical case discussion. No, she was a little girl whose eyes had looked into mine as if to plead: "Help me ... do something, Doctor." I was doing my best to comply but I knew I was failing her. I hoped it was nothing serious.

Maybe it really *was* just a virus.

I walked to the staff elevators to head to my office, lost in thought, completely distracted by my little patient. Just as the door opened, I had an irresistible compulsion to go back into the room. I am not a mystic, but I had the strong sense that a hand was on my shoulder and that words were being whispered into my mind: "Go back in there. You missed something." It was not palpable. It was not visible. It was not audible. But the encounter arrested me, and I turned around and went back in.

I knew exactly what to do.

After re-entering the room I did one more thing, knowing ahead of time what I would find. Without any doubt, I knew her diagnosis before I did this next thing. Some might call it prescience. Some might call it a gut feeling. Others would call it intuition. Call it what you will, but calling it anything other than this would be to call it the wrong thing: it was a gift from God. It was Providence. It was God's presence saving a little girl's life when her physician didn't know what to do. I asked the nurse for a Hemoccult card, donned a glove, and did a rectal exam. There was no gross blood in the stool, but the Hemoccult card turned positive for blood immediately, as I knew it would.

Mary Winn had an intussusception.

Intussusception is a life-threatening, often fatal, telescoping of the bowel on itself that left untreated leads to bowel obstruction and bowel death. Patients like Mary Winn come in to see their doctors with extreme irritability alternating with lethargy, all this a reflection of severe, crampy abdominal pain and intermittent relief.

I picked up the phone and called my good friend, pediatric surgeon Dr. Charles Howell, and discussed Mary Winn with him. I ordered a barium enema, a procedure that is diagnostic and can be therapeutic. Hers revealed the intussusception we expected to find, but it did not result in an ultimate cure. Dr. Howell took her to surgery and definitively treated the problem.

Mary Winn stayed healthy the rest of her childhood. She grew up (as my patients tend to do) and earned her MBA at Harvard University. She is now a management consultant in Boston and she is newly married.

I credit her survival to the hand of God on my shoulder, irresistibly leading me to the correct diagnosis and saving this little girl's life. I've experienced these moments of light—God's supernatural presence—at other times as I have taken care of other patients, but never any more powerfully than at this time. It is not a frequent occurrence for me. God usually uses more "ordinary" means to heal my patients, if "ordinary" is the right word to describe the ongoing outpouring of his grace and goodness at all times to keep us alive and heal us with or without the use of modern medicine. However God chooses to work, I know that my life and the lives of my patients are always in his hands, and that he is constantly, actively sustaining our lives, healing us, helping us, and supporting us. And I know I could never practice medicine without God's ever-present help, whether experienced in ordinary or spectacular ways.

I would never have the courage.

And your ears will hear a word behind you, "This is the way, walk in it," whenever you turn to the right or to the left.
   Isaiah 30:21

16

Casey

IT HAD BEEN a rough week. I was ten weeks into solo practice, and thus, ten weeks into being on call non-stop. I worked in my office, made rounds, and then, after hours and on weekends, I answered phone calls for emergencies (and often non-emergencies) twenty-four hours a day, seven days a week. It was getting a little tedious.

One Friday night, I went to bed after getting our four children tucked in. I hoped it would be a quiet night, one that allowed me seven hours of un-interrupted sleep, though I was used to fielding nighttime phone calls about any thing at any time.

"How do I get this lice medication out of Johnny's hair?" (at 11:45 p.m.).

"How much acetaminophen do I give my baby? He's teething" (at midnight).

"My little girl is constipated. What do I do?" (at 1:00 a.m.).

"I just thought you would want to know that my daughter is no longer constipated" (the same mother, the next night at 3:00 a.m.).

I had hopes of getting some sleep this particular Friday night, and I happily drifted off to dreamland.

Nancy was used to hearing my beeper go off. It hardly awakened her, and often I got up, answered the call from the kitchen phone, kissed her on the forehead, made my emergency room visit to handle the problem, and returned to bed without her even noticing it. The next morning, she would ask me how I had slept, not realizing I had spent half the night in the ER.

This time was a little different. At 1:00 a.m., my beeper went off. "Oh, no," I groaned. Uh-oh, a second beep.

I don't like pagers.

The beep had awakened my wife, and she mumbled, "Go ahead and call from the bedside phone." I rolled over, turned on the light, and made the call to Judy Wireman.

Judy was a new mother with a twenty-day-old baby boy, Casey. He was spitting his formula. "Okay, big deal," I thought, "every baby spits a little." How many babies with reflux had I dealt with already in my short career? And besides, most new mothers worry about all kinds of things. It was obvious that Judy was simply a nervous new mother. It soon became apparent, however, that the mere spitting was not the main reason for the call: she was just giving background information. I listened carefully as Judy went on rapidly: "He's vomiting, not just spitting up now. He just vomited, turned blue, and stopped breathing for about thirty seconds." Ooh, I wished she hadn't said that. Things like that don't make me feel good about my patients. She continued to explain more thoroughly. Judy and her husband, Roy, had gone out for a little break that evening while Roy's parents babysat. While in the elder Mrs. Wireman's arms, Casey had stopped breathing and turned blue; she had stimulated him by slapping his back and splashing cold water on his face to arouse him.[2]

I wanted to tell Judy she was over-reacting, that it sounded like a non-problem, a non-event. I was tired and sleepy. I wanted to tell her that he was fine. I tried to talk myself into thinking she was

2   Roy Wireman believes that Casey would have died then if he had not been in his grandmother's arms, yet another case of SIDS, or crib death. I think he is right.

just exaggerating. Parents always exaggerate their babies' problems when they're new, scared, and especially when it's after midnight. From midnight through 5:00 a.m., everything is magnified: seconds become minutes, gagging becomes vomiting, normal color in a darkened room becomes cyanosis, and the need to simply pick a baby up becomes the need for CPR. I wanted to talk Judy into just doing the routine things for reflux, calm her down, reassure her, and tell her just to watch him. I wanted to go back to sleep. I wanted to rationalize to myself that he was really all right.

But I couldn't.

Nancy was wide awake by now, and had been listening in to my side of the conversation. She said, "You should go see this baby."

I told Judy to hold on for a second and cupped my hand over the phone as Nancy and I had a brief exchange. "Huh? I thought you were asleep."

"I think you should see this baby."

"Yeah, you're right." Something in the conversation had bothered her. It was bothering me, too; I could not just ignore this problem hoping it would disappear. This is not a good strategy for patient care. In addition, I had learned early in our marriage to take my wife and her gut feelings seriously. She's usually right.

I should probably stop here and explain something. I love my wife, but Nancy has this problem that I don't like to talk about much. Her antennae are overdeveloped. Yes, it is embarrassing, but I like transparency; in the interest of full disclosure, I need to discuss this issue. She has a highly developed sense of smell, taste, hearing, sight, and touch. Her sensors regarding everything in life are finely and precisely attuned to her surroundings. Mine, alas, on the other hand, are barely rudimentary. We can walk into a room full of people, and something unremarkable (to me) may happen. When we leave, she'll say, "Did you see that?"

"What?"

"What just happened, of course."

"Huh?"

I had not seen a thing. I guess I should enjoy my inability to pick up on things; it makes for a more blissful life.

Her sensors usually are right on target but not always. I have been awakened by Nancy in the middle of the night because of her sensory acuity. Once, she slapped me on the side and said, "Are you awake?"

"Sure, I'm always awake at 2:00 a.m."

"Do you see that fire?"

"What fire?"

"The one down the block. Don't you see the flashing orange flames?"

"No."

"Well, I think you should go see what's going on."

"Okay."

I got out of bed, got dressed, and walked down the street.

The fire was the blinking caution light a block away.

Usually, however, her sensory perception is superhuman and in line with reality. Nancy smells toxic smells that no one else can smell. She sees danger that no one else can see. And she hears noises that are imperceptible to mere mortals. She is always on high alert. Her antennae are always up and hyper-functioning.

I'm glad they are, because she has helped keep me out of trouble on a multitude of occasions. This was one such occasion. It was nice to have a nudge in the right direction.

I told Judy to take Casey to the University Hospital ER. I quickly dressed and drove there. I expected to see a happy baby, a worn out mother, and an anxious, frustrated father. I would work my plan, developed as I made the ten-minute drive. I would do a brief exam, give lots of reassurance, and send them all home.

Casey was lying on a stretcher. He looked alright except that he appeared a little dehydrated. I decided that I would admit him for observation and some IV fluids. I discussed the admission with his parents, and as I was talking, Casey became dusky, then blue. I listened to his heart and couldn't count his heart rate—it was too fast, but I knew it was in the 250-300 range. He then became unconscious and unarousable. We gave him oxygen, connected him to a monitor, and noted that he was in ventricular tachycardia.

"Really, Casey? V. tach?" I thought to myself for a moment. Suddenly, he went into asystole: his heart had stopped! I could hear no heart sounds at all. I rapidy intubated him (placed a tube in his trachea) and began to ventilate him. My preconceived treatment plan was quickly falling apart.

Casey was not working with me. I don't like it when my patients do this to me. I was now very awake. Sudden terror has this effect on me.

We stabilized Casey and transferred him to the Pediatric Intensive Care Unit. Katherine Fulcher (now Katherine Pugh), a friend from church, was the PICU nurse. Casey was now in normal sinus rhythm. We began an IV, drew some lab work, and watched him. We kept ventilating him. He began to look better. I spent the next four hours with him; only after he promised me that he wouldn't die on me, I left to go home, eat some breakfast, shower, and go to work again, making rounds and seeing patients in the office.

At about 6:00 a.m. I was paged to call the PICU nurse who had replaced Katherine. Casey's lab work was back. The first set of labs had clotted, so this was the second set sent down.

I sat at the kitchen desk and recorded the values. His potassium was high, and his sodium was low. I was tempted to have the lab work redrawn and redone. There is always the tendency to think that abnormal laboratory values are simply laboratory error. You don't want to think your own patient has anything serious—that only happens to other doctors' patients! So, maybe this was a lab error. Or maybe the elevated potassium was due to hemolysis of the red blood cells. Ask any self-respecting doctor, and as the commercials on TV tell you, nine out of ten pediatricians will redo any lab value they don't like. Repeating lab work can be a way of avoiding two big traps: treating lab work instead of treating the patient, and chasing the wrong rabbit down the wrong trail. But it can also be a way of denying a real problem we don't want to think about. In this case, if the lab value makes the doctor uncomfortable, or causes anxiety, distress, or fear—repeat it. Thus, repeating a lab test can be a method of coping with a terrifying problem—coping by denial—much like getting in bed and pulling the covers over your head if you're scared.

The temptation was great.

I did not yield to the temptation. This whole scenario was beginning to feel very familiar. I sat there after the call and thought. Nancy was up by then, and she watched me think, always a very stimulating experience. All at once, I knew his diagnosis. Nancy saw the light of knowing wash over my face. I knew exactly what Casey's problem was, and it was obvious to Nancy that I knew.

Casey had congenital adrenal hyperplasia.

God had given me the diagnosis.

I immediately phoned Dr. Bill Hoffman, a pediatric endocrinologist, and told him the story. I consulted pediatric cardiologist Dr. William Strong (mentor, teacher, and friend) about his cardiac arrhythmia. We began Casey on a specific treatment plan, and he improved rapidly. That evening, I drove back down to check on Casey, taking my three-year-old son with me.[3] Casey appeared completely normal.

---

3   This was back in the days before HIPAA, and many times on weekends, I took my children with me for Saturday rounds. They enjoyed coloring at the nurses' station, and the staff were always kind to them. My son, Jeremiah, especially enjoyed making X-ray rounds with me because he usually managed to get a doughnut in the radiology suite. For many years he thought seriously of becoming a radiologist because in his way of seeing things, sitting in a dark room, drinking coffee, eating doughnuts, reading the newspaper, and looking at an occasional X-ray seemed a pretty good life.

Several days later, I discharged Casey from the hospital on a very strict regimen of medication. He is now a young man in his 20s, but he terrorized my partners and me many times during his childhood when he repeatedly went into adrenal crisis and shock, and repeatedly averted death.

Alright, I know. Any pediatricians reading this story may be thinking to themselves: "What was so difficult about this diagnosis?" Yes, Casey's story was classical for congenital adrenal hyperplasia, and every pediatrician should be able to make the diagnosis. It was obvious. But God gets the credit for this one, as he does for everything that goes right. I was exhausted and I was sleep-deprived. I easily might have gone the wrong way. It is not just this one instance, though. Every sick patient I see can die. It is only God's grace that keeps them alive. There are so many things that can go wrong—anything from a tired doctor trying to convince himself that a patient really doesn't need to be seen to a hopeful doctor who wants to repeat lab work until it's normal to an exhausted doctor misdiagnosing or incorrectly treating a patient.

God's grace saved Casey's life that night, and over and over again. God's grace gave me his diagnosis many years ago.

And God's grace gave me a wife with hyper-developed sensors.

> *I will instruct you and teach you in the way which you*
> *should go:*
> *I will counsel you with my eye upon you.*
>   *Psalm 32:8*

17

Matthew

JONATHAN DIED of fulminant liver failure at four months of age, and we did not know why.

He had developed jaundice soon after birth, and it never disappeared. It only worsened. Despite a major work-up, we could never determine what kind of liver disease he had, and so the disease persisted and it progressed. Jonathan never improved. He became gravely ill and as he lay dying in the hospital over the course of several days, many friends and family members came to see him and pray for him, and to try to provide comfort and love to his grieving parents.

There were lots of theories and lots of opinions about his disease process, but all we could say was that he had hepatic failure of unknown etiology. It was a frightening lack of clarity for his parents. His death was devastating enough, but it was compounded by the unknown specter haunting the future: Would all their subsequent children be afflicted with the same illness?

One Sunday afternoon, months after Jonathan's death, my wife and I had his parents over to our home for lunch. We discussed Jonathan for a long time. I remember encouraging Phillip and Pam to consider having other children. I told them the likely risk of having another child with the same disease was extremely small. It could not—it would not—happen again. I hoped they would have more children.

In retrospect, my encouragement was based solely on wishful thinking.

Pam and Phillip welcomed their second son into their family on April 3rd, almost exactly two years after his brother had died. Matthew appeared healthy enough. Before his birth, we had compiled a list of nationally known consultants, experts in hepatology, genetics, endocrinology, and metabolic diseases. I discussed with them how we should investigate this new baby once he was born, and we had a comprehensive plan in place. After his birth, we sent Matthew's blood and urine samples all over the country to these experts for analysis. I spent hours on the phone with them trying to prevent a repeat performance in this new baby.

Matthew appeared to be thriving. There was just one bothersome thing: he developed jaundice, and it persisted. By six weeks of age, it was apparent that we had a problem. He and his lab work looked exactly like his brother and his lab work had looked two years before.

He had the same disease. There could be no doubt about it. And no one but God knew what it was.

All we knew was that he would follow his brother to the grave if things went on as they were. I was scared. And I think that Pam and Phillip began to resign themselves to another funeral.

Matthew continued to deteriorate. He looked more jaundiced and his liver function tests were getting worse. The worse he got, the more doggedly I consulted the experts. Time was rushing toward a crescendo event, and as each day passed, my fears intensified. When Matthew was fourteen weeks old, frightfully close to the same age of his older brother when he had died, his most recent lab work came back. I didn't know how to interpret the results, so late that Friday afternoon after my staff had gone home, I sat in our front office, opened Matthew's chart, slumped down in a chair, and phoned Baltimore to speak with Dr. Richard Kelley, an expert in fatty acid metabolism. I had spoken to him before and he had recommended several tests in an attempt to elucidate the diagnosis.

Richard Kelley is a gentle genius. To this day, I have never met him in person, but he is always available to help. He cares about his patients, even if some of them are known to him only through lab work done by his laboratory. He speaks softly, calmly, and logically.

Now, as we discussed Matthew's latest results, we had a breakthrough. Dr. Kelley quietly and methodically thought about Matthew's serum fatty acid and urine organic acid profiles. Then he stated, still softly and unexcitedly, that he thought the lab work was consistent with long chain CoA dehydrogenase deficiency (LCHAD), an enzyme defect. The next step he recommended was an easy one: change Matthew to a special formula called Portagen, feed him only that, and repeat the urine test in about a week.

"That's it?" I thought. "You mean that's all we have to do?"

It seemed too simple.

But then, suddenly, it was all brilliantly clear to me. Still on the phone, I knew then, without question, that Matthew would live. I could see it all clearly in my mind. I had no doubt that this would work. It was as if God had spoken to me deep within my soul, had given me his diagnosis, and had given me supernatural assurance that Matthew would be all right. No, it was not as if God had done these things. He actually did them. I knew Matthew's diagnosis, I knew his treatment, and I knew his future (in part). I was relieved; I could not stand to see this boy die. After we finished our conversation, I made my notes in the chart as I smiled to myself, a burden lifted. Matthew would live. I knew it.

The breathtaking clarity of the diagnosis, treatment, and future was a gift from God. I was only a third-tier actor in the play, just on the edges of the action, maybe only a part of the audience, looking on as the events unrolled. God helped us all through the expertise of Richard Kelley.

I called Matthew's parents and explained what I had just discussed with Dr. Kelley. We decided to meet at their home the next night so I could go over the whole thing in more detail. I was far more optimistic than they were. I'm ashamed to admit that optimism is not my forté, so this was out of character for me. But here I knew the outcome: life.

I think Phillip and Pam were afraid to believe, afraid to hope that Matthew might live. They feared massive disappointment. Having seen this process play out before, they had accepted the very likely outcome of burying this infant son as well. It was not that their faith was defective, not in the least. They trusted God completely. Theirs was not a failure of faith but a huge affirmation of faith in God. They were able to entrust themselves completely to a loving and all-powerful God. They could say to God, "Thy will be done," and they meant it. They submitted themselves gladly and without complaint to God's sovereign goodness, trusting in him even though they could not understand why this was happening again. They were suffering extraordinary anguish, but they were at peace. They prayed for Matthew and left him in God's care. They knew God could heal him; the question was whether he would do it now on earth or ultimately in heaven. This much, however, was obvious: in the normal course of things, without something remarkable happening, Matthew would die just as his brother had.

Faith is simply trusting and resting in God that he will powerfully perform his good will, and that what he does is always for his glory and our good. Faith is in a person, not in a time-bound, desired outcome. We trust God; he handles the outcome.

Phillip's and Pam's faith in God was unshaken and strong.

Nancy and I went to their home as planned, and we spent an hour or so there as I explained what we needed to do and why. The week on Portagen would be both diagnostic and therapeutic for Matthew. We would recheck his organic acids in a week. We agreed to proceed with the plan. As we were leaving we prayed together, asking for God to heal Matthew and that this simple therapeutic maneuver would work. Pam and Phillip, as always, were grateful; I have never heard them complain about God's dealings with them. It was hard to see that a simple formula change might save Matthew's life, but in faith, they went on to this next step.

A week later, we did the lab work again. Matthew's jaundice had disappeared. His lab work began to normalize. The treatment had worked, and here was our answer.

We kept Matthew on Portagen and a strict diet as he grew older. He still requires a special diet and frequent lab work. It is still necessary for us all to maintain a high degree of vigilance. He had some setbacks as he grew, and we always kept in mind the fact that he had LCHAD. For many years, I kept two copies of his emergency treatment plan—one in my briefcase and one in a file at home—in case he ever got into trouble while out of town. I made sure my partners had a copy of the plan as well.

Matthew grew to be 6'3" inches, without a bit of fat on him. He played high school lacrosse. He is now a college student, a normal college guy, a fine man with big plans for the future. He has a little sister who did not inherit her big brothers' disease.

Matthew is alive today because although no else knew what disease had killed Jonathan, God knew. And late one Friday afternoon, he told us what it was.

18

John Benjamin

NAME TAGS.

Unless it's my Sears name tag, worn only in the gross anatomy lab, I don't like to wear them. It's not that I think everyone should know me without the aid of a name tag; I'm not that famous. I just feel silly wearing one.

I don't like name tags—unless someone else is doing the wearing. Now that is a different story.

I need more help than usual with names. I work hard to remember names, and I try to address people by their names. I hate to use generic greetings like "How're you doing, buddy?" or "Hi, dude!" or "Good morning, chief." (I never say "Hey, girlfriend! How's it going?" out of fear of being slapped.) These greetings seem a little impersonal. I like to look people in the eye and greet them by name. But I am just not very good at it.

Nancy, on the other hand, has a great facility with names and connections. It is one of my excuses for sticking close to her side at weddings and funerals. I can easily turn my head downward to her and hear her tell me "This is so and so." I don't even have to ask her. She knows I need her help.

In my ideal world, everyone would wear a name tag except for me. As you may have noticed, however, the world is not ideal.

One evening, when a tall, lanky, young man tapped me on the shoulder at church and asked me if I knew who he was, I was completely lost. He was rude enough to not have a name tag on—never mind that I had "forgotten" mine. Former patients often walk up to me and ask me if I know them. It can be difficult for me to recognize fully bearded young men that I took care of as children, or beautiful young ladies whom I saw as infants, now with babies of their own.

But I do my best.

When this particular young man approached me, I thought, "Alright, what do I do? Nancy's not here to help me." Some social experts would recommend saying, "Sure, but remind me who you are … " Then, if he gave his first and last names, I could have said, "No, I knew your first name … I just forgot your last name." Or vice-versa. I don't use this strategy; it requires a lot of fancy social footwork that I unfortunately lack. Besides, it is disingenuous and dishonest. I am terrible at faking it.

So, what did I do? I said, "No, I'm sorry, please tell me who you are," while thinking, "Please have the decency to wear your name tag next time."

"I'm John Benjamin Youngblood. Do you remember me?"

John Benjamin Youngblood? Oh yes, I remembered him all right. He had given me at least a few of my gray hairs.

John Benjamin was born twenty-three years ago on a Monday morning to Jerry and Virginia Youngblood, friends from church. Virginia had been the kindergarten teacher for one of our daughters. John Benjamin's initial newborn exam was normal though I heard a very innocent-sounding heart murmur. I told his parents he was fine, and I mentioned his murmur as being completely insignificant. We often hear murmurs in new babies, and they usually disappear very quickly.

The murmur persisted as I saw him again Tuesday morning. I was not alarmed and tried to assuage any parental anxiety. I could tell his mother was somewhat concerned, as parents usually are when I use the words "heart murmur." This murmur was trivial, I said (and hoped). I did my best to reassure.

When I made rounds on Wednesday morning, his murmur was still there. No, it wasn't "still there." It had changed as pressures in the circulation had changed, and it was different. It was louder, and it was harsher. It no longer sounded normal. John Benjamin looked fine, he was feeding well, his color was good, and he acted normal, but the murmur ... no ... we had a problem.

I went into his mother's room and discussed our new situation. I told Virginia I would order an electrocardiogram (ECG) to further evaluate her infant son.

I anxiously waited until the ECG was done and then immediately looked at it. There were no left-sided forces at all: the left side of his heart was almost non-existent. I was stunned. And I was afraid. I knew then that John Benjamin very likely had a serious and life-threatening problem: hypoplastic left heart syndrome (HLHS).

And I was thankful. The murmur had been God's way of prompting me toward a further work-up. The murmur had kept me from disastrously discharging John Benjamin.

We moved him to the neonatal intensive care unit where neonatologist Allen Blalock took over. I asked Bill Strong for a pediatric cardiology consultation and I ordered an echocardiogram. Dr. Strong confirmed my fears. John Benjamin had a hypoplastic left heart.

Hypoplastic left heart syndrome is a rare condition in which the left side of the heart does not fully develop during fetal life; this abnormality is not compatible with life. HLHS has killed many infants; I have seen babies die from it. Often, because of temporary collateral blood flow, these babies do fine for a few days. They may or may not have a murmur, and if they do, it is not diagnostic; *Nelson's Pediatrics* describes the murmur as "non-descript." Babies with HLHS often look and act completely normal—for a while. They might be discharged from the hospital appearing normal, and then go home with their mothers, where, once the collateral vessel closes a day or so later, they die. Or they may appear fine but then develop what appears to be an overwhelming infection; because the supposed infection distracts the doctor from the real problem, the baby may die before the actual diagnosis is made.

Twenty-three years ago, surgery for HLHS was just coming into its own, and it was not always the best thing to do. With John Benjamin's diagnosis established, the Youngbloods had one of three choices:

1. Do a heart transplantation.
2. Do a series of serious and dangerous operations.
3. Take John Benjamin home, love him, care for him, and allow him to die peacefully over the next few days.

There were major questions to be answered: How much suffering must John Benjamin endure? And for what outcome? Would surgery merely prolong his suffering and dying? Or would the surgical ordeal save his life? In coldly objective terms, it was classic risk/benefit analysis. As horrible as it seems even to consider, hospice care was not an unthinkable decision considering the surgical options then available.

After I discussed our choices with the Youngbloods, I went back to the newborn nursery and sat down to ponder what to do. As I was thinking, a good friend, obstetrician Gene Long came in and asked what was wrong. We talked about John Benjamin, and he encouraged me to start calling pediatric heart surgery programs across the country to discover all possibilities. I spent the next couple of hours on the phone.

The Youngbloods also investigated. They made their choice: to aggressively do all that could be done to save their son's life. John Benjamin was transferred to Emory University where his first operation was performed when he was twenty-two days old.

Many people in our church and across our city prayed for John Benjamin. We prayed for his survival, and we prayed he would emerge safely from surgery. People prayed he would grow to vigorous manhood, loving Jesus Christ.

John Benjamin had two subsequent major heart operations. His family moved away when he was five years old, and I lost track of him except for a few infrequent reconnections. Ultimately, he received his undergraduate degree in psychology from Bryan College.

Now he was back in town, tapping me on my shoulder.

When he told me who he was, I could only smile and hug him, and think to myself, "Thank God!" The reunion gave me encouragement when God knew I needed some. I am amazed at the little surprises God gives us along the way, tokens of his love, gifts of mercy, that keep reminding us that he is with us and that he loves us.

John Benjamin is a handsome, articulate, intelligent young man. He has excellent people skills. He follows Jesus Christ.

He worked at our office for a while, in the same pediatric practice where he was once cared for as a small child. He became a part of our staff. During that time, he would walk into an exam room where a baby with serious heart problems was lovingly being cradled in his mother's arms—the mother trying not to worry, but unable to escape it—the deep fear is always there, and it never goes away—John Benjamin Youngblood would walk into that room and offer hope and encouragement.

And, of course—he was always wearing a name tag.

19

Baby Rashes, Ecchymoses, and Petechiae

I SEE A LOT of skin rashes. All pediatricians do. Usually the rashes are not serious, and usually they are easy to diagnose and treat. But as with anything else in pediatrics, you never know what's behind the door to the next exam room. Danger and surprise are always lurking. "Don't get complacent, don't get arrogant, and don't be stupid," I remind myself all day long, especially the "stupid" part.

A rash can be as simple as a diaper rash, though even these can rarely signal something far more serious. But usually, diaper rashes are not a big deal. Some parents, however, get very upset over them. I have had parents come in, undo the diaper, show me a rash in the diaper area, and then ask me in very serious, funereal tones, as if they were asking about a deadly and life-threatening illness, "Doctor ... is this ... could it be ... is it ... a diaper rash?" (I await the shrieks and wails that are sure to follow.) They are almost afraid to mention the term. I think to myself, "Well, yes, this is a rash, and yes, it is in the diaper area, so, yes, it is a diaper rash." So I tell them that it is, in reality, a diaper rash and that we'll handle it. Diaper rashes are usually easily treated, so there is almost always a happy ending.

Good parents worry about their babies. And every first time parent worries about everything. I was the same way with our first child. It's normal to be extremely stressed with our first babies, often very anxious, often hyper-careful. That's a good thing, because that degree of worry wanes quickly as we get to our second, third, fourth children, and beyond. If we didn't begin at a high level of anxiety with baby number one, we might not care a bit by the time we got to number four or five. (My wife tells me that God gives mothers to children so someone will worry about them.)

During the summer I may see a baby who has generalized red pinpoint rash all over her trunk. It's a heat rash. No problem.

Sometimes I see a baby with a fairly nondescript rash that I know is not serious, and though I know its medical name, I jokingly tell parents that "this is a baby rash." I don't leave them there; I go on to explain what it is, how to treat it, and what to expect. But, the term "baby rash" often relieves the tension.

Or a five-year-old boy comes in with no fever and bright red cheeks. He feels great and wonders why he is in our office: he is not sick, and he tells me so. His cheeks look like someone has slapped him a few times (which I know is not the case), and he has a fine, lacy rash on his body. He has Fifth Disease. Again, no problem. (Fifth Disease, by the way, is not "Fifth's Disease," and it is not named after Dr. Fifth. It was thought by physicians many years ago to be the fifth infectious disease described that caused a rash—thus, the fancy, technical name. If you want me to sound medical, then we also call it erythema infectiosum. There. Now you know why I usually call it Fifth Disease.)

Sometimes rashes signify other things. Strep throat can cause scarlet fever and the rash is so typical that it helps us make the diagnosis. We see very little measles or chickenpox now in the United States since the advent of effective vaccines, but these rashes also are so characteristic that a visual inspection makes the diagnosis.

Most pediatric rashes are not serious.

But sometimes rashes can portend impending catastrophe.

Kiki was a cute six-year-old little girl. Her attentive mother and grandmother brought her to the office one morning. She had begun to feel sick the night before and had a fever and headache. Her head had hurt her so much the preceding night she had felt best watching TV upside down; this morning she had begged her mother to "squeeze" her hair in an effort to relieve her headache. Before the office visit, they had gone to her favorite fast food breakfast spot and she wouldn't eat. This was the telltale sign; they *knew* she was sick.

As I grabbed her chart from the rack to read the nurse's notes, I learned that she had a 103-degree fever and hardly any other symptoms except for the headache. This would be easy. This would be a viral illness, I thought. Most of what I see is viral, and I have often said that I could train a three-year-old to do what I do: give him a white coat and stethoscope, teach him to walk into the exam room, act serious, and then pronounce that the sick patient has a viral illness. He would be right ninety-five percent of the time. That does, unfortunately, leave another five percent, if my math is correct, and therein lies a small problem.

I walked into the exam room and greeted Kiki and her adult caretakers. (I often find that the number of adults who accompany the child is directly proportional to the degree of family anxiety over the illness.) I liked this family. The mother and grandmother were always pleasant; now they were worried.

Kiki looked like she felt terrible. She was lying on the exam table and was drifting in and out of sleep.

We were in trouble.

I began to examine her. Her neck was stiff and I knew she did not have a viral syndrome: she had meningitis. I untucked her shirt and slipped it up to her lower rib cage so I could examine her abdomen.

Uh-oh. A rash. And it was not a baby rash. I asked her mother how long she had had it, and she responded that this was the first time she had noticed it.

It was purple, and it looked liked bruising. As I continued my exam, I noticed she had the same bruising all over her legs as well. These were ecchymoses.

I don't like seeing rashes like this.

It was obvious she had meningococcemia, a life-threatening, often fatal, disease caused by a very dangerous organism. I sent her directly to the nearby emergency room, called ahead with orders for blood-work and IV fluids, ripped off my lab coat, and got in my car to follow her there. In the ER, I did a lumbar puncture, began IV antibiotics, and then transferred her by ambulance to a pediatric ICU.

ANOTHER TIME, I was on call. It was Friday afternoon, about 5:45. I was paged by a mother whose three-year-old son earlier that day had seen one of my call group partners. He had been sent home with what appeared to be (you guessed it) a viral illness. Except for fever of 104 degrees, his exam had been normal that morning. The blood count had been normal as well. Discharging the boy to his mother's care and careful observation had been the right thing to do. Now, as I talked to the young mother on the phone, I could tell she was worried. She said he was very lethargic. As I was preparing to give my stock speech on viral illnesses ("Anyone with high fever will be lethargic, etc."), she said something that terrified me: "By the way, he has this funny rash … " I don't like it when people say, "By the way … " I don't usually know what's coming next. This time, though, I knew, and I had a nauseating sense of foreboding. I knew what the rash was, but I asked her to describe it more completely for me anyway. I knew exactly what she was going to say, but I dreaded her pending answer: "It looks like little purple dots." That was enough.

I told her to come to the office immediately. When she

arrived ten minutes later, I saw she had not exaggerated. He was hot, he was extremely lethargic, and he had a petechial rash: little purple dots or pinpoints all over his body that did not blanch with pressure and that could not be felt. This combination is every pediatrician's nightmare.

He had meningococcemia.

I instructed her to go the emergency room across the street, where I would meet them five minutes later. I called ahead to the ER and told them he was on his way; I asked them to begin an IV stat.

Once I arrived in the ER, I did a spinal tap, I began high dose antibiotics, and I gave massive amounts of IV fluids to get his blood pressure up: he was in septic shock. I called for the transport team to take him downtown to the PICU. As we cared for him, I noticed that often, in his extreme obtundation, he would smile. I believe he was dying even then, smiling as he saw Jesus Christ welcoming him into heaven.

He survived in a comatose state for two days, and then he passed into the embrace of his loving Savior—forever.

KIKI, ON THE OTHER HAND, lived. Her disease caused long-term complications. She needed skin grafts on her legs due to meningococcal destruction. But she lived and she thrived. Her left foot is slightly smaller than her right, and that foot gets a little swollen when she is extremely active. But that did not stop her being a cheerleader in high school. She just finished college and will begin teaching school soon. She is also a new mother with a small baby who is a patient of mine. Kiki is a very cute and bright young woman.

Neisseria meningitidis (meningococcus) is a vicious little organism I despise, I hate, I loathe, and I fear. It causes meningitis and/or overwhelming septicemia often leading to death. It is difficult to escape this disease unscathed. We now give eleven-year-olds a vaccine to prevent this devastating illness, but thus far, younger children cannot be routinely protected. I hope that soon they can be.

I hate what meningococcus does to children. It maims and kills them. I hate the fact that it begins looking like a routine viral illness and then as it gathers steam and fully manifests itself, it causes devastation on a massive scale.

And I fear missing it. What if I had seen Kiki an hour earlier, before her neck had stiffened and before the rash had appeared? Would I have sent her home, assuring her mother that she had a virus? What would have become of her then? These kinds of thoughts haunt me. Thank God for that rash and for the timing of its appearance; it told me what she had, and it told me what to do.

" ... and, oh, by the way ... my child has this strange, purple rash ... " I never want to hear those words again.

Give me a diaper rash any day.

Or a baby rash.

20

The Exchange

WE HAD BEEN in Kenya for about two weeks and I was getting used to crises. I had at least one each day—usually more.

Nancy and I, along with our three younger children, Rachel, Esther, and Jeremiah, had come to work at Tenwek Hospital for a month. My job was to take care of sick children in the hospital. Nancy kept us going, as always, and helped out on the mission compound as needed.

Rachel, a college student on her way to becoming a teacher, assisted in teaching the missionary children and carried out research on the development of Kenyan children. Esther, then sixteen, became secretary to the hospital's medical director, and Jeremiah, fifteen, worked with the maintenance crew around the compound.

The hospital is located in the tea-country of northwest Kenya in a place of stunning natural beauty. The complex is surrounded by green mountains. The mornings are cool, but the near-equatorial noon sun is brutally intense. The elevation made the walks to the hospital each morning an aerobic workout. We awoke each morning to the sounds of roosters crowing and cows mooing. By the time the sun had risen over the mountains, and by the time we had finished our breakfast of Kenyan coffee,

U-Like-Me or Weetabix cereal, and boxed milk, the surrounding village was humming, and the butcher just behind us had slain his first cow of the day. Pungent charcoal smoke filled the air as breakfasts were being cooked.

It was June, their winter, and many nights we had a fire in the fireplace. Our drying laundry hung over lines stretched across our living room. When I went to the hospital to see patients at night, the guards often wore ski-caps and ski masks in the frigid fifty-degree weather.

This area of Kenya is home to the Kipsigis, the tribe mainly served at Tenwek, though we cared for many Maasai (always wearing red) as well. The Kipsigis are a handsome, tall, slender people with fine facial features; from them come many great world-class long distance runners.

The hospital itself had an open-air pediatric ward on the lower level, and it was here that I would live the next four weeks. As I walked in for the first time, I saw about fifty ill children in beds; their parents stayed near them to attend to their needs and at night slept on the floor beside or beneath them. Many of these sick patients would have been in the ICU in the United States. From the ward wafted the malodorous stench of human suffering.

My first day there, during morning report, I was called "stat" to the bed of a four-year-old boy with nephrotic syndrome and peritonitis. He was now in septic shock. He was arresting and he needed massive help. Despite our intensive treatment, he died the next day. This first day was a foretaste of what was to come: many extremely ill children under my care would die over the next month. Often, four or five of my patients would die each day. They had serious diseases like malaria, meningitis, pneumonia, tuberculosis, and measles, all compounded by underlying malnutrition. On top of that, the incidence of HIV positivity was at least fifteen percent in this population; AIDS was exploding across sub-Saharan Africa. Looking back, I realize that I pulled in and shut down emotionally that month; I talked very little to my wife. Experiencing so much suffering, dying, and death among my little patients while simultaneously knowing there was often little I could do for them—all this deeply grieved me and I subconsciously withdrew as a way of coping.

From that first day on, morning report hardly ever ended before I was called to the pediatric ward for some emergency. Often, the patient was a child having seizures, frequently from cerebral malaria or meningitis. I ordered many milligrams of IV lorazepam, phenobarbital and phenytoin.

Daily rounds rarely went uninterrupted. At each white steel bedstead, I removed the chart (a clipboard) from the metal hook. I had to be certain that patient and chart matched since there were often two children to a bed, feet to feet. As I looked at the child and parent, I smiled and asked in English, "How is Cherono (or Kiprono) today?"

The anxious mother or father looked into my eyes and smiled a worried smile. My Kipsigis nurse translated my question and their answer. The answer always came back: "He is bet-ter." Even now, I can hear the words, the pronunciation, and the inflection. No matter how the patient really appeared or really was, the words were always the same: "He is bet-ter." I think both parents and nurse colluded here to show courtesy and gratitude; they did not want to offend the doctor even if the child was really much worse. Unselfish and sensitive, they did not want to hurt my feelings.

Several of my sick children would have diabetes, having been brought in with ketoacidosis. We stabilized them and then sent them home with insulin and a management plan. Poverty and distance guaranteed that these children would be back within a few months—or not. Their families could not afford long-term insulin, and the fifty-mile walk made routine follow-up almost impossible. Diabetes mellitus was a death sentence.

As I began each day, I would discover that three or four new patients had been admitted overnight, frequently with high fever and seizures. They would usually have cerebral malaria or meningitis.

And, of course, there were my chronic patients with cavitary tuberculosis. They came to Tenwek with fever, weight loss, and coughing up blood and pus. They were emaciated, and their chest X-rays showed actual cavities, hollowed out areas of their lungs, filled with fluid and putrefaction. The TB was destroying their lungs—and them.

Then, there was the boy with the fractured femur. He was in traction and had a long stay with us. He was a joyful little boy, always happy and smiling. The rope of a mule had somehow twisted itself around the boy, and in the struggle to get free, the boy had broken his leg.

Rounds did not usually go smoothly. I would see five or six patients, and then handle an emergency. This was the pattern: do the routine until the next crisis arose.

Now the newborn nursery was calling me. This must be my "Crisis For The Day," I thought. The nursery never called me unless they had a major problem. All the routine care at Tenwek was handled by nurses or trained specialists; the handful of physicians and surgeons handled the serious problems.

As I picked up the phone and steeled myself, the nurse said, "Daktari, we have a problem."

I waited for the bomb to go off. "Go ahead, please," I said.

"Daktari, we have a baby boy with jaundice."

"Okay," I thought, "almost every baby gets jaundiced. Why are you calling me about this?" But what I said was different and polite.

"Have you checked his bilirubin yet?"

"Yes."

"Can you please tell me what it is?"

"Yes, Daktari. His bilirubin is 47."

The Kipsigis are a very dignified people, and the nurse showed no emotion. I, on the other hand, became very excited and could feel myself going into high alert. I tried to act as dignified and calm as the nurse.

"Forty-seven!!!??? Are you sure?" I don't like to hear things like this. I don't like bad news. Then I calmed down, moving into cynical mode to protect myself from my great fear. I began to talk to myself. "Sure," I thought, "47. Of course. We always see bilirubins of 47—especially in babies. This can't be right. Cool it, Jerry." (To place things in perspective, most adults have a bilirubin of 1, and often newborns have a bilirubin in the teens for a few days resulting from normal neonatal jaundice. But a 47 is not often seen, and I certainly had never seen anything more than the high 20s.)

Now shifting into denial mode, I decided I did not believe the number. For my own sanity, I could not believe the number. I went to the nursery and saw the baby. He had been born at home, and because of the jaundice had been brought to the hospital. He didn't look that yellow to me. He acted fairly normal. But he did have ABO incompatibility which can cause extremely high bilirubin levels. Since I didn't believe the lab report (or didn't want to believe the lab report), I did what any other reasonable doctor would have done: I ordered them to repeat it. Stat. If you don't like a lab value, repeat it. Hoping it was not really this high, I anxiously awaited the new report.

But I secretly feared this might be the real thing.

So why was I so upset? Here is the issue: Extreme jaundice can cause brain damage and sometimes death in newborns, an entity called kernicterus. The treatment for a number this high would be both cumbersome and dangerous. I might actually have to do something about this, and I did not want to.

The report came back a couple of hours later, and I held my breath as the nurse called me. "Daktari, we have the lab work on your baby."

"Please," I thought, "don't keep me hanging. Tell me what it is." I controlled myself and said patiently, since patience is one of my chief virtues, "Yes, what is the result, please?"

I was dying.

"It is not bet-ter. His bilirubin is 51." She said it so placidly and calmly.

I was not calm. Fifty-one!!! This had to be some sort of record. I had lost my bet, and I was stunned.

I was also very scared. A number like this required drastic treatment: a double-volume exchange transfusion. This treatment can be dangerous even under the best of circumstances, under controlled conditions and in the best hands. I had done exchange transfusions as a resident, but that was seventeen years before, and it was at the Texas Medical Center. But, now, as rusty as I was, to do it here in a remote Kenyan hospital seemed foolhardy. My first inclination was to do nothing—to just make a decision that we can't really safely help this baby. No one would know. The parents would not know the difference and would never know the reason for their son's mental retardation. The other doctors would cut me some slack. After all, I was the only pediatrician there, and they would trust my judgment. I did not want to do the exchange transfusion because it scared me to death.

I really wanted to land here and just let it go.

But I couldn't. God would not let me. I had to do something. Turning my rationalization on its head, by the mere fact that I *was* the only pediatrician here, I just had to try to help this infant.

I ordered blood from the blood bank. I ordered equipment to be readied. I needed some kind of central line[4] with a large bore-catheter for the exchange. Normally I would have used an umbilical line, but this baby had an infection of the umbilical stump, and inserting a line here would have killed him with infection as we cured his jaundice. Unable to get a large-bore catheter in, I consulted colleague and surgeon, Dr. Michael Johnson, who was able to insert a femoral line. Afterwards, he stated, "It's better to

---

4   A central line is a catheter inserted into a major, large blood vessel.

be blessed than good." I think he was surprised he got it in. We were both relieved.

At about midnight we started the procedure. We were in one of the surgery theaters, chosen because of its sterility. The only light was the surgical lamp overhead, and the darkness surrounding us was eerie. Two male Kipsigis nurses assisted me. We placed the baby on a heart monitor. Just before we began, and just after I had checked all of our equipment and supplies, the nurses both asked me, "Daktari, do you want to pray first?"

I sure did.

The three of us asked for God to heal and save this child, and to help us accomplish a successful procedure. We began. An exchange transfusion involves withdrawing small amounts of blood from the baby, and replacing it with new banked blood, thus removing the bilirubin: 10 cc. out, 10 cc. in. Babies can die during this procedure, chiefly from cardiac arrhythmias, but other things can happen as well, little things like hemorrhage or shock. I prayed the whole time. "Please, Lord, heal this baby. Please, Lord, don't let me kill him." It was a long two hours, and the procedure was tedious and laborious. We spoke only as necessary.

He survived. Thank God he survived.

The bilirubin came down, but began climbing back up later the next day. I repeated the exchange the next night. Same story, same result. I would like to say I was getting used to this, but I was not.

When we checked the result the day after exchange number two, the bilirubin was down to a more reasonable level and we simply treated with phototherapy. His numbers improved, he looked great, and he later went home to his parents.

I remember praying that this newborn boy would be normal and that God would use him in a great way in his country. Who knows? He is now fifteen years old. Maybe he will eventually become president of Kenya. Or maybe God will make him into a pastor. Or a teacher. Or a physician. Maybe he will be the next great businessman of Kenya who leverages his wealth to ransom African children from malaria. I won't know until I arrive in heaven.

An exchange transfusion is a good picture of how Jesus saves people. We have a fatal disease, sin, that will cripple and kill us, but we are utterly incapable of helping ourselves. Jesus performs the healing procedure. He exchanges his righteousness for our sinfulness; he bears our sins, and we receive his righteousness. Jesus shed his blood on the cross to make it all happen, so he is not only the operator: he supplies the blood as well. It seems like a dangerous and risky method of treatment; it was and it is. Jesus died to make it possible, trusting in God the Father to make him alive again. Jesus risked all for us.

And for us to trust in Jesus Christ alone for him to forgive our sins and reconcile us to God seems risky, as well.

But this exchange is the safest transaction in the universe.

He made Him who knew no sin to be sin on our behalf, that we might become the righteousness of God in Him.
II Corinthians 5:21

If we confess our sins, He is faithful and righteous to forgive us our sins, and to cleanse us from all unrighteousness.
I John 1:9

... and the blood of Jesus His Son cleanses us from all sin.
I John 1:7

21

Sweet Hannah

HANNAH WAS TEN years old when I first met her. Walking into the exam room, chart in hand, I introduced myself to Hannah and her mother. Hannah's face was simultaneously joyful and serious. She possessed a joyful seriousness, or was it a serious joy? She smiled a sweet, gentle, quiet smile that both belied and yet revealed her underlying strength.

I knew I was in the presence of no mere mortal.

She already had a thick medical chart, having already experienced more medical problems than most people do in a long lifetime. It was clear Hannah had suffered.

Hannah has unusual vascular (blood vessel) malformations in her brain as well as congenital heart disease. She has undergone multiple procedures and operations, but Hannah is resilient in every way: physically, mentally, and spiritually. She is a tough little girl.

I like Hannah. A lot. I always enjoy seeing her.

About a year ago, I noticed she was on my schedule and I was smiled to myself that morning just thinking about seeing her. She was then fourteen years old. At the appointed time, I entered the exam room and as always, she greeted me with her beautiful, serious smile. But something else was in the room that

I had never seen with her before and it was something I had not expected.

It was a walker.

And I grew sad and quiet from the obvious painful conclusion. Hannah had suffered a stroke.

Hannah was just as cheerful and optimistic as always. She was making good progress with her rehabilitation. And she still had her smile.

A few months afterwards, Hannah was selected to deliver a speech at her school awards ceremony. Here is what she said (italics for emphasis):

> *I can do all things through Him who strengthens me.*
> *Philippians 4:13*

> This is what keeps me going through each day. Every struggle, I don't worry, because I know God is always there, no matter what.

> This is what was going through my mind, when I was told that I had a stroke. This is why I wasn't scared. I knew God would be with me through every step of the way and that he would heal me, gradually, through time. That's why I think we all need to realize we are blessed, whether we see it or not and we don't need to take it for granted. This is why we should all live our lives to the fullest, and let him show his light through us and do what God would want us to do.

> Because, I can tell you, that I am so lucky, to have God show his incredible miracles through me. *If I had a chance to stop the stroke and my problems*

from happening, I wouldn't. Not that I would want everyone to have that pain of worrying about me and being scared for me. It's just that I wouldn't have this amazing chance to have the Lord inspire people and to let them know, that all things are possible with Him, through me. *I wouldn't change a thing.* Although this journey is hard, it is definitely worth it. To know that not only can God do absolutely amazing things, but also to know that so many people love you and to meet so many awesome people that have overcome great adversities.

So, what I'm trying to say is, even though there are some things in life you want, they may not be what you need. *God has these wonderful plans for us and he is always there for us, listening, helping and above all showing us we are never alone.* You can do things you never imagined. What we truly need to see is his plan for us. We just need to follow them and let them change our lives, to lead us through our paths.

I do not know many teenagers who have this perspective on life. I don't know many adults who do.

Hannah has learned by living life that God is both good and in complete control of all things. She knows it is safe to trust him and to follow him.

And that is why Sweet Hannah smiles.

Strength and dignity are her clothing,
And she smiles at the future.
  Proverbs 31:25

22

Sonny

"HERE STANDS A HERO."

This was not my first thought when I met Sonny.

Caring husband? Yes.

Committed father? Definitely.

Hard worker? Check.

Nice guy? Of course.

But hero? No, not really.

Sonny did not fit the cultural stereotype. As we all know, movies and television portray real heroes for us. But Sonny had no swagger. He did not strut. His biceps were not massive. He had no glint in his eye. It is easy to overlook the simple fact that courage and heroism are hidden traits, residing deep within the heart if they are there at all, invisible until they are needed.

I met Sonny for the first time when he and his wife came to my office with their premature baby, recently discharged from the neonatal intensive care unit. Sonny was a proud and engaged father. He listened carefully to my assessment of his new baby. He made certain that he understood the treatment plan and instructions. Sonny was attentive to his wife, looking to her needs and comfort, playing well his supporting role. He was unassuming and had a ready smile. My staff and I liked him immediately.

Sonny was a very happy man.

Over the next few years I became ever more impressed with Sonny's deep love for his family, doing whatever was needed to care for them. He provided well for them. He nurtured them. He protected them. He led them.

He seemed to actually enjoy his children's office visits. To him, these visits were not a burden to be endured, but a blessing to be relished. His love for his family was obvious and undeniable.

Sonny looked pretty much like a typical, average, ordinary, middle-aged guy who had a great smile. No, I'm afraid he did not look much like a hero.

Sonny just loved his wife and children. It was that simple.

And as I hung up the phone after talking with his widow, I could not speak. I tried to talk, but I couldn't. My wife asked me what was wrong and I could not answer. I was dumb with grief and shock and tears and anger and raw emotion. I had to go outside to be alone for a few minutes before I could tell her what had happened.

Sonny had been at home when the gunman came in. The man had brandished his sawed-off shotgun and threatened to kill Sonny's family. With unyielding courage, Sonny had defended his family. What was he thinking? Likely this: "*No one* will kill my family. No one will harm my family. No one will even *touch* my family."

Sonny had positioned himself between his family and the man with the gun. He had stalled and talked for a few minutes, trying to reason with the aggressor. Realizing it was futile to talk, and having accomplished his strategic goal, Sonny finally said, "If you're going to kill someone, go ahead … *kill me.*" Sonny's delaying maneuver had given his family just enough time to escape out of the back of the house. The killer aimed his gun at Sonny's chest and squeezed the trigger. Sonny crumpled in a pool of blood. He was dead.

Sonny loved his wife and children.

Greater love has no man than this, that one lay down his life for his friends.
   John 15:13

Husbands, love your wives, as Christ loved the church, and gave himself up for her ...
   Ephesians 5:25 (ESV)

23

Pooja's Redemption

I FIRST ENCOUNTERED Pooja when she was seventeen months old. She was a beautiful little Indian girl brought in by her parents for a checkup. She was tiny. Really tiny. She weighed seventeen pounds, about the size of an average seven-month-old baby girl. She remained small all her life; I predicted she would never become a giant, and my forecast was correct. She is now a very cute, petite, delightful eighteen-year-old young lady who stands a full 4'9".

Her birth parents abandoned Pooja when she was just an infant, wrapping her in a blanket and then leaving her in the street outside the gates of a police station in Bombay (Mumbai). After she was discovered, the police dispatched her to an orphanage. Pooja was adopted by her parents when she thirteen months old. As soon as this gracious couple received notification from the orphanage, her new mother quickly traveled to meet her baby. When she arrived, she was never allowed to see the interior of the orphanage, the hidden and likely unspeakable conditions inside being left to her imagination. Pooja was so tiny: she weighed a mere eleven pounds. She was weak and pale and fragile. She was malnourished and developmentally delayed. Her head was covered in boils. It was obvious to them that she had never been outside the orphanage since the day she had been discovered in the street. She was barely existing.

Her adoptive parents loved her the moment they saw her, and they have loved her ever since.

Pooja and her family eventually moved to Augusta, Georgia where I became her physician for many years. She grew and matured, and she became a typical American teenager. Friends were extremely important to her. She loved being on the flag team for her local high school. She had great fun as she planned the prom. Then she went on to college.

Each time I see Pooja, I like to tease her and joke with her. She has a ready smile and a happy laugh. And each time I see her, I think about her story and what it means.

Hers is a story of redemption.

Her adoptive parents went to great lengths to rescue Pooja. They expended extraordinary amounts of time, energy, and treasure to make it happen. Why? Because they wanted to save her from her stultifying existence in the orphanage, and more than that, to enfold her into their own home where she could grow and flourish. And because they wanted a daughter to love and one who would love them in return. When they first saw her and held her in their arms, they immediately loved her.

Life in the orphanage was one of mere survival. Pooja was not even conscious of her meager existence there and didn't know there was more, or that she needed more: it was all she knew. But her new parents knew there was more—much more. Pooja was completely unable to help herself, and besides, was not even aware of the need. But her new parents knew she needed help. They wanted to give her a new life, a life of freedom and plenty. They wanted to give her a loving home where there was opportunity for growth.

At great cost, Pooja's parents redeemed her from the orphanage. Her parents spent their money, their time, their energy, and themselves to redeem her life from a miserable existence that would have led to only more misery. They paid the price to free her. They rescued her, they saved her, and they adopted her.

God does a similar thing for us. While we were helpless and not even aware of our need, Christ died for us. And with that death, at supreme cost, he bought us out of slavery and mere existence to give us freedom and real life. Jesus freely offers to rescue us, save us, and deliver us. He offers to redeem us. And God the Father offers to adopt us into his family. Why does God do this? Because God desires a two-way relationship of love with us in which he loves us and we love him.

Pooja and her parents have taught me about redemption for eighteen years.

> *(The LORD) ... redeems your life from the pit;*
> *(the LORD) ... crowns you with lovingkindness and compassion;*
> *(and) satisfies your years with good things ...*
> *Psalm 103:4-5*

> *For He rescued us from the domain of darkness,*
> *and transferred us to the kingdom of His beloved Son,*
> *in whom we have redemption, the forgiveness of sins.*
> *Colossians 1:13-14*

24

Spitting Cobra

I HATE SNAKES.

I hated them before Indiana Jones hated them.

I don't like *any* snakes. I don't like green snakes. I don't like black snakes. I don't like garter snakes, and I definitely do not like poisonous snakes. Yes, I know, I should appreciate the "good" snakes. But as far as I'm concerned, the only good snake is a dead snake.

I am fairly certain I have ophidiophobia.

Before we got to Zambia, I knew there were plenty of snakes in Africa. I had heard of the black mamba; the very name is exotic and fearsome. I had heard of the cobra. These two were bad enough. But I had never heard of the spitting cobra. Spitting cobra? The mere idea terrified me.

We were in Zambia to care for patients at Mukinge Hospital for about a month. Our daughter, Esther, and her new husband, Daniel, then a fourth year medical student, had been at Mukinge for four weeks before we joined them there. Nancy and I arrived after landing in Lusaka, spending the day getting supplies, and then flying on to Mukinge. Our old friends Steve and Sherri Letchford had been at Mukinge for many years, and we went to assist and relieve them.

Mukinge is in the copper belt of Zambia, in the remote northwest corner of the nation. The children I cared for were extremely ill. Most were malnourished, and many were HIV positive. Many had malaria, meningitis or pneumonia.

Many die young in Zambia, including far too many children. We stayed in the Letchford home near the morgue and in the middle of the night often heard the wailing of families grieving the deaths of their children. They love their children as much as we love ours. In America, we are fairly insulated from death, and we don't think about it much. Americans tend to think that because it's Africa, they should expect and accept a high infant and child mortality rate. It is just the way of life there, we think. But I believe that because death is such a large part of their existence, they may view life much more seriously and realistically than Americans do. Life is short and life is fragile. They realize it, and we don't.

One Saturday night, I was on call and I was sick. I crawled into bed under the mosquito net, and within a few hours I had what I thought was a virus, but as it progressed, I began to wonder what was wrong with me. I'm usually fairly good at self-diagnosing, and I am not an alarmist, but here I was in the middle of rural Zambia and I worried that I might have something very serious. I began to think about how I could be evacuated.

And then the dogs began to bark. Outside our windows were dozens of wild, barking dogs that howled for hours. As we lived through the next few hours, my wife and I believed we were under satanic attack. We felt the presence of evil; it was palpable. The illness, the onset of sudden fear, the dogs, what I experienced afterwards—a long siege of spiritual warfare and demonic oppression—then and in retrospect, it all bore the marks of an attack from hell. I believe that it was.

(Lest you think me completely unstable, this night was not just a case of a pack of barking dogs. For the next two years, I was embroiled in a spiritual battle the likes of which I had never experienced before and hope to never experience again.

Emotionally, physically, and spiritually, I was barely able to hang on, or so it seemed. In reality, during that time, it was Jesus who was holding on to me. The events of that night seem to have set things in motion. Chapter 39 more fully explains the next two years.)

I recovered from the sickness, and the rest of our time in Zambia proceeded uneventfully. A few days after my illness, the Zambian eye specialist educated us about spitting cobras. He had treated patients who had experienced these serpents firsthand. The spitting cobra spits, or sprays, his venom into the eyes of his victim, up to a distance of eight feet with remarkable accuracy. This low dose of venom does not kill; it only blinds, often permanently. Afterwards, the serpent comes in for the kill, able to take his time before he sinks his fangs into the victim's body, injecting a lethal dose of venom that results in blood, organ, and neurologic damage and, eventually, death.

From that time on, I prayed that I would never encounter one or even see one.

I never saw a snake there at all, but I was always scanning the bushes and brush as I walked to and from the hospital, especially at night. God was gracious to me: he knew I couldn't handle it.

OUR GREAT ADVERSARY, Satan, the devil, that great serpent, works in much the same way as the spitting cobra. He attempts to spray blinding venom into our eyes, and if he is able to do it, rendering us temporarily and then permanently blind, the blindness eventually results in death. And as long as the victim is blind, it really does not matter when death occurs. Satan will come in for the final kill at his leisure. Who cares when the victim dies, as long as he is dying and eventually dies?

Satan's strategy is always based on blinding the eyes of his victims. His bag of tricks always includes deception and deceit; he is the father of lies, as Jesus said. He is also a murderer. So, lying and killing, blinding and murdering, are the strategies he employs.

Do I hate snakes because there is some primal fear deep within me dating back to the Garden of Eden and the serpent? Or do I simply fear snakes on a physical level? Probably both.

Did Satan take on serpentine characteristics in the Garden because God foreknew and foresaw that serpents would always be a good reminder of how Satan operates? Or did snakes take on satanic characteristics after the Fall to remind us of the same? Again, probably both.

I am certain, though, of these two things.

I hate snakes, and I hate that great serpent, the devil.

To combat Satan, we must know about him and his schemes in order that he not gain the advantage over us (II Corinthians 2:11). To learn more, go to www.campeadorpress.com and see the article, "Spitting Cobra."

25

Providence

SUNNY SUNDAY afternoons speak the names of boys and whisper irresistibly to them and inaudibly to anyone but them: "Come out and play."

It was a bright and warm Georgia winter day, and the school playground was nearby. It, too, was beckoning him to come.

In addition, a neighbor had just called, offering to take him and a few friends to the playground.

With a triple invitation like this, how could ten-year-old Matthew say "No"? How does a boy reject something that is so obviously meant to be? The gravitational pull of this confluence of circumstances was impossible to resist.

So Matthew yielded and went to the playground.

Matthew did all the usual things. He slid down the sliding board; he ran back up the sliding board. He climbed into the fort. He jumped into the sandpit. He went over the monkey bars hand over hand.

But what he liked most was the swings. He got into a swing, shoved off, and pumped his legs. He swung so high that the chains became a little slack. He threw his head back and gazed at the deep blue skies with their wispy cotton-white clouds. The sun on his shoulders and back was warm. It was a good day for a ten-year-old boy.

He and the girl on the swing next to him competed: who could achieve cruising altitude first? It was a good-natured, unspoken competition, but they both knew what they were doing. Having a pretty girl nearby enhanced his athleticism, and of course, he was winning the contest.

As he glided through the air, suddenly he felt an intense, stinging pain in his right cheek. His first thought was about the girl next door on the swing: "She must have just thrown something at me to distract me to keep me from winning." But she had not done anything.

The pain in Matthew's cheek forced him to jump out of the swing. He stood and felt his face, and it was wet. "Matt, you're bleeding!" shrieked the girl. Yes, it was true. The wetness was blood, and it was streaming down his cheek.

There was also something in his mouth. This was a little disorienting. "Hmm," he thought, "must be a tooth." He didn't remember any loose teeth but there was no doubt: there was now some hard object in his mouth, and it felt kind of round. He reached into his mouth and dislodged it. He spat it out onto the ground. It was a small, shiny metallic object in a mouthful of bloody saliva.

The parent overseeing the playground excursion saw Matthew's bloody cheek and realized something was wrong. It was time to leave. She calmly instructed Matthew to use his sweater to compress his facial wound, and firmly ordered the kids into the car.

Matthew entered his home and his father examined his cheek. Matthew's big sister, Meredith ran upstairs to deliver the news to his mother: "Mom, Matt's hurt!"

As they all gathered in the kitchen, Matt's father wiped away the caked blood, and for a second before the blood began flowing actively again, he was able to see a perfectly round four-millimeter hole in Matthew's cheek. He looked inside his mouth and saw the same thing: a perfectly round four-millimeter hole.

"Matt, what happened to you? You've got a hole in your cheek. Were you guys throwing rocks at each other?" his father asked. It was a reasonable question.

"I don't know what happened, Dad. We weren't doing anything ... just swinging."

"Did you hurt your face on the swing-set? Maybe on the chain? Was it sharp?"

"I don't think so. I'm not sure how I cut myself."

They thought in silence trying to solve the puzzle. The injury was real, Matt was bleeding, and yet no one knew how it had occurred. Just then, the mother who had accompanied Matt to the playground had an awful thought emerging from her subconscious memory. She began weeping, then crying "Oh, no!!" Between sobs, she said that she remembered hearing what had sounded like gunshots in the distance while the children had been playing. The terrifying conclusion was now almost too much to bear.

Matt's dad asked her to "Please, calm down." The crying was frightening Matt.

They called 911, and soon a deputy-sheriff arrived at their home. He heard the story, saw the wound, and questioned Matthew. "Were you and your friends having a BB gun fight?" Again, Matt pled innocent. After a brief visit, the deputy filed his report and detectives were dispatched to the playground.

Matthew and his parents got into their car and drove to the emergency room for treatment of the wound. On the way, his father kept the conversation light and joked with Matt, attempting to allay any fears and to keep his son from worrying. His father simultaneously fought back any disturbing ideas about the origins of his son's injury. They checked into the ER with the triage nurse, stating that Matt had a wound to his face. Then they sat in the waiting area, hoping to be called back soon for treatment and discharge.

About this time, detectives visited the school playground. On the ground beneath Matthew's swing, in a mass of dirt and clotted blood, they discovered a .22 gauge bullet.

A deputy soon burst into the emergency room and told the triage nurse that Matthew needed to be taken back immediately for treatment. He explained that the sheriff's department was officially handling his case as a gunshot wound. To this point, Matthew's father had mightily attempted to disbelieve it, but now the awful reality was undeniable: his ten-year-old son had just been shot in the face, and not by a BB gun. "Wow!" he thought.

Matthew's ER examination revealed a gunshot wound to his right cheek. It was through-and-through. A bullet had penetrated his cheek and settled harmlessly in his mouth. The only injuries otherwise were a few scraped teeth and a bruised tongue. No salivary glands or ducts were harmed, and no blood vessels were lacerated. The plastic surgeon glued his cheek wound shut, and Matthew was discharged to his home late that night.

About a quarter of mile away from the playground, investigators and ballistics experts soon learned, someone had been taking target practice with a .22 gauge rifle, just as Matt was swinging. An errant bullet had made it through an earthen embankment, skimmed off a pond, and penetrated Matthew's cheek, finally landing safely in his mouth.

Now, Matthew is twenty years old. He will soon finish college, a year ahead of schedule, with a triple major in genetics, biology, and chemistry. He plans to go to medical school and become an oncologist.

How many lives will Matthew touch because God kept him from serious harm the day he was shot? How many of his patients will be encouraged by the miraculous story of God's providential goodness to him? How many others will be amazed that he was not killed or brain-damaged or blinded? How many will wonder that the only tears he cried occurred the next day when food stung his tongue?

And how many will rejoice that a ten-year-old boy survived being shot in the face—now left with only a memory and a slight scar, tokens to remind him of God's personal grace to him—and was spared to enjoy a lifetime of irresistible sunny days?

For He will give his angels charge concerning you,
To guard you in all your ways.
    Psalm 91:11

... He [Jesus] ... upholds all things by the word of His power ...
    Hebrews 1:3

26

Auscultation

RENÉ LAENNEC, the famous French physician of the early 19th century, gave physicians the stethoscope, and thus birthed the fine art of auscultation: the expert use of the stethoscope. Laennec's first version of the stethoscope was very primitive; it was a rolled up piece of paper, one end on the patient's chest, and the other, smaller end in his own ear. Of course, the stethoscope has undergone numerous refinements since that time. Doctors all over the world and for almost 200 years have used this valuable medical instrument ever since to diagnose and treat conditions of the heart, lungs, and abdomen.

It is not easy.

Sometimes parents ask me whether they should purchase an otoscope from their nearest drugstore so they can diagnose their child's ear infections. It follows that they would then expect me to phone in a prescription for them. I try to explain to them that it is not that easy. Looking at an eardrum may appear to be the simplest thing in the world, but it is not. It takes years of experience to know what is normal and what is abnormal. Even physicians have difficulty with this diagnosis at times.

Likewise, learning to use an ophthalmoscope takes time and a lot of practice. Here, the objective is to shine the light through the patient's pupil to illuminate the retina, thus allowing the operator to examine the optic nerve, the retina, and retinal blood vessels. I rendered Nancy nearly blind when as a freshman medical student I practiced looking at her retinas using my new diagnostic kit. I was having fun; she was not. When my patient wife finally grew weary of this form of photo-torture, I practiced on our dog. She was very cooperative, and it was nice that her pupils were naturally dilated. I learned a lot about normal canine retinal anatomy.

Similarly, the stethoscope is not as easy to use as one might expect. You do not just slap the head on someone's chest and listen to determine if there is a heartbeat or if the lungs are there. Most of us get our first stethoscopes in our first year of medical school. For a while, our stethoscopes merely serve to improve our image: they make us look like real doctors, with the trademark medical instrument hanging from our necks, draped over our shoulders, or protruding in just the right way from our coat pockets. It takes a long time to become proficient at actually using them.

Becoming an expert in the use of the stethoscope requires many hours of practice, many years, many patients, much experience, and much concentration. Listening to the heart, in particular, is like listening to an orchestra play a musical piece. Truly appreciating a beautiful orchestral performance requires great concentration to distinguish the various instruments, the theme, the tempo, and so on. The same can be said of listening to the heart: it requires a finely tuned ear with well-honed powers of discernment.

It can be especially difficult to listen well to an infant's heart. Here, the baby is often screaming, the heart rate is 160 beats per minute, and my goal is to simply hear the heart well for a few seconds unencumbered by crying. I spend much time agonizing over infants' hearts: I don't want to miss a big problem.

Once a doctor is competent, many diagnoses are possible by simply using this method of physical diagnosis called auscultation.

I can diagnose pneumonia, a pneumothorax, and specific heart lesions. I can gain a clue as to whether someone is in heart failure, or if they have fluid surrounding the heart.

A good physical exam with a stethoscope is efficient and money-saving if artfully done.

In medical school, I noticed that the high-powered internal medicine professors all carried expensive Sprague-Rappaport stethoscopes. These things had three heads and two large black tubes the size of garden hoses, held together by an engraveable stainless steel clip. They were wondrous to behold, as the doctor slowly and ceremoniously drew it from his white lab coat's pocket and made an impressive diagnosis. I used to covet these great stethoscopes; I thought I needed one, at least to show I was serious about medicine and maybe even to demonstrate that I, too, was a superb diagnostician. Sadly, my medical student's budget did not jibe with my champagne taste, so I stuck with my Littman, not an inexpensive stethoscope, but not a Ferrari either.

I felt better about my stethoscope a couple of years later when I spent time with Dr. Dan McNamara, chief of pediatric cardiology at Texas Children's Hospital. He was an international star; he introduced me to Dr. Helen Taussig, his mentor and a pioneer in pediatric cardiology. I had the privilege of working with Dr. McNamara for a month or so. After I saw one of his patients, I would go into his office to present the patient to him: give a status update, review historical and physical findings, and then review my recommendations for his comment. I should have been intimidated. He was an important man, but he was so humble and welcoming that I had only due respect for him and no fear. He never made me feel like an idiot. He brought his lunch in a brown paper bag and munched on it at his desk as I talked about the patient. He taught me a lot about pediatric cardiology, about auscultation, about life, and about brown bagging—it saves time and money. He also used an adult Littman stethoscope, just like mine. He recommended using the adult size because of the increased surface area of the diaphragm which he said increased his auscultatory acumen. I have continued using an adult size Littman ever since. It did not make me into a Dan McNamara, but it has served me well.

For many years, I've noticed an interesting phenomenon; I call it the "stethoscope conversation." I've observed that, often, at the very moment I begin to listen to my patient's heart, that is precisely the time the patient or parent wants to chat with me or divulge some important bit of information. Or, that is the exact moment that the family in the room feels liberated to begin a noisy conversation about anything and everything. It is possible that once my earpieces are placed in my ears, a circuit is completed that causes a sign in the room to light up, announcing, "You are free to talk now." I don't know. I've never seen the sign, so it must be invisible to physicians. But the chit-chat is distracting in the extreme, and I completely lose my focus after having struggled to "tune-in" to the heart sounds. I have to begin again.

I've also noticed that if I listen to the heart for a prolonged time, usually trying to be sure everything is completely normal, or trying to prove to myself that a child's murmur is normal and not pathologic, or simply attempting to hear the heart in a crying baby, I receive one of several responses. A young child may say, "What's wrong, Dr. Miller? Can't you find my heart?" I assure her that it is really there. The second is that the parent is very appreciative that I'm so thorough. The third is fear. In this case, the parent believes I've found some serious heart problem. That usually not being the case, I explain that everything is normal, that I was just being careful. It takes some time to reassure these worried parents.

Once, I listened to a child's heart for awhile, and after the "You are free to talk now" sign came on, another must have come on a few minutes later that said, "You may shriek if you're worried." The nervous grandmother in the room let out a scream that startled me, interrupted my auscultatory meditation, and scared me to death. I ripped my stethoscope out of my ears, looked at her and said, "What in the world is wrong?" I thought she was having a heart attack right there in my office; I'm just a pediatrician, and I do not do heart attacks. She told me she was just frightened that the cardiac exam was taking so long; she explained she was a nervous, high-strung person. I asked her, "Please ... never do that to me again."

Sometimes listening to the heart gives me a chance to think about what to do with the patient when I have no idea how to proceed; this is a brief respite of quiet in which I'm not expected to talk and in which I can try to order my thinking. And once, as an intern in the emergency room, when closing my eyes while listening to a patient, trying to look impressive in my deep concentration, I went to sleep—standing up. After all, it was 1:30 a.m. I'm not sure how long I stayed that way, but no one complained.

Deafness is an occupational hazard of pediatrics. No kidding. The noise in the exam rooms, listening to the hearts and lungs of crying babies, and the occasional bright idea kid who takes the end of my stethoscope and shouts into it while it's in my ears—all these things may damage our hearing. So far, I'm okay, I think.

I've seen the recommendation that a pediatrician should leave the stethoscope in his ears during the entire physical exam, even after the heart and lung exam are completed. The idea is to use the ear-pieces as a kind of ear protection from crying babies during the ear, throat, and abdominal exams, thus conserving the pediatrician's hearing.

But one of the most unusual uses of a stethoscope I have heard of, but have never tried, is this one. I heard of a pediatrician who routinely walked into his exam rooms and never removed the stethoscope from his ears. Never. Not once. This maneuver insured that he never heard any questions that he did not want to answer, he never heard any complaints he did not want to deal with, and that he wasted very little time in the exam room. He was not a good listener, but he was in and out in a blitz.

It is highly doubtful that Dr. Laennec ever dreamed of such a creative use of his legacy.

27

Rounds

ROUNDS ARE A TIME-HONORED tradition among physicians. It's the way we are trained, and it's the way we work.

Rounds began many years ago when the local doctor visited his patients in their homes. A family member became ill, the rest of the family notified the doctor, and the doctor came to the home to evaluate and treat the patient. He might see the patient every day until the illness resolved. To maximize efficiency, the doctor planned his course of travel and went house to house, then back to his home or office.

Rounds.

We still make rounds. Now, we go to the hospital and see our inpatients there before going to our clinics or operating rooms. We go room to room, checking progress, making treatment decisions, refining therapy, discharging patients.

Rounds.

In medical schools all over the country, medical students and residents rise early, arrive at the teaching hospital (if they haven't spent the night there) and check on their patients' overnight progress and current status. These are *work rounds*. Students and residents make certain orders were carried out, that lab work has been done and results checked, that procedures have been scheduled. They prepare for *teaching rounds*.

Teaching rounds occur at about 10:00 a.m. when the attending physician calls the troops together to go around the ward once again—seeing patients, making decisions, and teaching the residents and students. Every attending has a different style of seeing patients and teaching. Most are truly there to care for patients and to teach. Most use the Socratic method, asking questions, and getting students to respond in order for them to think their way through to the answer.

A few attendings are insecure, and they nervously blame any problem on anyone they can pin it on; the problem is always someone else's fault. A few really don't want to be there; they are in a rush to get back to their research. Some are arrogant; they strut around as if they were the only intelligent beings in the hospital. A few are belligerent and love nothing more than to humiliate others.

But in my own experience, most medical school attending physicians are excellent at what they do, and these excellent attendings are physicians who are superb clinicians and teachers. They want to pass their knowledge on to the next generation of doctors while caring for their patients using a team approach. Most are pleasant and good-natured. They are also dead serious about the care of their patients; the attending physician is where the buck stops. And they are dead serious about the knowledge and integrity of their young students. They have a responsibility to their patients and to future patients who will be cared for by these doctors in formation.

Beneath it all is the unspoken but understood message emanating from the attending physician: "Do not mess up with my patients."

Thus, in academic centers, each morning at about 10:00 you'll see crews of medical personnel slowly meandering from room to room as they make their rounds with the attending physician. The attending physician is the general, the team of residents and medical students his army, and the hospital the battlefield. The general takes the field and directs strategy and tactics. The residents and medical students discuss the patient with the attending physician and together they create the differential diagnosis (more below) and treatment plan. It is usually the job of the third or fourth year medical student to present the patient, offering a clear and concise summary of the patient's history, physical exam, lab work and X rays. The attending questions the medical student to test his knowledge, ability to think, and courage under fire. This is his time to shine ... or not. Making rounds as a medical student or resident requires good roundsmanship.

A medical student learns early what roundsmanship is. Roundsmanship is like a game. There are several keys to being a good roundsman, and these are actually keys to survival:

1. If the attending poses the question to the entire group, speak up if you know the answer to the question. Get it on the table if you know it; you may be clueless on the next question.

2. If you don't know the answer, keep your mouth shut. "Silence is golden," I learned from Dr. Julian Hutchins, Sr. Let others answer and take the initial bullets for you, then jump in with the right answer which you have arrived at by a process of elimination. You will look brilliant.

3. Don't get rattled. Don't lose your cool. Don't sweat. But if you must sweat, never let them see you sweat. If you start to panic, some attendings will start directing every question to you, looking for a chink in the armor. If you can't stand up to tough questioning on rounds, what will you do when you are alone at midnight with a dying patient?

4. Never, ever tap dance. If you don't know the answer, and the question is directed to you, just say, "I don't know." Or if you have failed to do something, or have done the wrong thing, tell the truth. Don't lie, and do *not* start making

things up. The attending is not stupid. Some attendings delight in allowing med students to tap-dance, to keep going in this foolish direction, digging their own graves deeper and deeper, the attending all the while offering them a bigger shovel. At the end, all the attending has to do is blow a puff of air, and the student crumples over into the hole just dug. This degree of self-humiliation and self-destruction is cause for eye-aversion by the other students and housestaff.

ROUNDS IN THE INTENSIVE CARE Units (or "Intentional Care Units," as I have heard them described) can be ... well ... intense. They are frequently interrupted by emergencies. For example, simultaneously, a new patient is being transferred into the unit, the patient in bed #3 is arresting, the patient in bed #7 has just developed a pneumothorax (blown a lung), and the patient in bed # 8 is in septic shock. Any one of these patients can die at any moment. For both doctors and nurses, working in such a high-stakes, rapidly changing environment makes for a combustible combination of stress, fear, anxiety, and uncertainty. The intense pressure in the Intensive Care Unit is not easy to bear; a good intensive care doctor must possess the ability to thrive under this pressure, must be able to make good decisions quickly, and must have a high degree of self-control.

On call as residents, we made continuous rounds all night long in the NICU. Every baby there was my responsibility until the rest of my team arrived the next morning at 7:00 a.m. Every hour or two I made my way through the intensive care nursery to be sure all the babies were behaving. At each bed, as needed, I ordered ventilator changes, follow-up blood gases, new IV fluids. Nothing could be left to chance, and nothing was on autopilot. We got very little sleep. One resident was found at 2:00 a.m. standing over a two-pound baby with an IV needle in his hand, ready to start a new IV; the nurses noticed that the resident was not moving. On closer inspection, he was asleep—on his feet!

Grand rounds originally began as a conference in which the patient was presented, including the history and physical exam, lab work, and so on; then the patient discussed was actually brought in for all the attending doctors, residents, and medical students to see, question, and examine. Over the years, grand rounds has evolved into a conference without the actual patient's presence, so it is a misnomer now. Usually a patient is presented *in absentia*, and then the illness is discussed by an expert in the field.

Case conferences are a little different. Someone presents and discusses a patient, his symptoms, his physical findings, and his laboratory work; the diagnosis is not revealed. Then, an expert discussant asks questions, draws conclusions, and demonstrates the diagnostic process, showing how an experienced clinician thinks, and how to drive for the final diagnosis so that appropriate treatment may be initiated. The key to the whole process is the differential diagnosis, a traditional diagnostic model, a method of listing all reasonable diagnoses that may fit the particular patient's clinical picture. Physicians use the differential diagnosis when treating real patients in real time. If the actual diagnosis is not in the list of the different diagnostic possibilities when the patient initially is seen, there is often a delay of days before the true diagnosis comes to light, if ever. The excellent physician knows that the initial differential diagnosis must include the actual final diagnosis, or the patient may likely suffer or die.

Once in practice, physicians continue to make rounds on their inpatients. Each morning, we arrive at the hospital to check on our patients, hoping to see some improvement; we correct course if needed, write new orders, and eventually discharge the patient to home when well. Rounds give us a way of following a patient's course as the disease process evolves. Rounds allow for continuity of care and coordination of care.

Rounds.

A good way to work. A good way to take care of ill patients. A good way to train young physicians.

I'm just glad that roundsmanship is no longer required of me.

28

The Stench

"WHAT IS THAT AWFUL SMELL?" I thought to myself as I entered the exam room.

The young mother sat there quietly with her baby girl in her lap as her three-year-old son, Oscar, rampaged around the ten by eight foot room. He made all the noise expected of a little boy. "Noise" and "boys" rhyme, and they therefore go together. I wondered if the mother smelled the foul odor that I smelled.

And I wondered where it was coming from.

My office was in an old converted house, and I thought possibly there was a dead animal in the crawlspace or even in the walls. Maybe the smell came from the little boy's sneakers—I have had my breath taken away by sweaty tennis shoes. Maybe someone had forgotten to take a bath.

I smiled and greeted the mother as I closed the door, suppressing all of my distracting thoughts about the odor that had flashed through my mind unbidden, and I proceeded to the reason for the visit. Little Jessica had a cold and was now running a fever of 102. I examined her, found that she had an ear infection, and prescribed amoxicillin. The unpleasant (and unhealthy?) atmosphere I was breathing motivated me toward the goal of a speedy exam and exit. I was in and out in five minutes. I said my goodbyes as I quickly backed through the doorway and walked into the hallway, and there I took a deep breath and inhaled some wholesome air.

Moving toward my next exam room, I was still puzzled about the smell. I hadn't mentioned it to the mother for six reasons.

First, maybe she hadn't noticed it. No reason to address an issue that was not an issue for her.

Second, maybe she had anosmia. She was unable to smell anything. Period. Again, the smell was a non-issue.

Third, maybe she had smelled it and, thinking it was emanating from our building or even from me, she had been too polite to mention it. It might be uncomfortable for me to mention the unmentionable.

Fourth, for me to bring it up if she had not noticed it might cause her to lose confidence in my new practice. She might smell it if I mentioned it. Maybe she would then think, as in Reason Number Three, that it was coming from my office or me. A doctor's office should smell clean and sterile—like isopropyl alcohol—or at least like Lysol. In addition, I did not want her to wonder about my personal hygiene.

Fifth, I didn't want to embarrass her. What if she were the source of that awful stink? For me to mention it might be rude.

Finally, maybe there was no smell at all. Maybe I was having olfactory hallucinations. I didn't want to appear unstable.

So, I kept my mouth shut and we both acted as if we smelled nothing but gardenias and roses. The invisible, malodorous elephant in the room went unrecognized.

A week later the mother and her two children were back again. During the intervening seven days, I had not given any thought to the stench at all, mainly because it was not there. I had discarded the idea that I might have a dead rat or dog under my office.

But now, I walked into the exam room and I smelled it again—it was unavoidable. The stinking elephant had returned. This time the mother brought it up.

"Doctor, I'm worried about Oscar, my three-year-old. I've noticed that for several weeks he's smelled really bad. It's not his shoes, and he's not dirty … I bathe him every day. He seems fine otherwise. He just stinks. Can you smell him?"

Oh, yeah, I could smell him all right. The stench was nauseating. As I drew nearer to Oscar to examine him, I was completely repulsed by the malodor radiating from him.

I had an embarrassing thought, long kept secret, but now, at long last, revealed. I should probably check with my attorney before I say this—it might be a HIPAA violation to reveal my thoughts about a patient. But I can't keep it in. Come see me in prison.

I wondered how in the world this mother could possibly come close enough to Oscar to kiss him. Did she ever really kiss him? Or did she simply blow him kisses from ten feet away?

I wisely decided to keep this sequence of thoughts to myself and rejected the idea of verbalizing it.

I talked with Oscar as I examined him. He was a nice little guy. He was well groomed, and he was clean. I had him drop his sneakers to the floor, and they did not have any off-putting odor. I looked in his mouth for dental problems, for evidence of tonsillitis, for ulcerations, for anything. He was fine. I had him lie down so I could look in his ears, listen to his heart, and feel his abdomen. All clear.

He did not have anything to suggest a sinusitis, though sinus infections can cause halitosis. And, it was becoming clear that his breath was horrible. It was sickening. It stunk like putrefaction. His breath was "the smell."

I tilted his head back a little and noted that his right nostril had a greenish, purulent discharge; his left was clear. That was unusual.

I shone my light up both of his nostrils and found the answer to the puzzle, the key to life, the buried treasure I was so longing to find: Oscar had something up his right nostril, occluding it, oozing green mucus, and stinking like putrid pus.

He had a foreign body in his right nostril.

I asked my nurse for some forceps, and I gently reached up his nose and grasped the mysterious object. As I withdrew it, I gagged at the magnitude of the cloacal stench; I have never experienced an odor worse or even equal to this smell of all smells. From his nostril, I pulled a three-inch mass of rotting foam rubber, all held together by tenacious green gunk.

I pitched it in the trashcan and looked again at Oscar's nose to be sure nothing else was there. He was clear.

As we discussed the now-resolved problem, Oscar's mother told me that she had seen Oscar pulling the foam rubber from a hole in his stuffed bunny as he sat and watched TV. Oscar was a great believer in ergonomics. He sat with his left thumb in his mouth, his left index finger in his left nostril, and his right hand and arm hugging his stuffed bunny. This was his idea of comfort as he watched his favorite TV shows. His beloved bunny had a hole in its chest, and from that Oscar had often, against maternal advice, extracted chunks of foam rubber. His mother knew all of this. But what she had not seen was that Oscar had not only removed the stuffing, but he had secretly placed it in his right nostril (the only one not occupied) for safekeeping; one never knows when one will need some foam rubber.

The family left the office, yet another miraculous cure having occurred from my hands. I dumped the trashcan in the main garbage can as soon as I could and asked my staff to spray both Lysol and air freshener in the room and hallway. The stench never reappeared.

Oscar's halitosis disappeared also, and I never had to remove anything from his nose again.

And I never had to wonder again if his mother could stand to kiss him.

29

Miller's Laws: My Contributions to Science

I'VE NEVER REALLY enjoyed bench science.

After my first year of medical school, I did a summer research project on breast cancer in mice. It was a forgettable bit of research, yielding no useable information to the world except for one thing: it proved that I was not made to do research in the basic sciences.

However, clinical research is another story altogether. Here, I have been extremely successful. By careful clinical observation over many years, I have unearthed two scientific principles of epoch-making proportions. Some jealous peers may say I simply happened upon them, that it was merely serendipity. They say I'm lucky. Lucky! As if I haven't paid my dues. I say to them, "If you were as observant and diligent as I have been, maybe you would have accomplished something great, too!" It is just a case of sour grapes. They're jealous. Some people can't stand to see others succeed.

Miller's laws are my contribution to the world of medical science, my legacy, my gift to the all the citizens of the globe. The NIH, never able to have the vision to value my research, and thus, never having funded me, now wishes it had. It's okay. I'm not bitter. True science always triumphs. The truth always comes out, with or without funding.

Here are Miller's Laws.

1. Miller's First Law

This is my life work, my claim to fame. For this I may one day win the Nobel Prize.

In children less than two years old, skeletal muscle strength is directly proportional to the amount of cerumen in the external auditory canal.

Just think about this statement; feel it in all its weightiness. It possesses both depth and simplicity. It is inspiring. It lays the groundwork for future studies. Its elegance reflects the elegance of my scientific work itself. And it has a clarity rarely found in medical investigations.

Since I am a big proponent of translational research, I'll translate the italicized statement above. In simple lay terms, Miller's First Law states: "The more ear wax a small child has, the stronger that child is."

How do I know this? The obvious answer is evidence-based medicine. After more than thirty years in practice, I have accumulated more evidence than anyone should ever have. After churning the data from a randomized series of slightly less than a million children, I have found that when I need to see the eardrum with my otoscope, and the ear canal is plugged with massive amounts of ear wax, and I therefore must curette out the wax in order to visualize the eardrum, it is always, without fail, the strongest kids who have the most wax. Three of us, the mother, my nurse, and I then engage in baby wrestling with the child to get the wax out. Two of the combatants often emerge from the fray crying (mother and baby), and all four of us emerge utterly spent and perspiring. The baby often has ruptured capillaries on his face. It is not a pleasant experience.

For more information you may read the entire groundbreaking study: Miller et al. Is there a correlation between the amount of cerumen and childhood muscle strength? Miller's First Law. *The International Journal of Cerumenology*; 28 (1): 1197-1205, 2009 (www.IJC.org).

Phase II of my longitudinal study will look at this intriguing and not less important question:

In children less than two years old, does the amount of cerumen in the ear canal accurately predict future success in professional sports?

I have developed an extremely accurate computer model for answering this question for which the world is anxiously awaiting a final word. Look for me soon on the cover of *Time Magazine* when I announce the final results. In the meantime, follow our study's progress on our website at www.followthewax.org.

Finally, for those of you who secretly harbor embarrassing capitalistic instincts and are wondering, "What is the cash value of this information?" but are ashamed to ask, I will reveal this much. My spin-off biotech company, HumanCerumen, is investigating the commercial uses of human ear wax. We are looking to answer many questions which are both translational and transformative (and enriching). For starters:

Is it possible that ear wax is actually the source of human strength?

And, if so, is it possible to increase the amount of endogenous ear wax? Is there a heretofore undiscovered circulating cerumen stimulating peptide (c-CSP) that is modulated by the pituitary and hypothalamus?

What about exogenous ear wax? How would one go about harvesting enough to market it to athletes? Is it possible to produce it in the lab by genetic engineering? Or might it be manufactured using 3-D printing?

How about the questions and quandaries raised by increasing ear wax by endogenous or exogenous means? Would it be safe? Would it allowed? Would society approve? Would it be legal? Would it be ethical? Would it be moral? Would ear wax be considered a performance enhancing drug?

And here is the most vexing question of all: what about the route of administration? Is it best given IV? Is cerumen most efficacious if taken in capsule form by mouth? Or is it best just to stick it in your ear? All these provocative questions and more are discussed in detail at humancerumen.com under FAQ's. Investors are welcome. The limited IPO is set to launch soon. On the website, click on the "Gullible Investors" tab, fill out the online form, and be certain you include your bank routing number (a required field). We will be happy to transfer your funds electronically to our offshore bank at an undisclosed Caribbean location (HIPAA regulates all these secrets) if you qualify.

2. Miller's Second Law

The number of bruises on a boy's shins is directly correlated with the amount of fun he has, and inversely proportional to his time on the couch playing video games.

This law is self-evident. Others may have observed this (though I doubt it), but I am the first to formulate it formally. I may as well claim it as my own and slap my name on it.

DISCLOSURES:
1. I'm a spokesperson for HumanCerumen, where I am also the chairperson of the board. Compensation consists only of reimbursement for expenses. I should also mention that I have a generous stock option bonus set to activate when the limited IPO launches.

Well ... alright ... I want to be completely candid and transparent ... HumanCerumen also gives me a few free pens and notepads each year but you have my guarantee that these neither affect my prescribing habits nor skew my research.

2. To be fully forthcoming, at national medical meetings, I occasionally partake of free coffee and frozen yogurt, but never in Massachusetts, where it is strictly illegal.

3. I think I may own a few shares of Solyndra and General Motors, courtesy of the U.S. government. And my share of the national debt is more than $100,000.

PART THREE

30

Helen

THEY SAY THAT the face of Helen of Troy launched a thousand ships.

I knew a Helen whose heart helped launch a myriad of lives.

She was my grandmother, my father's mother.

It wasn't that my grandmother's face wasn't beautiful. No, she was beautiful all right—it was just that her heart was more beautiful. But the odd thing was this: no one seemed to want her.

Helen was born in 1904, the third child of Charles and Miriam Sands. Her parents divorced when she was just a little girl. Divorce was rare in those days, almost unthinkable. Helen and her family bore the shame, the misery, and the ongoing disruption of a failed marriage.

Her parents didn't want her, or at least it seemed that way to her. What else could she read from the events of her life?

After the divorce, adults shuttled her from foster home to foster home. As a five-year-old little girl, she was forced to mop floors and perform other arduous tasks while under the loveless glare of her foster parents. She never spoke of it to me. I hope she was not physically abused, but I know she was psychologically and verbally abused. "What is wrong with me?" Helen must have thought. "Why doesn't anyone love me? Why doesn't anyone want me? Why are they mean to me?" Did she wonder if God loved her? Did she even know that God existed? I don't know.

The abandonment by her family marked her for life. She finally landed in a home on a Maryland farm where she was treated with kindness and dignity. The Zouks were her surrogate parents, and she called them "Auntie" and "Uncle" all her life; they even gave her a room of her own. But she never again lived with either of her parents—until she later took in her own elderly father when he needed her help, the same father who had deserted her so many years before.

Helen was a beauty. She was nineteen years old when my grandfather noticed her. Edward Israel Miller was no fool, and he had great visual skills: he knew a pretty girl when he saw one.

I should mention here that Miller men may not always be the smartest men around, but we are inherently blessed with finely honed discriminatory powers when it comes to selecting beautiful women to marry. It must be some genetic thing; I am not sure if my grandfather was the first in his family to have this gene, it thus being a new mutation, or if he was simply continuing a long line of Miller men who had this gift. I have inherited this genetic trait as well.

There are two unwritten, unspoken rules for Miller men, but we all mysteriously know what they are: 1. Marry a pretty wife, and 2. Don't be stupid. We are all very good at living by the first rule. I find I am not so good at Rule Number Two.

My grandfather pursued Helen and convinced her that she should marry him. That's another family trait all Miller men share: once we identify our future brides, we pursue and persuade them to marry us until they finally surrender. We are very persistent. Some people may call this characteristic "stubbornness" or "hardheadedness" or even "pigheadedness." Why must they be so negative? We prefer to be more positive and call it stick-to-it-iveness, unwillingness to give up, a never-say-die spirit, or just ... persistence. Perseverance is a nice word for it, also.

Ed persisted until Helen gave in and thus they married soon after they met. Both lied to each other about their ages, both pretending to be older than they were. It was a fair deal.

Helen had little formal education, and she never finished high school. That did not mean she was not smart. *Au contraire, mes amis*, she was extremely intelligent. All her life, she had an endless thirst for knowledge and self-improvement. She read constantly. Her grammar was flawless and her vocabulary voluminous. She educated herself. She once made the mistake of telling me that many careless and uneducated people in her hometown, Baltimore, called it "Ballimer." I, of course, called it "Ballimer" at every possible opportunity just to tease her.

Helen wanted her family to have what she never had. My grandparents had three sons, two who served in World War II in the U.S. Navy, and a third who later joined the Army. All three sons finished college and went to graduate school. The sons went on to have a total of ten children. I am one of those children.

Because of her harsh and unhappy childhood, Helen knew what it was like to be unloved and unwanted. Suffering and rejection thus rendered her heart tender, loving and gentle to everyone, especially those who were poor, needy, and disenfranchised. I never saw her angry, though I did see her hurt.

After my grandparents and their sons moved to a different section of Baltimore, a neighbor invited them to her church, Arlington Presbyterian Church. On the roof of the church was an illuminated sign that read in bold letters: GOD IS LOVE. "Could this really be true?" Helen thought to herself.

Here, for the first time, my grandparents heard the gospel of the grace of Jesus Christ. The whole family received God's free offer of forgiveness and redemption. My grandmother became an ardent student of the Bible. She loved the Bible. She read it, she heard it preached and taught, and she studied it. She believed it. She took the Bible for what it is: the very Word of God. And she began to feel loved in a profound way; she experienced the love of God, the unchangeable, accepting, understanding, gentle, faithful love of God. She realized someone wanted her, desired her, and loved her in a way that she had before thought impossible. Her years of rejection and desertion were replaced by an eternity of infinite love. And Helen loved Jesus Christ because she knew he loved her beyond all her imagining.

She now knew by experience that the church sign was not lying to her. The statement on the sign was absolutely true: God *really* is love.

Helen's loving heart worked itself out in practical ways. She took in strays, as my father says. Any member of the family, including her father, was welcome to live with them. The Great Depression was a time of now almost unthinkable disruption and poverty. In spite of limited funds, my grandmother freely offered shelter to her suffering family, and many lived with my grandparents during this time. My unsophisticated grandmother really thought Jesus was serious when he said things like " ... I was a stranger, and ye took me in ... inasmuch as ye have done it unto one of the least of these my brethren, ye have done it unto me" (Matthew 25:35, 40 KJV). And of course, Jesus *was* serious— dead serious.

My grandparents were not known for their business acumen. After World War II, they opened a Maytag franchise in Vinton, Virginia, just outside of Roanoke. These were boom years for our country. We had just triumphed in Europe and Japan, America was now the world's superpower, our economy was humming, veterans were returning home and marrying, and the mind-set of our nation was pure optimism. Miller Maytag should have been a roaring success, an almost effortless success. My grandparents mismanaged the business, much of this due to their love of people. If someone bought a washer on credit, and later couldn't pay the bill, my grandparents covered it. They loaned cash from the cashbox to needy people. These kinds of things occurred repeatedly. Eventually the business failed. Helen didn't really care much about money. She cared about people.

My grandparents struggled to make a living all their lives. They worked hard. They had little money. But they were generous.

Helen loved cats. Any stray cat had a home with my grandmother; as I said, she took in strays. The feline star of the home was Snowball, a little cat surrounded by a great cumulus cloud of white fur. I never inherited her love for cats, maybe because of my allergies to cat hair and dander.

In addition, Helen loved clouds, any kind of cloud (was this why she loved Snowball?), but especially pink clouds, and she loved sunsets, especially pink sunsets. She loved the color pink.

Sitting on her back porch, she wistfully enjoyed the infinite spectrum of the variegated sunsets as day turned into dusk over Virginia's Blue Ridge Mountains. Then, with the full shroud of darkness, the Mill Mountain Star brightly shone white against the black sky, signifying that there had been no automobile deaths in the area that day. The infrequent red-colored star told my grandmother that the opposite was true: someone had died from a car accident that day. And her tender heart became sad.

My father used to half-seriously tell my grandmother that she would eventually land a coveted seat on heaven's "Cloud Committee." Who knows? Maybe God gave her that honor, and maybe some of the multi-colored sunsets we now see are the result of my grandmother's input—especially predominantly pink sunsets.

Helen loved her grandchildren. I was the oldest, in her terms, "the eldest grandson." Of course, I always thought I was her favorite, but Helen made each of her grandchildren feel like a favorite, so I am sure my sister and all of my cousins think they were her favorites also.

My grandmother was always kind to me, always patient. My sister, Becky, and I eagerly anticipated spending time with my grandparents in Roanoke when we had the chance; it was a world of love and acceptance. Besides, my grandfather had somehow accumulated a pool table, a pinball machine, and a jukebox in the basement. Add to that dozens of old comic books, a collection of Hardy Boys books, and my grandmother's gourmet fried chicken, and it was a young boy's paradise.

I loved the fact that Helen was always proud of me, and I'm glad she was able to see me graduate from medical school. She enjoyed hugging me and saying aloud to herself (and to me and to others who overheard): "My grandson ... the doctor." It was a little embarrassing, but it gave her pleasure.

My grandmother loved my wife from the moment they met. She was accepting, kind and encouraging to her; they connected from the start. Helen loved my children.

When I think about Helen, I remember her smile, a smile tinged with sadness that had been overmatched by joy.

I remember that my grandmother loved God, and she loved people. To her, what else in life could possibly be very important? God used her suffering to produce a joy and love that could not have developed otherwise.

Helen was never rich, never powerful, never famous, and never thought to be important.

Yet, Helen's heart helped launch a thousand ships, lives that have been touched directly or indirectly by her love for God and people.

That's not a bad legacy for a little girl whom no one wanted.

31

Pop

THE EXACT LOCATION and date of my grandfather's birth have always been a little mysterious. Whether he was born in East Prussia or on the ship making its slow crossing through the Atlantic Ocean to the United States, we are not certain. Maybe he was born just after his parents arrived in America. Our best theory is that his mother carried him as a baby off the ship once they disembarked in the Land of Opportunity.

Edward Israel Miller grew up in Baltimore, the son of immigrants. He was my father's father. Friends called him Ed. I knew him and loved him as Pop.

We are also not certain of Pop's European ancestry. Were the Millers Prussian, or were they Cossacks? We don't know. I have heard both sides, and maybe both are true. I like the idea of the Prussian military tradition, but I also like to think there is something to the Cossack story. An ancient Cossack symbol pictures a stag pierced through with an arrow. The stag is still standing, and the accompanying motto reads: "Wounded but not conquered." This motto seems fitting for Miller men. We are able to absorb a lot of punishment, we tolerate pain well, and we keep standing. We are not easy to kill.

What we do know for certain about Pop is this: he was a kind-hearted man who loved God and his family.

He also loved being an American.

During World War I, he volunteered at age fifteen for the United States Army, passing himself off as an eighteen-year-old and joining the cavalry. Though he never saw action in Europe, he was honorably discharged as a veteran of that great war. I'm proud that my grandfather had the courage to fight for his country and risk death when he was a just a boy.

He later worked as a rivet bucker in the Baltimore shipyards. A rivet bucker stood behind huge steel plates, and bodily and manually gave resistance to rivets being driven through them. This task required no ordinary strength. Even as an old man, my grandfather always had huge and muscular arms, I think mainly from his labor in the shipyards.

An exceptionally nice looking man, he went on to work as a model for clothing catalogs. He cut a dashing figure, his black hair parted in the middle, occasionally sporting a mustache.

When he met my grandmother, he swept her off her feet with his striking good looks. He exhibited the trademark manly Miller traits I have already discussed in the chapter on Helen: the ability to choose a beautiful wife, and persistence.

Pop enjoyed tools and working with his hands. He enjoyed giving his work away. We still have some furniture he crafted. I also have many of his tools from the early 20th century, and I prize them as I use them. My favorite is an old socket set; they don't make tools like this anymore. In addition, I have Pop's coal shovel; I don't often need to shovel coal in 21st century Augusta, Georgia, but it has other uses.

I'm sorry to confess that I never inherited my grandfather's expertise with tools, nor did I inherit my father's. Both had far more finesse than I. My default setting seems to be this: if something doesn't work, any tool becomes a hammer, and thus, it follows that everything else becomes a nail. And the corollary is that if something doesn't work, hit it hard or if it still doesn't work, hit it again harder. I still struggle mightily against my innate tendency to hammer harder when things go wrong—with tools or in life. This does not usually work as desired. It often breaks things—and people.

As children, we loved spending time at my grandparents' home. Pop had an old, green Chevy pick-up truck that the grandchildren played on, crawling all over it. He never minded. His collection of toys in the basement (jukebox, pinball machine, pool table) was there for our enjoyment. He never seemed worried that we would break or ruin anything. He just wanted us to have fun.

I never saw Pop get upset.

Pop was active in his church and community. He taught Sunday school. He sang in the choir. Once, when my mother was convinced he had dozed off in the choir, he replied that he had merely been resting his eyes. He then recounted point for point the sermon just preached. Weekly, he visited men in the Roanoke, Virginia jail to encourage them and share the universally-needed gospel of Christ with them.

Pop was very good to my mother as she entered the family. She reciprocated by making him banana cream pie every time he visited.

As Pop lay dying, unable to communicate because of a massive stroke, my parents played recorded hymns for him. Tears in his eyes gave evidence to the fact that the hymns had reached his heart.

The last time I saw Pop, he was lying in bed in a VA hospital, unable to move and unable to speak. I was saddened to see this end to a vigorous and strong man's life. My wife, children, and I went to the hospital with my grandmother on a Sunday morning. There, we all said our goodbyes. I lingered behind to spend time alone with him for a few minutes. As I held his hand, I thanked Pop for being a good grandfather to me. I talked about Jesus Christ and his love for us. I prayed with him. I spoke to Pop as if he heard and understood everything. I believe he did. The expression on his countenance changed, and his look told me he had taken everything in. There was a slight increase in the pressure on my hand as well.

He had heard and understood everything.

I left my grandfather with a kiss and the words: "I love you, Pop."

I regret not having had the opportunity to spend more time with Pop. Because I lived only briefly in the same town with my grandparents, my visits with them were short and infrequent.

I also regret that in the times I actually had with Pop, I never really got to know him very well as a man. Maybe that is just the nature of children and young people. One of the sad ironies of life is that we often do not realize the value of our elders and their stories until after they are dead.

My grandfather enjoyed simple pleasures: family, friends, hard work, and good food. He loved God. He loved his country. Pop was humble, he was gentle, and he was kind. He provided for his family. He safely navigated his family through the storms of the Great Depression and World War II.

I still have a little red New Testament that my grandparents gave me for Christmas when I was eleven years old. I've had it for fifty years. It is worn, and the leather is crumbling around the edges. Inscribed in the front in blue ink is a note from Pop with the reference Psalm 39:4. This verse reads:

> LORD, *make me to know my end,*
> *And what is the extent of my days,*
> *Let me know how transient I am.*

This is sage advice, given to me when Pop was about the same age as I am now. I hope to pass the same counsel on to my grandsons.

Pop's EXACT PLACE of birth and family origins remain mysteries to us, but not to God—though God doesn't seem to place much importance on these things. What matters to him is whether we are citizens of heaven. Pop is such a citizen.

The Kingdom of God is very different from the kingdoms of men.

> *But of Zion it shall be said, "This one and that one were born in her"; And the Most High Himself will establish her.*
> *The LORD shall count when He registers the peoples, "This one was born there …"*
> *Psalm 87:5-6*

> *So then you are no longer strangers and aliens, but you are fellow citizens with the saints, and are of God's household, having been built upon the foundation of the apostles and prophets, Christ Jesus Himself being the corner stone …*
> *Ephesians 2:19-20*

32

Ezra

Who, after all, speaks today of the annihilation of the Armenians?
Adolf Hitler, 1939

UNBELIEVABLY, even now, there exist deniers of the Holocaust.

This denial is inexplicable and irrational. These deniers of reality state that six million Jews during World War II were never really exterminated by Hitler's Nazis. They claim there was no genocide, there were no death camps, there were no gas chambers, and there were no furnaces. They say none of it ever happened.

Just as unbelievably, there also exist deniers of the Armenian Genocide. Between 1915 and 1923, 1.5 million Armenians were wiped out in an ethnic cleansing that occurred at the bloody hands of the Ottoman Turks. Yet, Turkey still denies that it ever happened; of course, some Armenians died during World War I, they say, but only as a kind of collateral damage that always occurs in war. Sadly, even now, only twenty-one nations have had the courage to call it what it was: genocide.

Humans are very good at hiding facts, at least for a while, though the truth always eventually emerges. We brazenly lie. We subtly recruit words and redefine them. Just look at the situation that exists now in the Western world with the issue of abortion.

In the United States alone, one million babies each year are killed by abortion. One million. Various smoke screens are used to hide the essential facts. Euphemisms are employed: the baby is actually only a "fetus," or an "embryo." And, of course, the twisted logic goes, fetuses not really fully human. The term "abortion" is sanitized and becomes "termination of pregnancy." The aborted baby is really just one of the "products of conception." Justifications are invented to attempt to give moral cover. "A woman's body is her own," goes the argument; therefore, she can do what she wants with her own body. Or an abortion is a "woman's choice," and since we are Americans who are big on freedom, of course, no one should stand in her way. Or "the fetus is really only part of the woman" as if the baby were an organ that can be discarded at will, much like an appendix, or tonsils. The procedure is said to be merely a simple surgical operation without any repercussions; this wording never mentions the baby's present suffering, or the mother's dehumanization, complications, and future anguish. It all sounds so urbane, high-minded, and clinical. All these things serve to obscure the fact that a baby is being murdered. This is high-order denial of reality.

Humans are adept at denying reality and at attempting to hide what we don't like to admit. Such was and is the case in the Armenian Genocide.

Yet, if there were no Armenian Genocide, then how do I explain this about my friend Rick Keuroglian's grandfather? Why, as a two-year-old Armenian boy, was he smuggled out of the Middle East rolled up in an oriental rug?

And if there were no Armenian Genocide, why did my own grandfather, Ezra Deter, spend a year in Beirut and Aleppo doing relief work among Armenian refugees?

IN THE EARLY 1900S, Turkey was the "sick man" of Europe. The glory of the Ottoman Empire was a flickering memory, and now young military officers, the "Young Turks," had taken control of the country. In an effort to restore former Islamic glory, the Young Turks embarked on a policy of Pan-Turkism; this left no room for Christians, and it gave opportunity to expropriate lands and wealth from the Christian Armenians. This policy also invoked the name of Allah to justify all manner of evil.

Armenia had been the first Christian nation on earth. The lands they held had been in their families for millennia. Many of their people were among Turkey's elite. And on April 24, 1915, Turkey unleashed a era of fiendish brutality hardly discussed now, barely even remembered. In too many polite or political circles, it is not mentioned, or it is spoken of in obfuscating euphemisms, or it is just flatly denied.

That April night, 300 Armenian men were rounded up and murdered. These were leaders of the Armenian people and of Turkey, men of wealth, status, and education. Quickly, the pogrom was rolled out. Armenian soldiers in the Turkish army were forced to give up their weapons and were given jobs reserved for slaves. Armenian civilians were likewise disarmed and required to surrender their guns. Death units composed of criminal goons massacred thousands of Armenians at a time, mainly men. Most men under fifty years of age were slaughtered.

Physical and psychological cruelty reigned; it was a reign of terror. Women were raped as their husbands were forced to look on, unable to aid their suffering wives. Men and women were mercilessly whipped or beaten to death as family members helplessly watched, their tormentors satisfying their bloodlust.

Deportations began. By this time, survivors were chiefly women and children. Railroad boxcars were overstuffed with suffering humanity; often their transport led merely to death after days dying of thirst and hunger.

Long treks were organized. The Turks lied to the Armenians, telling them that they were being relocated to safety. These treks were in reality death marches into the desert. Women and girls were humiliated: they were often forced to march completely naked. Hundreds died of starvation, dehydration, and exposure. Demonic orgies of unspeakable abuse and degradation occurred nightly. Women often committed suicide rather than endure the brutality inflicted upon them. Worse, to prevent suffering of their own children, mothers frequently killed them by drowning them in rivers along the way to their own deaths. Other mothers simply went insane.

As the marches progressed, young girls and women were sold to Turks and Arabs to be their slaves or concubines.

Armenians were killed and tortured in unthinkably sadistic ways, methods that come from the fires of hell. Humans can be surprisingly cruel, but these methods of torture were so heinous that mere mortals could not have dreamed them up: they were demonic.

A Turkish official, Jevdet Bey, was known as the "horseshoe master." Why? Because of his penchant for nailing horseshoes to Armenian feet.

Aurora Mardiganian escaped with her life from her Turkish masters, later publishing *Ravished Armenia* and still later contributing to the documentary film "Auction of Souls." In both print and film media, she presented first-hand evidence of Turkish brutality. She describes girls who were ravished and then nailed to crosses. Others were burned alive.

Henry Morgenthau was the American ambassador to Turkey during this time. One of his many comments: "The gendarmes would nail hands and feet to pieces of wood—evidently in imitation of the Crucifixion, and then while the sufferer writhes in his agony, they would cry, 'Now let your Christ come help you.'"

Some Armenians were made to participate in an especially gruesome and grotesque game. Men on horseback planted their swords, points up, in rows in the ground. Young women and children stood nearby, secured by their tormentors. Each horseman then galloped toward his chosen victim, picked her up, and tossed her onto an upright blade, impaling her. If she died, good. If not, she was picked up for another try. The terror itself was unimaginable.

Soldiers scooped Armenian infants off the ground and then tossed them into the air, catching them and skewering them as they descended onto a vertically held bayonet.

Armenian heads, severed from their bodies, were used as footballs.

Hellish varieties of torture and killing were nearly infinite.

But as many now say, it never really happened, or if it did, it does not really matter now. "Let's not talk about it," people say. "It's in the past. Let's move on."

Hitler counted on the Armenian genocide not really mattering in 1930s Europe. He knew that people forget history, and they especially forget history if it did not happen to them. Thus, he was emboldened to proceed with his own genocide, and he even built much of it on the platform the Young Turks had provided. Look closely, and you will see many similarities, not only in strategy but in specific tactics. Guns were removed from German homes. German arrogance gave them the right to commit murder and expropriate wealth, thus yielding room for the German *übermenschen*, the Aryan super-race. It was all justified by the "fact" that "Germans deserved to rule." And, unimaginable horrors resulted: the death of six million Jews, and the near annihilation of a people.

When human beings ignore or forget any episode of genocide, it opens the door to future genocides. If there is no admission of guilt, no declaration of evil, no outcry or outrage, no justice for victims, and no retribution—future malevolent humans are made bold to do it again. Then again, even with all these things in place, we humans still have an inborn perverse propensity to naturally hate and kill each other. Yet, the guardrails of justice and acknowledgement of absolute right and wrong help us avoid falling prey to our own evil tendencies.

AFTER THE ARMISTICE of November 11, 1918, World War I ended. But it did not end the plight of thousands of Armenians in the Levant. It did not end the massacres. And there were still Armenian refugees, orphans, and widows scattered all over the Middle East. They were dying of hunger. They had no homes. It was a humanitarian tragedy writ large. Here is where Ezra Deter comes in.

MY MOTHER'S FATHER was born in Iowa in 1892, later moving to western Illinois as a child. His entire family were farmers, and they were Mennonites. Ezra had a thirst for knowledge and eventually went to Goshen College; his terminal degree was an MA from Northwestern University.

During World War I, he was drafted by the United States to enter military service but because he was a conscientious objector (CO), he never went to war. Instead, he was assigned by the government to a farm and served his country there providing needed food to our troops on the front. He endured much criticism, mockery, and taunting for his status as a CO.

I disagree with my grandfather's position on the use of lethal force, but I respect and honor him for his courage in standing up for his beliefs. My own view is that Scripture gives individuals a mandate to defend our families and selves, gives legitimate governments the right to "bear the sword" to uphold justice and punish evil, and gives us all the responsibility to protect the helpless and weak. I believe there is such a thing as a just war.

My grandfather was not a coward, however; his CO status did not arise from fear. He simply had strong convictions—so strong that when he heard about the Armenian humanitarian disaster as it was coming to light after the war, he quickly volunteered to serve there with the Near East Relief (NER). He saw a great need and he was moved to help, not with only a nominal contribution, but with his life. It was not a safe place to go. He went just after his service to the government had ended.

Ezra arrived in Beirut in 1919 and spent the entire year there, at Aleppo, and in between the two cities. He was twenty-seven years old.

It seems he had a great gift for organization and administration. He spent most of his time in support roles, repairing and installing things, keeping the supplies rolling out to the orphans and refugees, and managing a staff of nationals.

As I read his diary, it is obvious that he was often frustrated and impatient with people and processes. He had a temper. He was honest enough to admit his failures. And he was always conscience-stricken when his anger had erupted. I can identify with his frustration, impatience, and anger, because every day, I, too, fight against these tendencies in my own life.

Family lore tells of his going out in a truck, picking up Armenian orphans off the streets of Aleppo and then carrying them to security.

His diary often mentions orphanages and refugee camps, each containing thousands of displaced Armenians. He frequently discusses his fears of more massacres; the political climate after the war was far from stable, and the hostilities against Christian Armenians had not ceased, only decreased.

In his letters and diary, he comments on Muslim culture. On one occasion, taking an evening walk with a female friend, they come upon a farmhouse on a hill that makes him homesick for his Illinois farm. He remarks to his friend that he imagines there is a happy man and wife inside. To which the friend answers: "Yes, perhaps a happy man but about four unhappy women."

Ezra reports on a vital role of their mission: rescuing Armenian girls who had been sold into harems. They saved at least 250 of them from this sexual slavery.

He describes the rescue process in a long passage in a letter written from Aleppo to his family; it is dated October 12, 1919.

Our rescued girls, about 250 of them, gotten free from the harems (Arabs) will soon be moved to Aintub. You should see Mr. Dunaway and Miss Shyab come home at night with their big load of girls which they got that day. It's some sight. Some are crying, others laughing … others are too frightened to do either.

This is the way they get them. These two Americans jump in the Reo (truck) in the morning …. and drive across the plains until they come to an old village with houses made of mud … It is a dirty, filthy place and the people are dressed, or half dressed as the occasion may be and as dirty as one could imagine. They all come out to meet the rare sight and wonder what is to happen. In several cases, the men ran and got their guns and the "would-be rescuers" had to retreat for safety. But as a rule, they first go to the Sheik's tent and produce a list of Arab names which they of course had gotten sometime previously so they know just who they want. Mr. Dunaway says: "These men have girls hidden in their homes and we want them and we are going to have them." In the meantime, Miss Shyab who is a Syrian by birth and speaks Arabic …. is jollying the old Sheik with her jolly good way and he sort of takes a liking to her. She is a very striking little girl but has tact and grit that most girls do not possess. She says in her good humored way, "Now, Mr. Sheik, we've got to have those little women of these men," as she drinks the native coffee with him. In most cases he'll say, "If you can find them, they are yours."

So, they make a beeline for one man's house. He sees them coming, smells the rat, and hides the girl. They go to the door and ask for the man but he isn't to be found or at least the woman says he has gone to a nearby village, but upon investigating you will find him beneath a trap door in the floor or buried under some blankets, hiding, etc. Well then Mr. Arab comes forth, when asked where the little girl is which he has married and is Armenian, he says, "I've never had any." They know he has so feel free to press him. They insist and search the village. Pretty well discouraged, Miss Shyab walks up to the man, draws her revolver which she has strapped around her and gives him one more chance to lie, which he usually refuses to do, and the little girl comes forth, right out of a stone wall where she was hidden. She perhaps is 12, 13, 14 years old, haggard-looking and poorly clad.

So goes the story. Some days they bring home 3, 4, 8, and one day 16. You see when the Armenians were deported from their country, they of course had to go thru this Arab territory and when the Arabs saw a girl they wanted, they kept her. We keep the girls here and try to get them back to their people in Armenia, which we have been quite successful in doing recently.

MY GRANDFATHER worked for the NER all of 1919. He returned to the U.S. for a brief time, and soon returned to Beirut to live for three more years, this time starting an automobile dealership. He seems to have fallen in love with the Middle East, and he seems to have had a love for adventure. He was by now an entrepreneur.

He met my grandmother, Edith, in Beirut during this stint. She was an Indiana girl working for the YMCA as a secretary. They married in America a few years later.

Ezra and Edith settled down in Chicago and reared their two daughters, Virginia and Dorothy. Virginia would become a missionary in Japan after World War II; Dorothy would become my mother. My grandparents both taught school, and both were active in their church. They lived a simple and humble life. Ezra was an upright man who took care of his family well.

My grandfather died at age sixty of a massive heart attack. He never made it to the hospital.

I was not quite two years old when he died.

Thus, I never really knew Ezra Deter. It is one of my great disappointments in life not to have known him. I think I would have liked him; I would have enjoyed him. I think we would have understood each other well.

I'm proud of my grandfather. I'm proud he was intimately involved in taking relief to the Armenians. He braved danger and isolation. He gave a year of his life to assist those who had been nearly exterminated and who were still suffering the ravages of their ordeal. I admire his courage and willingness to take risk. I admire his sense of adventure. I admire his honesty, and I admire his convictions that led to action.

All I know about him is what others have told me and what has been handed down to me from other sources. I know his two daughters greatly loved and respected him. I hear his friends from his college yearbook tell me about his laugh, evidently an identifying characteristic. I look at old faded, wrinkled photographs and see the serious, smiling young man wearing glasses. I read his journals and letters and gain a fleeting glimpse inside of him, seeing through a glass darkly. But the special relationship between a grandfather and his only grandson is missing.

But, yes—I do have one more thing: I have a letter from him to my mother. In it, my grandfather tells my mother that he was praying for me. I'm grateful to know that. When I couldn't pray for myself, my godly grandfather prayed for me, taking me to Jesus when I had no idea he was doing it.

Who knows what God did with those prayers?

ACKNOWLEDGEMENTS:

1. I am indebted to Marvin Olasky and his article "Prove Hitler Wrong" (World Magazine, October 23, 2004) for stimulating my interest in many of the particulars of the Armenian genocide. From his article, I made a wider search for specific incidents and learned much more about Aurora Mardiganian.

2. I owe my cousin, Hazel Nice Hassan, a debt of gratitude for her book, *Moved with Compassion*. This book contains a history of Ezra Deter based on his journals and letters. Her hard work of reading, compiling, editing, and organizing his written legacy made my job much easier in writing this chapter. The letter on pages 227 to 228 is a quotation from Hazel Hassan's book and is a distillation of my grandfather's letter home.

33

Appomattox 1956

I WAS FIVE YEARS OLD, living in Norfolk, Virginia. During a shopping trip to Ward's Corner in downtown Norfolk, my mother, three-year-old sister Becky, and I needed to find a restroom. Since I was the alpha male while my father was at work I made it my job to find one for us. I did.

There was, however, a problem. My mother informed me we couldn't use the one that I had found. I asked why, and she patiently explained to me that it was only for "colored" people. That was my first conscious encounter with the segregated South, more than ninety years after the War Between the States had ended.

I later learned that there were water fountains for whites, and water fountains for colored people. There were signs that I couldn't read above the water fountains and on restroom doors clearly announcing who could use which.

It didn't make much sense to me, but that was the way it was. I wish I could say that my child's sense of justice was provoked, and maybe it was. I hope I was outraged, but I cannot remember for certain that I was. All I can remember was that it seemed very strange.

The term "colored people" was the preferred and respectful term for blacks (later shifting to "blacks" and "Afro-Americans" and still later "African-Americans"). On official forms that asked for race, the choices offered were "Caucasian" or "Negro" or "Oriental," but in daily conversation, the term "colored people" was used for blacks. (For example, the NAACP was the National Association for the Advancement of Colored People, and the name was self-chosen.) We used that term at home. My family never used the "n-word." It was considered a bad word, derogatory and demeaning. I heard it some in school, but not at home.

America ran along two parallel tracks, one for whites and one for blacks. This was especially so in the southern U.S. but was true in the North as well. Not only were there separate water fountains and restrooms, but there were separate schools and even (paradoxically and wrongly) separate churches for whites and blacks. Churches should have been the one place, at least, where blacks and whites were together, irrespective of color. Believers in Christ should be expected to worship together in unity.

Society was divided along racial lines.

In second grade, while we lived in Baltimore, I began going to school with a few black children. It seemed normal and natural. I remember one black classmate who helped me find my way around the new school and later helped me find my lost gloves; race did not matter to us. My square-dance partner was a pretty, vivacious black girl who patiently put up with me as we do-si-do'ed and as I swung my partner.

Schools in the South were pretty much segregated until 1967, when, by court order, the "separate but equal" myth was destroyed and schools were integrated by law. Prior to integration, there were schools for whites and schools for blacks, two separate systems, and anything but equal. I was in tenth grade, my first year at Winter Park High School (Florida), when a few courageous black kids from Hungerford High School, the local black high school, braved public opinion in exchange for a better education and entered the previously all-white school. Some in the community predicted violence. It never happened. My first encounter with some of these black students was in football two-a-days in the 100-degree humidity of Orlando. Enduring this type of physical torture melts away superficial differences and bonds you with your teammates quickly, and I don't think either the white or black guys cared what color anybody else was. When we looked around, all we saw were teammates, guys who had suffered together and would play together in common cause. Later in the year, we would play basketball together, as well. Our coaches and players welcomed these guys from Hungerford, some of whom would prove to be fantastic athletes. We were happy to have them, and there were no problems ... none at all.

I didn't realize until recently how close I was as a small boy to an historic period in race relations in the South. In 1956, before I lived in Norfolk, I lived in Appomattox, Virginia, where, in 1865, the War Between the States had ended. I remember visiting the McLean House at Appomattox Courthouse where General Lee had surrendered to General Grant. This surrender should have been the beginning of the end of slavery and racial oppression in our country. Yet, deep evil dies stubbornly. When slavery was declared illegal, the deep evil was only weakened and unmasked; it retreated to more subtle, less overt, more legal, and less blatant forms of racism. Legislation outlawed slavery, but it could not outlaw the maneuverings of some men to legally accomplish their own ends and to keep others under their control; it could not outlaw or change the fear, pride, greed, hatred, and selfishness in the hearts of men. I do not mean to imply that all white men are or were bigots, or that only whites can be prejudiced. All men have elements of fear, pride, and hatred in their hearts to larger or lesser degrees. But whites were in control then, and the whole structure of our country in the 1950s had been actively designed by some to legally continue the subjugation of black people; this structure was passively accepted as a way of life by most of the others, many of these being overall "good people." Yet, how often are "good people" willing to perversely accommodate ourselves to systematic injustice or other evils? Here is the thought sequence:

1. The injustice has been handed down to us in the system.
2. We feel no responsibility for having created the evil.
3. We see that it may even benefit us (a secret, unarticulated thought).

It is thus easy for us to conveniently turn a blind eye to the wrong and to rationalize that it is not our business or that we have no time to deal with it.

Oppression and racism loomed large in 1950s America.

Virginia public education during this time was a hotbed of white-black conflict after the *Brown v. Board of Education* decision was handed down by the United States Supreme Court in 1954. The Southern Manifesto and Massive Resistance resulted in temporary school closings in several Virginia counties to avoid integration. Prince Edward County resisted integration of black students into white schools to the point that eventually, in 1959, the county chose to shut down the entire county public school system indefinitely. The Prince Edward Foundation was created, out of which private schools for white children were formed. These schools were supported by government funds, yet they excluded black children. For five years, from 1959 to 1964, there was no public education for black children. And so, for five years, many black children received no education at all in Prince Edward County.

In 1956, a group from Prince Edward County paid a visit to the teachers of adjacent Appomattox County in the library of Appomattox County High School. That afternoon meeting was designed to convince and urge the public school teachers of the county to follow the course embarked on by Prince Edward County. There was a lot of discussion. The plan made sense. The white and black schools were separate and unequal anyway. They were so unequal that in some black schools of Appomattox County, records were not even kept. Consequently, the reasoning went, closing the county schools really wouldn't affect things much for the black kids; they would simply go from a bad education to no education. And the public school teachers would continue receiving paychecks in the new private system where the white kids would continue to get a decent education.

The argument to shut down the schools was persuasive.

A twenty-eight-year-old teacher who was new to the school sat in the back of the library, listening. He had a wife and two kids. He had determined to keep his mouth shut. Since he was new, he thought he should just stay out of this battle. Just sit there, learn what was happening, be polite, stay out of trouble. That was the idea.

He listened. He kept his seat. But he was boiling inside, and his stomach began to hurt. His stomach always hurt when he got upset, ever since he had developed peptic ulcer disease following the death of his infant daughter a couple of years before. His ulcer had bled then, and now it only hurt. His stomach pain was his constant companion, sometimes more and at other times less present. His stomach was also a good warning system for him. It even helped him to stay out of some trouble—sometimes. Now his stomach was burning and it was gnawing. No, now it was killing him. But he listened and stayed seated. He stayed seated—until he couldn't stand it anymore. He rose to his feet and spoke.

"Look, I'm new here. Most of you don't even know me. And I don't know much about politics. All I know is this: I have a contract to teach students at Appomattox High School. That means I'm here to teach. My contract doesn't state whether I'm supposed to teach white kids, black kids, or green kids. It only says I'm supposed to teach high school kids. I'll honor my contract. And I'll vote to keep the schools open. And I intend to stay and teach."

He sat down. The mood in the room changed quickly. The teachers voted to stay and teach, and the schools of Appomattox County never closed. Ultimately they were integrated.

And the new, young teacher?

He was my father.

I have a dream that my four little children will one day live in a nation where they will be judged not by the color of their skin but by the content of their character.

    Martin Luther King, Jr.

    August 28, 1963

34

Sylvester

AT A CHURCH MEETING, leaders discussed a new church initiative in another city. We were cooperating with other churches to jointly begin this new ministry. Our pastor called on Sylvester Brown, one of our elders and a member of the church planting committee, to give a report.

Sylvester started by explaining the vision for the new church: it was meant to be an African-American church planted by our denomination. He reviewed all the comments of other committee members. He discussed all the logistics and the finances.

I was getting uncomfortable with the whole thing the more he discussed it.

Being a fair-minded man, Sylvester had given generous representation to all other views. Now, he finally told us what he had said and what he thought.

"Why not just plant a church? You know, a *church*. Why do we need to plant a *black* church? What's wrong with just a *church*?"

Wow. That did not sound very politically correct. But he said exactly what I had been thinking, and he was right. I felt better.

Let me explain something about Sylvester Brown.

He is a black man. He is a black man in a mainly white church. I don't think we ever notice. We're family.

I love to hear Sylvester pray. Why? Because he talks to God like he knows him well; that's because he does.

He is a man of quiet wisdom. He speaks gently and humbly, yet with authority.

Sylvester Brown grew up in rural Texas in the 1940s and 1950s. There, he experienced both overt and subtle forms of racism common across our country in that time. Some whites spoke to him disrespectfully, and some spoke down to him, as if he were a lesser human. People called him ugly, hateful, racist names. What hurt the most was when children treated him in cruel, disrespectful ways. The white-dominated society expected certain things of a young black boy and man, and Sylvester knew exactly how to "play the game." He knew "his place." One small detail is very telling: blacks in his town were said to be "uppity" if they wore dressy clothes anytime except Sunday. And being accused of "uppitiness" was never a good thing. When I ask him now if he was ever bitter or angry toward those behind the racism, Sylvester says, "No, I felt sorry for them." Of course, the names and injustice hurt, but bitterness and resentment never became a part of his character. He credits God for working in him to prevent these natural human responses.

Sylvester began following Jesus Christ while in college. He later served in the U.S. Army and still later became a teacher. He eventually led a school as principal for many years.

God has used Sylvester many times and in many places to break down racial barriers. It was not something he set out to do; it just naturally and normally occurred wherever he went. Sylvester seems surprised that God would use him as an agent of racial reconciliation, but he has. It has happened repeatedly. It happened in Vietnam; even his base's commanding officer noticed his influence. Sylvester often spoke at chapel services there where both black and white soldiers worshiped together. On one specific occasion, as Sylvester spoke to the other soldiers, a young white man came to Christ and eventually became an evangelist. I wonder how many people (red, brown, yellow, black and white) have followed Christ as a result of that evangelist's ministry; these are all Sylvester's multi-racial spiritual descendants, just one branch of his life of cross-racial evangelism.

God used Sylvester again when he and a fellow principal, a white man whose father had been in the Ku Klux Klan, began their long friendship. Over the years, they did many things together socially and professionally. And their friendship helped to transform the county principals' association. No longer would white and black principals sit on different sides of the room.

Sylvester was not afraid to begin attending our "white" church twenty-eight years ago when he was decidedly in the racial minority. It took a lot of courage. He did not really fear rejection. It was just that it might be a little uncomfortable—it was a step into the unknown. He was accepted with open hearts and open arms, and he accepted us in the same way. He says he felt a little like he was some kind of "oddity" at first, but very quickly, any unease disappeared. He jokingly recalls his black friends asking him, when he joined our predominantly white church, "Sylvester, what's wrong with you? Haven't you noticed that you don't quite fit in there? That maybe you're a little different?" He laughs as he tells the story.

He and his family fit in just fine and have for twenty-eight years.

Sylvester Brown understands that the gospel of Jesus Christ is the great equalizer of all men. Every human needs forgiveness and redemption, and only Jesus is able to give both. At the cross of Christ, superficial things like race, color, origins, social class, appearances, and status … these things all melt away. All that matters here is our need and Jesus' love.

Sylvester also understands that what is needed in a ministry and a church is this: to preach the gospel of Christ. Certainly, we should be culturally sensitive. But, in America, it seems to me that we've outsmarted ourselves. We've created divisions of all kinds where God intended none. The gospel creates unity, not divisions.

Sylvester simply wanted to plant a church.

This is God's way. Jesus taught it. Sylvester knew it.

Hold out the gospel of Jesus and all people will be drawn to him.

> ... I, when I am lifted up from the earth, will draw all people to myself.
> John 12:32 (ESV)

> .... behold, a great multitude that no one could number, from every nation, from all tribes and peoples and languages, standing before the throne and before the Lamb, clothed in white robes, with palm branches in their hands, and crying out with a loud voice, "Salvation belongs to our God who sits on the throne, and to the Lamb!"
> Revelation 7:9-10

35

Appearances

My son, Jeremiah, was three years old. The two of us were wandering the halls of our church one late, dreary, winter Sunday afternoon after we had dropped off the girls in our family at their respective activities. This gave the males, Jeremiah and me, a chance to spend some time together.

We walked into the dark church sanctuary and heard organ music. From the front of the church, we looked up to the rear balcony and saw our organist practicing his music for the evening worship service. He was illuminated by the light on the organ just over his sheet music, giving him a beatific and other-worldly appearance.

Jeremiah saw him and made a reasonable deduction, voiced in a question. He looked into my face, his own face placid and serious and guileless, his eyes shining with deep thought. He put the question:

"Daddy ... "

There was a long pause. Whenever Jeremiah said "Daddy ... " like that, with a particular intonation, I knew something profound was coming. He was thinking.

I waited for him to order his thoughts.

"Daddy ... is dat ... Gawd?"

Was that really God in our church balcony playing the organ, surrounded by a halo? It was very good question. Here Jeremiah was in church, the place he knew God was preached and worshiped, and there above him was a person surrounded by light. Was this God?

No, of course he was not God, but it was easy to understand how it might appear that way.

And I think to myself, how often do I misperceive God? How often do I misread him and misjudge him? How often do I not see him when he is right there? How often do I misunderstand him? How often do I misinterpret my circumstances and what God is doing through them? How often do I fail to trust him and believe he really loves me? How often do I wonder if he really cares about me?

The Bible answers all these questions and more with three more questions.

> *What then shall we say to these things?*
> *If God is for us, who is against us?*
> *He who did not spare His own Son, but delivered Him*
> *up for us all,*
> *how will He not also with Him freely give us all things?*
> *Romans 8:31-32*

36

Susanna Nancy

SUSIE IS OUR TENTH grandchild—a California girl. Of course, it goes without saying (but I'll say it anyway), that two-year-old Susie is preternaturally beautiful, intelligent, athletic, well-rounded, articulate, and altogether superlative—just like all my granddaughters. My grandsons are just as remarkable. Amazing.

But there is something else that is remarkable about Susie, and that is the way she came to us.

In May, almost four months before she was born, God gave me the idea that our church should set aside a day to pray and fast for his special blessing upon our church.

On July 12th, church leaders agreed and decided that the day of prayer and fasting would occur on September 17th.

On September 11th, we announced in Sunday school that as part of our church's day of prayer, our class would gather in two separate groups on September 17th to pray from 10:00 a.m. until 11:00 a.m., one group at our home and another group at the home of our close friends, the Jeffcoats.

And as planned, on September 17th, many of our congregation prayed and fasted. At 10:00 a.m., four of us gathered at our home and several others gathered at the Jeffcoats' house.

Now, what we did not know when all this planning was going on was that our son's wife, Kate, would go into labor in San

Diego on September 16th, and that she would have some serious problems. We received phone updates from our son, Jeremiah, several times that night and early on the morning of the 17th. We were all concerned for our daughter-in-law and her baby. We knew that both lives were threatened. Through the night and into the early morning, our family all prayed for Kate and Susie.

The birth process is not without great risk to mother and baby. I've attended hundreds of deliveries, always prepared to resuscitate or do whatever was needed for my new patient. Even "routine" deliveries cause me to fear for the mother and her newborn, and some deliveries deeply terrify me. I know what can happen. I have seen the worst. Standing by the infant warmer, gloved, gowned, and masked, impatiently waiting for my little patient, I have often prayed for both mother and baby. It's always a great relief to have the baby in my arms, and to hear the first great wail, while simultaneously seeing the mother's tears of joy and hearing her laughter.

Things can go badly very quickly. It's remarkable how fear focuses my prayers.

At about 10:50 a.m. on September 17th, the group at our home prayed in earnest specifically for Kate and Susie.

Just after 11:00 Eastern Time (8:00 Pacific Time), an ecstatic Jeremiah called to tell us that Susanna Nancy Miller had arrived and that both mother and baby were well. With relief and joy, we thanked God.

God did something wonderful the day Susie was born. He brought her to us safely and he protected Kate. But beneath all of this, something else had occurred, something even more wonderful. God had arranged for this all to happen precisely as it did: the date, the time, and the circumstances. At some point in eternity past, unknown to us, God had planned to give us the privilege of praying for Susie at the exact time she was being born, on a day of extraordinary prayer involving our entire church when we were asking for God's blessing.

When God gave me the idea for our church to pray and fast, and when he gave us the date to do it, and when we decided the time to meet at our house, and when we prayed for Susie and Kate just as Susie was arriving, we had no idea that events would come together as they did. And I had no idea in May 2011 that my desire for our church to pray and fast would result in my praying and fasting for my own daughter-in-law and granddaughter at the exact time of their great need. I could not have orchestrated this. God did it.

God works everything for his own glory and for our good. He is always at work in us, around us, and through us. He gave Kate and Susie safety that day, and he gave Nancy and me the privilege of praying for them in real time at a pre-planned point in time of concentrated prayer. He showed us again that he always is with us to help us and guide us and to protect us.

Susie's birthday was a miracle of God. I can't fully understand it, and I can't fully explain it. But it was a miracle of God, and as God loves to do so often, he allowed us to participate in it.

O LORD, Thou art my God; I will exalt Thee, I will give thanks to Thy name;
For Thou hast worked wonders,
Plans formed long ago, with perfect faithfulness.
   Isaiah 25:1

It will also come to pass that before they call, I will answer; and while they are still speaking, I will hear.
   Isaiah 65:24

At the beginning of your pleas for mercy a word went out [the command was issued (NASB)], and I have come to tell it to you, for you are greatly loved.
   Daniel 9:23a. (ESV)

37

Robin

MY MOTHER was twenty-four years old when my youngest sister, Robin, was born. My father was twenty-six, a high school teacher in Berryville, Virginia. Becky was a one-year-old, and I was three. We lived in a little rented house on Page Street, called "Page Alley" by the locals.

Berryville and the surrounding area had seen much military action during The War Between the States. This had been Stonewall Jackson territory. Berryville's Grace Episcopal Church, built in 1831, had been badly damaged by occupying Federal troops.

Our next-door neighbors were the Drs. Barlow, Canadian physicians who wintered in Virginia each year in their retirement, living in a simple stone cottage. They took a special interest in us, acting as surrogate parents and grandparents. They visited often, gave us free medical care, and offered good counsel. They frequently asked what we had had for supper, and then shared their meals with us: they wanted to be sure the school teacher's family was getting enough to eat. After all, my father received a salary of $3,800 per year. Money was tight, but we never went hungry.

My mother's third pregnancy went well, and there was nothing in her prenatal course to suggest anything but a healthy baby. The entire family was excited as we anticipated the birth of the new addition. Of course, then, in the 1950s, no one knew whether this would be a boy or girl. My parents made all the usual preparations, organized logistics, and finalized plans. They were ready.

Robin Allyson Miller was born on December 17, 1954, in the nearby town of Winchester. She was a beautiful little girl with dark-brown hair. She weighed nine pounds. She appeared to be healthy. Assured that his wife and new daughter were safe and resting well, my father left the hospital for a short time to check on his two older children and to do a little work at school.

He received a call at the school soon afterwards asking him to return quickly to the hospital. His new baby was in trouble.

It had soon become obvious to her young physician that Robin was gravely ill. This was not supposed to happen.

But surprises often occur.

Robin was pale. She was in marked respiratory distress. She was swollen. She was jaundiced. Her heart, liver, and spleen were enlarged.

Her doctor did not want to believe what he knew her diagnosis to be.

Lab work revealed severe anemia. And the clincher was Robin's blood type: Rh positive. My mother's is Rh negative.

Her doctor's fears were confirmed. Without doubt, Robin had erythroblastosis fetalis. Hydrops fetalis. Hemolytic disease of the newborn. These are all names reflecting different aspects of the same disease. My mother's blood type was Rh negative, and Robin's was Rh positive. In those days, this blood group incompatibility in a second or third pregnancy could spell catastrophe.[5]

---

5   RhoGAM (Rho (D) Immune Globulin) was first used in the 1960s (ten years after Robin's birth) to prevent a baby from developing hemolytic disease of the newborn. It was a major development, the culmination of many years of research. It is still used today in Rh negative mothers to prevent their future babies from developing this severe disease.

My mother's antibodies to Robin's Rh + red blood cells had initially been activated by me, the firstborn. I'm Rh +. My mother's second child, Becky, is Rh -, so there had been no immunologic stimulus or booster effect. But, now, with Robin being Rh +, my mother's immune system was stimulated exponentially. With each successive pregnancy with Rh + babies, the antibody levels had increased dramatically, attaching themselves now to Robin's red blood cells and destroying them. Rh isoimmunization caused the symptom complex Robin now exhibited. The profound anemia led to her severe heart failure and respiratory distress.

Robin's doctor consulted the experts, his former professors, at the University of Virginia School of Medicine in Charlottesville, and did exactly as they said. They placed Robin under an oxygen tent and eventually she underwent two exchange transfusions with O negative blood. All the while my parents and others were praying for a miraculous healing.

Her healing did not come, at least not in the way they hoped it would.

Robin died on December 18th at slightly more than twenty-four hours of age. My mother had held her twice, and my father only once. They would never hold her again.

My shattered father then shouldered the strain of caring for and comforting his heartbroken young wife. He and my mother carried the burden of grief for their living children, shielding us from having to bear it.

Life had to go on: there was a family to raise and work to be done.

And so, as the leader and protector of his family, my father did the next necessary things. He made the funeral arrangements. He chose Robin's casket. He bought her tiny burial plot for fifty dollars. He selected a white marble lamb to mark her grave.

On a wintry day, Robin was buried in a graveside service at Green Hill Cemetery in Berryville. My mother, still hospitalized until Christmas Eve, was unable to attend her daughter's funeral.

And my parents wept tears of anguish that flowed from breaking hearts.

How DID MY PARENTS handle Robin's death?

Did they deny reality, and act as if nothing had really happened? No. A daughter's death is not nothing.

Did they deny their deep pain? No. A stiff upper lip doesn't work very well as a means of coping. God never expects us to deny our suffering.

Did they anesthetize their pain? There are many ways to do it: turning to chemicals, busyness, overwork, and on and on. No, they faced the pain and felt it as it lacerated their hearts.

How about blame? Bitterness? Anger? We love to blame someone or something when disaster strikes. It is a very human response.

Did they blame themselves for some imagined "defective" faith in God? Was that why God had not healed Robin? I hope no one told them the hateful lie that they had not had enough faith, thus making them the murderers of their daughter. Our faith is in God, not in our own puny faith.

Did my mother blame herself for generating antibodies against her own baby? No. She realized that we live in a fallen world; the fallenness manifests itself in all of life, even in diseases involving the immune system.

Did they blame me for inciting the antibody production in the first place? I could have been a good scapegoat. They could have made me feel guilty over Robin's death for the rest of my life. One could logically and correctly conclude that if I had never been conceived, then Robin would never have died. No, they never blamed me or even suggested any such thing.

Did they blame the doctor? How about the hospital? No. They had done all they could.

Did they blame God? No. They trusted God. They trusted

in God's goodness and omniscience and, therefore, never complained about God's providence in their lives.

What did my parents do? My parents took their sorrows, their tears, and their broken hearts to God. They openly told their Father in heaven how they felt, and they asked for mercy. And the God who is near the broken-hearted, and Jesus, the man of sorrows who is acquainted with grief, gave them healing comfort. Only God can heal a broken heart.

DID GOD HEAR my parents' prayers? Or did he turn a deaf ear to them?

I think he heard and answered. Must God answer our prayers exactly as we pray them? No. Would he even be God then? I don't want to have authority over God to tell him exactly what he must do.

God did not heal Robin in this life. He healed her in heaven where she does not suffer as she did here. Why was she not healed on earth? I don't know. I'm not the God who knows the first from the last. I do know that God is good, and God is sovereign. That's enough.

I don't like it when I hear would-be (well-meaning, I suppose) comforters uttering inane things to grieving parents like: "It's okay, she's in a better place" or "It's all for the good" or "I know just how you must feel" (unless they actually do know from experience). I hope no one said these things to my parents. I think these trite expressions ignore and minimize the bleeding gash in a mourning parent's heart. It is better to sit and weep and grieve with them. It is often better to say very little and simply show that we love them.

Yet there is truth in saying that God does all things well, and that now, Robin is healthy in heaven with her Maker.

EVERY DECEMBER 17TH, my father and mother quietly remember Robin's birthday and mourn her death. From her dresser drawer, my mother takes out a baby rattle, the only thing remaining that belonged to Robin. The rattle had been purchased before her birth as a present to be given to her for her first Christmas. It had been bought in the joyful hope of welcoming a healthy baby into our family and then shepherding her through childhood and into vigorous adulthood.

My mother leaves the rattle on her dresser all day to remind my father and herself of the deep valley that God brought them through, of the great comfort that God gives a grieving heart, and of the little girl they will see at the side of Jesus … very soon … when they, too, are made completely well.

The LORD is near to the brokenhearted,
And saves those who are crushed in spirit.
   Psalm 34:18

The LORD gave, and the LORD has taken away.
Blessed be the name of the LORD.
   Job 1:21b.

38

Children and Fathers: Buried Treasure Here Awaits the Persevering Reader

I MISS my children.

I miss every one of them. I miss every age and every stage.

I miss having babies and little kids around the house. And I miss my teenagers.

Now, all four of our children are married, all four have children of their own, and all four live far away.

I miss seeing them. I miss being with them.

I miss coming home to my children after a hard day at work and receiving a conquering hero's welcome. They somehow had it in their minds that their daddy was some kind of champion; Nancy did nothing to dispel that generally held household opinion, and everything to create, build, and polish it. I miss chubby little arms around my neck as I, bending and kneeling, swept up and embraced each child, receiving in return loving, willing hugs and sweet-smelling, innocent kisses.

Often I was late to dinner. I was a busy, young pediatrician, and in those days, call could be brutal. There was scant buffer between patient phone calls and me. By mutual agreement, Nancy began dinner at 7:00 p.m. whether I was home or not—usually not. Too often I was late to dinner, too often I was late to concerts or sports events because of emergencies, and too often I had to rush away from the same events for the same reasons.

My wife and children forgave me. They knew I was doing it for them and for other children that needed my help. They thought I was a good and loving daddy and husband. I hope I was.

Our children gave me almost constant joy, and they still do. I love each of them.

I miss them.

Our Children

Nancy and I married young: I was twenty and she was eighteen. This is not what the experts recommend. Were we nuts? I wasn't; I'm not so sure about Nancy. We knew we loved each other. We look back and wonder at God's protection and providence all these years. Nancy took a big chance when she married me; she had unwavering confidence in me and she believed in me. Her trust rested on little more than promise. After all, what had been my biggest accomplishment up to that time (besides the fact that I was basketball legend)? I had been a student. That was all. I was still a student. I had never really done anything. Yet Nancy was willing to follow me anywhere and attach all her earthly hopes to me. Nancy was completely committed to me; she was all in. Nancy's confidence in me was like oxygen for my soul: it gave me life, it nourished me, and it fueled the fire that blazes in every man's heart, that burning desire to provide for, protect, and lead his family. Without her trust and confidence, the deadly cares and worries of living would have drowned, suffocated, or strangled me; life has many ways of asphyxiating men.

We have had a long, surprising journey together, a surprisingly good journey.

We wanted a large family, and wanted to have our children while we were young. We did not buy into Zero Population Growth (ZPG was a faddish, pseudo-scientific, pseudo-intellectual movement of the 1970s which wanted to limit couples to two children or less—for the good of the planet, of course). We did not believe in a scarcity mentality. We did not ascribe to weird, dystopian visions of the future. We had hope. Our four children were born before Nancy was thirty years old.

Rebecca, our oldest daughter, was born when Nancy was a mere twenty-year-old. I was a twenty-two-year-old sophomore medical student. I had never been to a delivery before, and when Rebecca appeared, I was terrified that she had something dreadfully wrong with her; her head was so misshapen that I was certain she must have had a serious problem. Dr. Dottie Hahn attended the delivery and reassured the new father that everything was fine.

Rebecca was a delight. She was a beautiful little girl with her bouncing, curly blonde hair, often in ringlets. After crying with colic for her first three months of life, she became a happy, joyful child and adult. She was a smart little girl, unusually precocious. (I know, everyone says this about his child. In her case, it was true.) She began five-year-old kindergarten when she was still four years old; thus, she graduated from high school and began college as a seventeen-year-old. I grew to regret that we started her early in school, not because she had any problems, but because it meant she left our home a year earlier than she would have otherwise. It meant that I had one less year to enjoy her.

Rebecca was an easy child to rear. She has always had an extraordinarily sensitive spirit. She tried hard to please us and obey us. She has always had the desire to do what is right in any circumstance, sometimes almost eternally agonizing over decisions (an unfortunate tendency she learned or inherited from me). Her joy was overflowing. She made friends easily, she loved life, and she flourished.

Rebecca had the fortune and misfortune of being our first child. There were many perks associated with being the first child and the first grandchild on both sides of the family.

And there was a downside; she had to endure and survive the neuroses and mistakes of first-time parents. Rebecca experienced almost everything Nancy and I did. She went to Haiti with us. She moved three times with us. She even attended my medical school graduation, when, as a two-year-old, she watched the whole procession as she rummaged through her little purse and finally found an old piece of cheese to snack on, placed there for safekeeping weeks before.

Rebecca was the ultimate big sister, and she welcomed each new addition to the family with unfettered joy. She was dependable and mature for her age, so we relied on her to help us care for and corral her younger siblings. She was the third adult in the family, our secret weapon.

Rebecca was in third grade when her last sibling was born, a little brother. I wanted to be the one who told her about him, and I wanted to do it face to face. I looked forward with eager anticipation to the moment I announced her baby brother's birth to her. Rebecca was in school when I left Nancy's bedside at the hospital. When I arrived at her school, I walked into her classroom and asked to see Rebecca alone in the hallway. When I gave her the good news, her face beamed with gladness and excitement. Her response was exactly what I had hoped for, and her response was my rich reward for being my eldest daughter's personal messenger. Her beaming face has been my great reward over and over again for many years.

Rebecca still gives me great joy.

Rachel came next, born when I was an intern in Houston. Since I was working at the hospital when Nancy went into labor, and since Nancy is an independent woman, she drove herself to the hospital. I met her there, and soon thereafter, Rachel arrived.

Rachel was a beautiful, dark-haired, chubby baby. She was a happy little girl despite the fact that she was a constant "spitter" her first year of life: she had gastroesophageal reflux. Her spitting offered one big advantage: we always knew exactly where in the house she had crawled. All we had to do was follow the puddles on the floor. It was like a primitive tracking device.

For many years, I have risen early each morning, before anyone else is up, to read my Bible and pray. Why? Because I'm religious? Or because I like rituals? Or because I want to impress God, or maybe earn his favor? No.

I know I need help from God to get me through the day. It is a simple formulation: I need help and God offers it. He is my only hope for sanity and survival. Is there anything intrinsically heroic or noble in the fact that you and I eat food and drink fluids to survive physically? Of course not. Daily nourishment for the spirit is much the same. Knowing God and gaining strength from him makes complete sense to me. Not doing so is suicide.

As a little baby, Rachel often joined me in my morning times with God. She woke up soon after I did, and before she aroused the rest of the household, I went to her crib and quietly and gently took her into my arms. We went back to my chair in the kitchen where she sat in my lap as I read my Bible and drank my coffee. God poured out his grace upon us both as we sat together. I cherished those minutes with Rachel.

Rachel eventually became the middle sister. This placed Rachel in a tough position, as all middle children are. She felt unavoidable pressure to be like her big sister, and she felt unavoidable pressure to make way for her little sister. She has developed a comprehensive philosophy of life rooted in her "middle childness."

Rachel was a bright girl with a gift of great common sense. She has always had an acute sense of justice. Rachel has always had the courage of her convictions and she has always had a strong will. She is willing and brave enough to pursue her own path; she does not mind doing things differently from others. Her willingness to blaze her own trail showed up early in life; as an infant, she had an uncanny ability to locate any toxic plant or chemical that could be ingested. She alone among our children was well known to the Houston Poison Control Center.

Rachel is affectionate, generous, and sensitive, and she has always loved having friends. Rachel was an entrepreneur from a very young age, and has carried that trait with her into adulthood. Even as a child, Rachel had the ability to make money, and she never feared hard work. She created earrings and sold them, she decorated trash cans and marketed them, and she babysat. As a teenager, she ran a mothers' day out at our home one summer. She recruited and hired her younger sister and brother to be her employees. Each day for two weeks we had twenty small children at our house as Rachel and company entertained and cared for them.

Rachel still gives me great joy.

Esther was born during my last year of residency in Houston. Nancy was in labor all night and she gave me a scare for a few hours after delivery when her blood pressure remained dangerously elevated. I was relieved when it finally came down, and when I could relax with my new daughter. A father experiences uncontrollable terror when his wife delivers a baby; two precious lives are on the razor-thin border between life and death.

Esther was the easiest of our children. She was a beautiful baby with a full head of dark-brown hair. She was slender and slight. She seemed so frail and fragile.

We moved from Houston to Georgia when Esther was two months old. During the long drive east, Nancy drove our air-conditioned car with the girls, and I drove our Volkswagen (without air-conditioning), accompanied by the houseplants and our dog. I led the way on interstate, all windows down; I unable to hear much of anything because of wind noise. At one point, Nancy honked at me for a few minutes, signaling that we needed to pull over (there were no cell phones then, and if we were separated, we would never have seen each other again until we finished the trip). Esther was hungry and was blowing her top; it was time to nurse her. Unable to get my attention, Nancy finally did what she had to do: she asked Rebecca to extricate Esther from her car seat and hand her to Nancy. Nancy then proceeded to nurse her on I-10 as she drove 70 mph.

Esther was a typical third child: she was just happy to be around. Nothing seemed to upset her. Noisy big sisters, being carried around like a little doll, going to all her older sisters' events—it was all fine to Esther. She enjoyed her status as the baby sister. She was a lightweight; I teased her that she had hollow, bird-like bones. She was also the queen of nicknames, and accumulated more than any of our children. At different times and in different phases, she was known as Es, Essie, Little E, Esther Bunny, Queen Esther, Queenie, Little Nan, and The Skinny Kid.

When she was two, Esther developed pneumonia. I worried like any other father as I watched my sweet little Esther languish for days without eating and hardly drinking. Maybe I worried more than most; I knew what could happen. I felt like I should do something more for my little girl, but there was nothing more to do. I did not like to see her suffer. Being a pediatrician does not make one immune to anxiety over a loved child's illness.

Esther cares about people. She freely and often puts herself out for others, and she looks for ways to help others. She is happy to do it.

As Esther grew and matured, it was apparent to us that she had special gifts of intelligence, perseverance, and organization. She never gave up, and she kept going until she had accomplished her mission. She could organize anything; I am certain she could even organize and harmonize a bunch of doctors, a nearly impossible task.

Esther is the best shopper in our family. She can always find a deal, and she gets better deals than anyone I know.

Esther still gives me great joy.

Jeremiah is our youngest child and our only son. We were living in Thomson, Georgia when he was born, and when Nancy began having contractions, we left home without wasting time and raced to Augusta, thirty miles away. A mother delivering her fourth baby can go extremely rapidly. Call it respect for the birth process, call it common sense, or call it fear—okay, call it fear, or call it dread—I was not about to deliver my own baby in the bleak mid-winter on the side of the road or at the local fast food place. We got to University Hospital Labor and Delivery in record time, and in plenty of time.

We did not know whether this baby would be a boy or girl. I was getting used to having girls at home. I like girls, I loved my own little girls, and I fully expected that Nancy would give me another beautiful little Miller daughter. I was getting used to this. There was one thing that concerned me: we had run out of names for girls. We were still working on our new daughter's name when Dr. Gene Long announced that we had a son. I was surprised and I was overjoyed. He would be Jeremiah Allan Miller III, named after my father and me. My nurse had an illuminated sign placed conspicuously in downtown Thomson announcing, "Dr. Miller has a son!"

Jeremiah enjoyed (usually) having four mothers. His big sisters babied him, and he learned a lot about females. They called him things like "Gravy Train." And "Meatball" (I'm not sure where that came from). And "Montur" (translation: "Monster," as in "Jeremiah Mill, you are a Montur!"—it is tough to articulate all these words when you are a two-year old-big sister). It was a good life for him.

As the only two males in our household, Jeremiah and I spent a lot of time together. We played ball together. We surfed together. We worked together around the house. I taught him everything I could about sports and girls and life and God. We are a lot alike in appearance, personality, and mannerisms, yet we are different. Jeremiah has better street smarts than I do. He is a better writer than I am. He is a far better golfer and tennis player than I am. He made his own choices about school and career. I'm glad he's his own man. He serves other people humbly, quietly and hidden from view. He is a man of unusual wisdom and uncommon integrity.

Jeremiah and I have some things in our lives that are eerily similar. He and I both spent a year at Wheaton College and then departed. He and I both married girls from Cobb County, Georgia, and they both have striking Celtic looks. He and I both attended medical school at the Medical College of Georgia. He and I both took a small detour in our career paths, he to dermatology, and I to pediatrics. He and I both have sisters and daughters named Rebecca. We both moved far away for our training, and we both returned to the Southeast.

Jeremiah still gives me great joy.

I have discovered, surprisingly, that our adult children still seem to need me as an advisor and counselor. I'm grateful for that. And I have discovered that our adult children are now my friends and peers, and I rely upon them for advice and counsel. I'm glad for that as well.

All of our children, and all of their spouses, and all of their children—all of them—follow Jesus Christ.

I have no greater joy than knowing that my children walk in the truth.

Other Things I Miss

I miss meal times with our children. Despite the fact that I was absent many times, we enjoyed talking and sharing as we ate together.

I miss family devotions. We read the Bible and prayed individually with our children when they were young. Later, we did it all together. We tried to keep it brief; we tried to use these times to teach them, show them their need for a Savior, and urge them to go to Jesus who would welcome and receive them. We prayed for their needs and for the needs of others.

I usually questioned the kids as we discussed the Bible; I wanted them to think for themselves, and to discover what God was saying to them. We had some lively discussions.

When she was little, Rachel had the best stock responses when I asked questions during devotions or after church. To my most profound questions, if she did not know the answer or if she had been daydreaming, she put on her most serious expression, dramatically paused for a few seconds, and uttered an all-purpose answer: "God." She was always right. The ultimate answer to all questions really is God. But it was not quite the specific answer I was looking for.

If she got tired of answering "God," Rachel employed the second response in her repertory. Then, when asked a question, thespian-like she flopped her arm on the table, laid her head on her arm, and plaintively uttered the sad, sad words, "I ... am *so ... tired*." How could a sympathetic father be harsh with that pitiful reply? It always worked.

I miss going to church with my children. I miss sitting in the same pew and worshiping God together, singing, praying, and receiving the preached Word of God.

Frequently, Nancy had to get everyone to church by herself. It was not an easy task. We tried to get everyone up early enough on Sunday mornings to have breakfast and get dressed without rushing around and getting stressed. Rachel nicely solved the problem of being ready and dressed on time: she bathed and dressed the night before, sleeping in her Sunday dress. Jeremiah never quite solved the problem, and usually was the last one out the door, dashing to the car with his shoes and socks in hand, arriving seconds before I pulled out of the driveway.

I miss being together on family vacations. We went to the beach for a week each summer, and there, we left all responsibilities behind. It was a time to pull away and regroup. It was a time for fun. The children slept late, they ate a leisurely breakfast, and each morning they watched Chicago's *Bozo Show* on cable TV;

life does not get better. They ate their fill of junk food that week, and since I'm an easy mark and have no idea what I'm doing while shopping, they loved to go the grocery store with me that week; I said "yes" to any food request. Esther's favorite was Klondike bars. And of course, we spent many hours on the beach and in the water together. Rachel grew to fear the unseen critters in the ocean, and so she stayed out of the water more than the others, but all the children loved using floats and boogie boards as they caught the waves. In the evenings, we watched movies during beach week. Old family movies from the archives were most favored, even over great Hollywood productions. Any viewing of *Jaws* was strictly forbidden.

At the beach, away from distractions and interruptions, we were able to spend deep, concentrated time with each other and with God. We reconnected, and we built and repaired relationships.

I miss little things like teaching each of our children to drive. They all first learned to drive in a 1973 Volkswagen Beetle using a stick shift. The car smelled like a gas can, and by the time the younger kids got to it, it was on its last lap. They began referring to it as "the hunk of junk," or "The Hunka."

I miss going to our children's piano and violin recitals, and I miss their concerts. I miss watching them play basketball, baseball, softball, tennis, and soccer.

I miss laughing with our children. We laughed when Rebecca and her friend Stephanie Johnson fell into Rae's Creek one January afternoon after an attempt to swing across on a vine. Rebecca came running to me to help Stephanie who was still waist-deep in the water.

We laughed that Rachel spent so much time at the home of her best friend, Alison Blount. Alison had no siblings, and Rachel liked Alison's house because she and Alison had no other children to compete with; besides, it was peaceful and calm at Alison's house. Ironically, Alison loved being in our home, where something was always happening, and where life was not quite so peaceful and calm.

We laughed when Esther and I secretly bought our family's first video camera as a Christmas present. I experimented on Esther, aiming the camera at her and letting her talk. She rocked back and forth in her little rocking chair, asking me to talk back to her: "Talk to me, Daddy! Well … why don't you say something?" I kept quiet, I kept filming, and she kept talking. The recorded segment is a classic piece of videography.

We laughed about Jeremiah's lunch-making abilities. Each child took responsibility for a week at a time for preparing and packing the entire family's lunches. The girls gave him failing grades for his lack of creativity and imagination in food preparation and presentation, but he made up for it with speed.

We laughed when we played ball together. We laughed when we worked together. We laughed as we watched old reruns of *I Love Lucy* and *Leave it to Beaver.*

Regrets

I loved my children and did my best for them. But I have some regrets, two in particular.

First, I was not as understanding as I should have been. I failed to realize that each child, though arising from the same genetic pool, was unique, and therefore required individually-tailored care and handling. In addition, I tended to view all their experiences and thoughts through the lens of my own experiences and thoughts; this was a mistake. I should have been more careful to understand what was happening inside of them, their motivations, their intentions, and why they did what they did. I failed each of our children here to a larger or smaller extent.

Second, I regret that, too often, I disciplined my children out of impatience and anger. I should have offered them much more grace and patience.

I have asked for and received my adult children's forgiveness for my failings as their father. I find that children are usually ready to forgive their parents' faults and shortcomings.

What Children Need From a Father

Children do not demand or even expect their fathers to be perfect; they know that we cannot be perfect. They want us to humbly walk with them and before them.

Children need fathers who love them, who tell them that they love them, who back up their words with objective acts, and who assure their children of their love with hugs and kisses. Children need fathers who understand them and who encourage them. They need fathers who accept them for who they are. They need fathers who are gentle, patient, and kind with them. They need fathers who lead them, who protect them, and who provide for them. They need fathers who nourish and nurture them, and who create an atmosphere of grace in which a child flourishes. They need fathers who teach and discipline them. They need fathers who fiercely defend them. They need fathers who courageously suffer for them, dying for them at any level as the need arises. They need fathers who pray for them. They need fathers who humbly repent of their sins, and who humbly ask for forgiveness. They need fathers who will never desert them or abandon them, and they need the security of living in the reality of this assurance.

Children need fathers who live openly before them and who allow them to see their victories, their defeats, their weaknesses, and their struggles; they need to see that their fathers need Jesus, too.

And children need fathers who take them to the same Lord Jesus Christ.

And they [fathers] began bringing children to Him, so that He might touch them ...
Mark 10:13

PART FOUR

39

The Sting

SOMETIMES GOD breaks into our time-bound, natural world with astonishing clarity.

It is not that he hasn't been there all along; it is simply that sometimes he makes himself known in an unusual way to our limited human perceptions, and thus, gives mortals extra gifts of encouragement and assurance.

For seven miles, the Greeneway in North Augusta, South Carolina, rolls along an old railroad right of way that has been repurposed with asphalt for recreation. Every day, and especially on weekends, scores of walkers, runners and cyclists spend their mornings there, exercising, enjoying God's creation, and clearing their minds.

The Greeneway begins at the Savannah River, then gently slopes uphill as the coastal plain meets the piedmont at the fall line. As you ascend from the river, it is easy to get the impression that you are really in the mountains; all is quiet and still, lush vegetation surrounds and engulfs you, and there is a peace not to be found in the busyness of everyday life.

My eight-year-old grandson, Michael, and I had traversed the Greeneway the day before, and now, on Saturday morning, we wanted to initiate his grandmother. Nancy loves to ride bikes and delights in being outside in a beautiful, natural setting. We ate an early breakfast, loaded our bikes, and crossed the river to our entry point.

The day's ride would be a leisurely one that would not require much expertise and only moderate exertion. We would make a few stops for water breaks and snacks (Michael's favorite stuff). My neighbor, Daniel Metzel, had recently given me the FATS experience: FATS is the Forks Area Trail System, a well-known local mountain-biking trail where you have to watch out for the trees that constantly jump into your path; I never knew that trees could move so fast. I had survived FATS with exhilaration, and even more importantly, with my skull intact. Today's ride would be a piece of cake, a walk in the park … a cruise on the Greeneway.

What could possibly go wrong?

The early morning was cool and tranquil. We rode uphill away from the river. At times I led, at others, I trailed behind Nancy and Michael. A couple of miles into the ride, with me bringing up the rear, I heard an ominous snapping sound and then a loud thunk as a large missile dropped from the sky and landed just behind me. I was twenty feet away when I realized that a ten-pound limb had almost speared me as it fell seventy-five feet from the trees above. One or two seconds had been the margin between safety and harm. As we rode, Nancy and I discussed with Michael the kind providence of God. One of us could have been severely injured by the falling limb, and God had protected us. This was not a lucky break: it was God actively protecting us from harm.

We completed our ride uphill and turned around for the easy downhill return. I led our trio, with Michael between Nancy and me, traveling single file. We commented to each other that someone had cleared the limb out of the path.

Halfway to the river, I had a sudden pain in my left hand: something was stinging me. I tried to swat it away, but it would not go away; it was a persistent little thing. Was this a bee or a yellow jacket? Or had a snake dropped from the overhanging trees? I didn't know, but I did know it really hurt. I smacked the offending organism again, this time quickly glancing at my hand to see what was biting or stinging me.

I never saw what it was. The next thing I knew was the strange, sickening sense of foreboding we often have before something bad happens. "Uh-oh," I thought in an instant. "I'm going down."

Yes, indeed.

I went down hard. I may have hit a rut or a root, or I may have simply jack-knifed in my attempts to be free of the sting. I felt as though an invisible force had swiftly given a mighty downward jerk on an invisible cable attached to an invisible steel hook stealthily inserted into one of my helmet's air-holes, pulling me straight down to the ground. I hit the asphalt with all my 180 pounds directly concentrated in one spot, and I did not bounce very well. I landed on my left shoulder, with my left arm tucked under my body. I was stunned for a few seconds.

I got up slowly and was on my feet by the time my wife and grandson arrived at my side, but I was, as they say, "shaken up on the play." Nancy helped me right my bike, and I made it to the side of the bike path to prevent further injury to myself or others. Once there, I leaned over my bike for a few minutes, experiencing that delightful, noxious combination of pain, dizziness, and nausea.

Just then, a nice older woman riding from the opposite direction arrived at the scene. She was worried that somehow she had caused the wreck. I assured her that I was fine, and that, no, she had not been at fault. I was just happy she had not run me over and then caused a twenty-bike pile-up.

As my head cleared, I examined myself to check out my condition. "How's it going in there?" I thought. "How're you feelin', Big Guy?" My head was fine. My bike helmet was still on, and I had not hit my head. My cognition was no more abnormal than usual. My left elbow was bleeding, but it was only an abrasion, a flesh wound. I was worried about my shirt, though. I was wearing my favorite T-shirt, the yellow one with "Mitch's Surf Shop, La Jolla" emblazoned on it; I was relieved to see that it was neither torn nor bloody. It's important not to ruin a good shirt. My sunglasses had flown off, but despite their crash landing to the path, they were still okay except for a few scratches. I would still be able to wear them and look cool. My watch was chipped but still ticking.

However, my left shoulder was throbbing; I palpated the lateral margin of my collarbone with my right hand and made a diagnosis. I turned to Nancy and told her, "Nancy … I've just fractured my clavicle."

Oh yeah, I was feeling good now. I was also peeved at myself: this stuff happens to other people—like my patients—not to me.

I was able to get back on my bike and ride the three miles to our car, but I was unusually cautious and we pedaled slowly. Arriving at our car, one-handed and with assistance, I loaded the bikes back on the rack. I didn't feel much like driving, so Nancy drove home for us.

Back home, we unloaded the bikes, and I called my neighbor and friend, orthopedist Mark Fulcher. He was in Atlanta but talked me through an exam and helped clarify if anything needed to be done immediately. In children, we usually just let the clavicle heal, but I'm no child. Besides, I'm a pediatrician—I don't do adults; I needed some input from a real expert. He agreed that even if the clavicle were fractured, there was nothing to be done just then. He recommended icing my shoulder and taking ibuprofen, and said he would be over early the next morning to examine me.

Mark walked over to my house at seven thirty on Sunday morning to look me over. Shirtless, I met him at the door, my shoulder, arm, and chest revealing some dramatic, large-scale bruising. We both felt a hint of crepitance over my clavicle, a sort of crunching, unstable sensation that is a reliable sign of a fracture here. But since most clavicle fractures require nothing more than symptomatic treatment, we went forward with the plan: ice and ibuprofen. I appreciate Mark's good sense and clinical judgment.

I was not able to raise my hand over my head and had a tough time getting dressed, combing my hair, tying my tie, or doing much of anything with my left arm. Sleeping was a challenge. Simply getting into bed required serious planning and elicited a lot of pain. In private moments, I groaned and moaned; I could control that. In public and private, however, I winced—involuntarily. In addition, I began to notice a fair amount of chest wall pain.

I finally surrendered to pain and curiosity. I asked radiologist Jimmy Davis, an old friend, to do some X-rays. For my self-esteem, I wanted to determine if I was just acting like a baby over nothing, or if there was really something wrong.

Well, okay, maybe I *was* acting like a baby. But there was also something wrong, in fact, at least two somethings. The X-rays revealed a fractured clavicle, not surprisingly, but also a fractured rib. It was all becoming clear to me now. My shoulder pain was not just the clavicle. And my chest pain was very likely three or four more rib fractures. I didn't bother to get any more films taken; it didn't really matter now. There was nothing to be done except to give these fractures time to heal.

Something else was occurring in the background the whole time this little drama played out, something at least as real as hitting asphalt and breaking bones. The night before the wreck, I had a phone message from a pastor friend of mine, Mike Dann. His message said that he was thinking about me and just wanted to check on me. Since it was late when we arrived home and retrieved his message, I decided I would return his call the next day, after the planned bike ride.

After the surprise bike accident the next day, I called Mike and told him what had transpired. I thanked him for his thoughts and prayers. My vision was becoming a little clearer now as I thought about the sequence of events. Mike makes it a habit, as God brings people to his mind, to pray for them. I believe that God heard his prayers and then mysteriously answered them to protect me that Saturday morning. I could have been injured much worse than I was; I am not a dramatic person (I'm pretty boring), and I am not a kook (usually), but I might even have died.

We live a very fragile existence. How many "freak" accidents and incidents occur, things that are completely unexpected, in which people die suddenly? The sting could have sent me into anaphylactic shock. The bike accident might have sent me tumbling to my death into the thirty-foot deep ravines that lined the path. The crash to the pavement could have killed me or severely injured me. It could have kept me from doing something important. And God had something important for me to do. That important thing coming up very soon was this: the very next day, Sunday, I was scheduled to teach some essential truths that everyone needs to hear, things that God had been teaching me, to our young couples at church.

I had been thinking about my talk for days, I had thought about it on the bike ride, and I continued mulling it over in my mind that afternoon and evening. We went to a wedding Saturday night, and I took care that no one slapped me on my left shoulder as men are prone to do with good friends; it happened only once. We came home, I studied a little more as I iced my shoulder once more, and then went to bed.

Because of the pain, I slept fitfully. I awoke several times but drifted back to sleep quickly. At about 2:30 a.m., I awoke again and this time a verse from Isaiah was in my mind: "You have given me the tongue of disciples to sustain the weary one with a word." This kind of thing doesn't usually happen to me. It was unusual. I went back to sleep, grateful that God had encouraged me with his words even in my sleep. He was saying to me, "Don't worry, I'm with you. I have a task for you to complete. I have a message for you to deliver. I'm going to encourage some weary people today through you." Glad to have received such a clear supernatural sense of God's blessing, and eagerly anticipating being able to teach his Word a few hours later, I stayed on my right side, draped my left arm over my chest and abdomen, and slept a few more hours. I awakened again at about 5:00 a.m. and slowly and gingerly slid out of bed, keeping my left arm pressed to my chest and aching as I walked to the closet to dress.

I poured myself a cup of strong, black coffee and picked up my Bible. Getting to the table took a little longer than usual since I was doing everything with one hand and one arm. I sat down to read and pray. I opened my Bible to the bookmarked spot, the next chapter I was due to read for my daily Bible reading. It just happened to be at Isaiah 50. And here I read these words in verse four:

> *The Lord God has given Me the tongue of disciples, that I may know how to sustain the weary one with a word. He awakens Me morning by morning, he awakens My ear to listen as a disciple.*

Was this a coincidence? A random confluence of events? Was my mind playing tricks on me?

No.

Awakening me early that morning, God was again assuring me of his presence and blessing. I had not read this chapter for a long time. Isaiah 50:4 was not even on my radar screen, yet God had awakened me in the middle of the night with this verse impressed upon my heart. Now again, as if to say, "Hey, don't miss this," he had graciously awakened me early to give me the whole verse again. The same verse. It had come unbidden at night. It had come unexpected in the early morning. It was clear to me that God again said to me, "I'm with you, and I will bless you today as you teach."

If it is true that God at least kept me from serious harm, or at most, saved my life that Saturday in order to preserve me until Sunday to teach important truth, and that he kept encouraging me in ways that were supernatural, what was it that I said to the group? What was so important?

I taught three vital truths that God had taught me through

his Word and Spirit as I had walked through life with him. They may seem simple, but I think they are profound.

First: The most important thing about God is his goodness.

What do we think of when we think about God? What first comes to mind when someone mentions God? What does God want us to know about himself, if there is only one thing we can know? The answer lies in Exodus 33:18-19 and Exodus 34.

In these verses, Moses asks God to show him his glory. God answers that he will show him his goodness. God's glory is his goodness.

God's glory is his goodness; this seems to be the most important thing God wants us to know about himself. His goodness encompasses his lovingkindness, faithfulness, gentleness, understanding, forgiveness, mercy, grace, acceptance, and love. God is essentially good: his very essence is goodness. At his core, all-powerful God is good, and this sovereign goodness informs every aspect of his character, words, and deeds. If we can comprehend this, it changes our view of God, and our view of God determines how we view life, ourselves, and others. We begin to read God's Word and life circumstances through the lenses of God's goodness, his mercy, and his unfailing promises. This changes everything.[6]

Second: Jesus saves sinners.

This also seems fairly simple. Everyone knows that Christians believe this. Who hasn't seen a "Jesus saves" sign somewhere? Yet,

---

6   The first time I clearly saw this major implication from Exodus 33 and 34, that is, that God's glory is his goodness, was when my pastor, Dr. George W. Robertson, pointed it out in a sermon a few years ago. I have thought about it often since then.

this simple phrase is freighted with infinite significance. This is the gospel of Christ.

Sinners desperately need aid. We are all sinners. We are all guilty before God and each other. That lurking sense of guilt inside each of us is not merely some psychological construct, but the sign of true moral guilt. We desperately need to be rid of it. This is why we are prone to run from it, anesthetize it, deny it, suppress it … do anything but face it. There is a real answer, a true cure, a way to be free of our guilt both objectively and subjectively. And this is what Jesus offers us: freedom from guilt through his blood.

Salvation from this guilt means healing, rescue, and freedom from our sins. We need to be rescued and freed from ourselves, our sins, our guilt, and hell.

Jesus Christ alone is able to save us. He does it by his death on the cross and his resurrection from the dead. He offers his salvation, rescue, healing, and freedom to each of us. All we must do is turn to him and say, "Jesus, have mercy on me." He never turns us away.

Jesus saves sinners. That means we trust in him alone. We stop trusting in anything we can do because there is nothing we can do to save ourselves, and nothing we can add to his salvation freely offered. He causes us to turn to him in the first place, awakening our darkened hearts. He gives the gifts of faith and repentance. He holds on to us until the very end. We do not depend upon ourselves to hang on to him. No. He holds on to us. He takes us through life and into heaven, guiding and supporting us all the way.

Jesus saves sinners. A simple phrase and a profound truth. A comforting truth. I don't have to trust myself, I should not trust myself, and I can't trust myself. Why would I ever want to trust myself, a weak and changeable mortal, when I can trust the all-powerful, unchanging, unfailing Son of God? This is a relief. No more pretending. I am who I am, a sinner in need of the mercy of Christ. He receives me as I turn to him and he says to me, "Don't worry. I save sinners."

Third: The dark night of the soul can happen to real people.

It is important for followers of Christ to realize that we will all suffer in this world, sometimes because the world is fallen and broken, sometimes because of our own folly or sin, sometimes because of our status as followers of Christ. We in America tend not to talk much about these sufferings for Christ, but the Bible does—a lot. Peter tells us in I Peter 4:12 not to be surprised at our fiery trials. Jesus anticipates for us that in the world, we will have tribulation, but he tells us to be of good cheer because he has overcome the world (John 16:33). Yet, practically, we are often surprised that we suffer.

A distinct category of suffering is the "dark night of the soul," a phrase coined by St. John of the Cross and used by most (and by me) as shorthand for a time in which one perceives that God is completely absent. (I do not know enough about St. John of the Cross to recommend his writings, but this term is useful.) The phrase is an accurate description of a seemingly horrible reality. In this intense crisis, one has the feeling that he is abandoned by God and that God is hiding his face (as the Psalms describe it). It is a time of deep confusion, dark disorientation, and profound hopelessness. The person experiencing this dark night feels utterly unable to connect with God; it feels like hell.

I should know: I have experienced the dark night. I was there for two years, from 2005 until 2007. I believe it had its beginnings the night of my illness in Zambia (Chapter 24). Before I arrived in Zambia, on the long flight over the Atlantic Ocean, I had prayed for a closer relationship with Jesus Christ; not as I might have expected, God answered that prayer by allowing me to experience a dark night of the soul. During those two years, I felt utter despair because I perceived that God had abandoned me. I never knew then that others had experienced it, as well, so the impression that this was a unique thing known only to me further tortured me and isolated me. Not everyone undergoes such a time, and maybe only a few do, but if one ever experiences such a thing, it is important to know that the Bible has a category for it.

I cried out in desperation to God for rescue and I sought the aid of others. Through God's mercy and through the patient help and prayers of my wife, parents, sister, and close friends, I slowly began to come out of this dark time in my life. I found that it helped me to talk honestly of my struggle with those closest to me; bringing the lies of the devil into the light of truth destroys the power of lies.

As I ascended from the dark night, I found Luke 22:31-32 to be especially meaningful. These verses helped me make sense of what had happened to me. Here, Jesus is talking to Simon Peter as he foretells Peter's future denial and failure.

> *Simon, Simon, behold, Satan has demanded permission to sift you like wheat; but I have prayed for you, that your faith may not fail; and you, when once you have turned again, strengthen your brothers.*

From these verses, I see that Satan wants to destroy all followers of Christ, but he may do only as much as God allows. God seems to allow these situations so that we are sifted to the point that we depend upon God alone, and not at all upon ourselves; we are stripped of any desire to trust in ourselves because we see ourselves as we are: utterly weak and undependable. Human pride is crushed. During the crisis, Jesus prays for us (it is comforting also to note that in Romans 8, Paul tells us that Jesus and the Holy Spirit pray for us). Jesus' prayers and presence assure us that our faith will not fail, and that when the process is complete, we will strengthen our fellow believers.

I have found all of this to be perfectly true in my own experience. The dark night of the soul does not last forever. And in my case, in the end, God gave me what I had asked for: a closer relationship with Jesus Christ, a deeper love for him, and a new humility.

Is God really absent during the crisis of the dark night? No. God never abandons us. He is there all the time, secretly supporting and protecting, despite the fact that the one undergoing the crisis perceives only what feels like God's terrifying absence. In the end, God gives more of himself to the sufferer, and after all, isn't God exactly who we need?

> *But as for me, I will watch expectantly for the Lord;*
> *I will wait for the God of my salvation.*
> *My God will hear me.*
> *Do not rejoice over me, O my enemy.*
> *Though I fall I will rise;*
> *Though I dwell in darkness, the Lord is a light for me.*
> *Micah 7:7-8*

Hebrews 7:16 reveals that Jesus Christ possesses the "power of an indestructible life." If Jesus is indestructible, then so are his followers, since we are joined to him in inseparable union.

We do not need to be surprised or discouraged at anything that might happen to us, realizing two things:

1. Nothing may ever occur outside the circle of God's sovereign goodness.
2. Followers of Christ can never be ultimately destroyed. We may suffer, we may bleed, and we may die. But we can never be destroyed.

GOD ALLOWED me to teach his Word the day after my wreck. If I had died immediately after I taught, I would have died happy and fulfilled. But I'm still here. God must have more for me to do, and thus, there are more reasons he spared me on the day of the bike accident.

Does God still work? Does God still protect us? Does God still move in our lives in surprising and supernatural ways? Does God still answer prayer?

Yes.

God is always there, always with us, though we may see him more or less clearly at different times.

I'm convinced that the sting and the wreck were only surface events, and that below them and around them and in them was a much deeper battle raging between God and Satan.

God won.

O death, where is your victory? O death, where is your sting?
The sting of death is sin, and the power of sin is the law:
But thanks be to God, who gives us the victory through our
Lord Jesus Christ.
    I Corinthians 15:55-57

40

The Champion Who Bears
Unbearable Burdens

Come to me, all who are weary and heavy-laden, and I will give you rest.
Take my yoke upon you and learn from me, for I am gentle and humble in heart, and you will find rest for your souls.
For my yoke is easy and my burden is light.
  Matthew 11:28-30

Blessed be the Lord who daily bears our burden,
The God who is our salvation.
  Psalm 68:19

Surely he has borne our griefs [sicknesses]
and carried our sorrows [pains] ...
  Isaiah 53:4 (ESV)

... and the LORD has laid on him the iniquity of us all.
  Isaiah 53:6 (ESV)

I HAVE NEEDED someone to be a champion for me. I have needed God, and he has been my Champion all my life.

I could not be my own champion. I could not carry my own burdens ... not really ... not without being crushed in the process. I could not bear the massive weight of my sins, my guilt, my failures, my weaknesses, my sorrows, my disappointments, and my fears. I could not endure my shattered relationship with God, yet I could not heal it. These are all weights that individually crush and destroy humans; how much more does the sum total crush the life out of us? Attempting to bear them never works. They are unbearable burdens for us. We are not designed to bear them.

God gave me someone to be my Champion. He gave me Jesus Christ. And Jesus bears my burdens—all of them. Here is a fantastic thing. Jesus, the only Son of God, the second person of the Trinity, knowing that I cannot possibly take on the burdens each of us encounters in life, takes my sin, guilt, worries, cares, and problems, and he bears them all for me. He is able to do it without being destroyed himself. And he heals my estrangement from God.

My unbearable burdens are not unbearable for Jesus.

My Champion is for me, and he is with me. I know this because God promises it. I know it because he sent Jesus to die and now to live forever as Savior and Redeemer. I know it because of the continual presence of the Holy Spirit in my life telling me God loves me. I know it because God has proven it to me in my own experience for many years. In truth, God has carried me, he has borne me—all my life. I am his problem. It is my Champion's problem to take care of me, to lead me, to protect me, to defend me, and to provide for me. It is my Champion's problem to bear my sins, my guilt, and my fears. I cannot do it. He can and he does.

Here is another amazing thing: Jesus does not grow weary of bearing my burdens, and he does not get tired of me.

I have a Champion. His name is Jesus Christ. Jesus invites us, no, he commands us, to "Come." He tells us to lay our burdens down, to let him bear our unbearable burdens, and to allow him to be our Champion. And he will do it—if we only ask him to.

The Lord is with me like a dread champion ...
Jeremiah 20:11

... Whoever believes in Him will not be disappointed.
       Romans 10:11